NAPOLEON AS A GENERAL

Napoleon in his Study by Hippolyte Delaroche © Private collection Bridgeman Art Library.

Napoleon as a General

Jonathon Riley

hambledon
continuum

Hambledon Continuum is an imprint of Continuum Books

Continuum UK
The Tower Building
11 York Road
London SE1 7NX

Continuum US
80 Maiden Lane
Suite 704
New York, NY 10038

www.continuumbooks.com

First published 2007

British Library Cataloguing-in-Publication Data
A catalogue record for this book is available from the British Library.

ISBN 978-184725-180-0

Typeset by YHT Ltd, London
Printed and bound by Cromwell Press Ltd, Trowbridge, Wiltshire

Contents

Maps

Figures

Acknowledgements

As far as possible I have verified my assertions by reference to Napoleon's correspondence and the writings of his contemporaries. I would like to thank the following: the staff at the University Library in Tampa, Florida, who gave so much of their time in obtaining this source material for me while I was working on this book when stationed with US Central Command; the graphics office in US Central Command which produced the maps; Lieutenant Colonel Phil Bates, who advised me on logistics and made many helpful suggestions; and Mr Stephen Petrie who gave me valuable advice. There are a few footnotes in the book; however, where I have quoted or referred to secondary sources, I have acknowledged the author in the text, and cited the work fully in the bibliography. In particular, I would wish to acknowledge the works and influence of Martin van Creveld, Michael Broers, David Chandler, Alan Forrest and J. F. C. Fuller. The maps were drawn by Mr Steve Thwaites of the Graphics Office, Joint Services Command and Staff College.

Introduction

What is the world, O soldiers?
It is I.
I, this incessant snow, this northern sky:
Soldiers, this solitude
Through which we go
Is I.

Walter de la Mare
Napoleon

Walter de la Mare's epigram speaks of something that every general knows: loneliness. Surrounded as he is by his staff, his aides, his subordinates and his men, he is, nonetheless, alone; for he is the one man, regardless of the level of command, who is responsible for the conduct of battle, for the behaviour of his force, for spending his country's blood and treasure. He is, moreover, accountable for both success and failure. His responsibility and accountability are neither negotiable nor transferable: he cannot shed them either up or down the chain of command. He can, indeed he should, delegate authority over parts of his command to his subordinates, but it remains the general who ultimately takes credit or blame. Thus we speak of Hannibal who crossed the Alps, not the Carthaginians; Caesar who conquered Gaul, not the legions; MacArthur who landed at Inchon, not the US Marines.

When I was invited to write this book, I did so with all that in the back of my mind. My first reaction, though, was that the last thing the market needed was another book about Napoleon. But on reflection and investigation I changed my mind. There are, indeed, plenty of books about Napoleon's career; many excellent biographies; shelves of chronological histories of his campaigns – including Graf Yorck von Wartenberg's work that bears the same title as this book. Separately, there are a few books about generalship, and a few more about command: J. F. C. Fuller's incisive *Generalship: Its Diseases and their Cure*, and Martin van Creveld's *Command in War* being of particular note. What there is not, however, is a book about Napoleon *as a general*.

I am not entirely clear why this is so, but there is one possible explanation: lack of qualified authors. Most books about Napoleon are written by academics or historians. They are well placed to write on historical events, and interpret them, but few have any experience of generalship. Then again, there are many generals, but a minority of those who wear the badges ever exercise generalship in terms of strategic, operational or tactical command. Of those who do, few write. Those who do write, usually confine themselves to their memoirs, and are not in any case historians in the accepted academic sense. There are a few exceptions: Michael Carver, Shan Hackett, Rupert Smith and Julian Thompson, for example. But the fact that one can so easily name them proves how few they are. The list of qualified authors is thin, therefore. Moreover, writing such a book, even if one is qualified, is risky, given the huge amount of knowledge of, and interest in, Napoleon.

This book is not a biography, nor is it a chronological history. It does not examine Napoleon as head of state, and it excludes maritime and naval affairs. It is a thematic examination of Napoleon's generalship, using subjectively chosen examples rather than every one of his campaigns. In form, it opens with a short treatise on generalship, in order to define the examination of Napoleon's achievements. It then moves on to the man himself in a series of related essays on Napoleon's generalship at various levels, as well as an examination of two areas often ignored in the context of pre-industrial age warfare: logistics, and counter-insurgency. It proceeds to three case studies which illustrate the general theses made and ends with a general concluding chapter.

I

Generalship

Napoleon and Generalship

This is a book about Napoleon as a general. If we are to assess his success or failure as a general, then we must first establish what we mean by a 'general', and 'generalship'. At the outset, one must be clear that this is not a discussion about the peacetime role of general officers, since they will be judged by standards of professional competence; this is a discussion about generalship in war, where generals are judged by results. Because war remains an art, rather than a science, generalship too remains an art, although tempered by science, rather than a straightforward exercise in professional competency. There are, therefore, no simple criteria for assessing great generals or, at least, for what makes a great general.

A common dictionary definition of a general speaks of one who holds 'extended command': not helpful in itself. Moreover, generals come in different sizes. A brigadier, the smallest kind of general, commands a brigade of three or four combat units and supporting arms, engaged in close, tactical, battle and unable to influence anything beyond the range of his organic weapons. A major general commands a division. In Napoleonic times this was often the basic tactical formation, composed of several brigades, and was again confined to tactical manoeuvres; in modern times, a division is the lowest level of command that plans and carries out operations simultaneously, and conducts the close, deep and rear fight. A lieutenant general commands a corps. In Napoleonic times this was considered the smallest command capable of acting independently; today, a corps is more an operational than a tactical level formation. Thus, the first aspect of generalship is command of a fighting formation, of combined arms, engaged in war. Above formation command, generalship encompasses the planning and execution of campaigns, or the command of an extended theatre of operations. At the highest level, a general will be responsible for managing the military aspects of his country's policy and strategy, and the spending of its blood and treasure in war.

Considerable care is needed, therefore, when discussing generalship in a historical context. The responsibilities and required competencies of a general have changed in the intervening years, and one must be careful not to judge Napoleon by modern standards. Our understanding of strategy, the operational art, and battlefield tactics are also different, and more will be said of each of these in the appropriate chapters, especially III, IV and V. Complex, modern, war – sometimes referred to as 'Fourth Generation War', or 'Three-Block War', was far in the future. Technology, too, has advanced in the intervening period: the full effects of the Industrial Revolution had hardly begun to be felt by 1815, and technology then was little different from what it had been 100 years before. Nor is it right to judge a field commander with the benefit of hindsight, because he made his decisions based on the information available at the time: our lives and experience go forward, following what Steven Hawking calls 'the arrow of time'; we are able to review those experiences by looking back, but we cannot change them.

So if the context has changed, how is it possible to assess Napoleon as a general? First, perhaps, according to those principles of war that have not changed – even though Napoleon himself would have disputed that such enduring principles exist. There is some variance between different nations as to how many these are, but those which are generally agreed, and which will recur time and again in this book, are the need for good intelligence; the selection and maintenance of the aim; economy of effort; concentration of force; sound administration and logistic sustainability; flexibility; co-operation between arms, services and allies; security of one's own force; surprise and unpredictability; the maintenance of morale and what the British army refers to as 'the moral component of fighting power' – that is, *why* an army fights; the maintenance of good communications; and the primacy of the offensive. The ability to comprehend the political dimension of war is also implicit and unchanging. Those who rail against 'political generals' fail to understand that war is a political act, and that every action in a theatre of operations will have political consequences for the general's own masters, his opponents, or both. The successful general understands this, and does not fall into the trap of entirely separating what he does from its context.

The second yardstick for assessment is by reference to the human condition. In terms of our evolution as a species, we are no different now from what we were in 1815. Our mental processes are the same; our decision-making abilities, likewise, are the same. Armed with the knowledge of what the general did or did not know, one can understand and analyse his successes and failures.

What is the essence of generalship, therefore, at any level? In the Napoleonic period, just as now, the general had to be the man in a military organization who could recognize any problem at issue, in its entirety; define those things which were likely to be decisive (very rarely that one event or action only); and having done this, change the situation to advantage in order to *win*. General Rupert Smith says of this that the general must 'employ *force*, by *design*, to achieve required *objectives*'. Put yet another way, he must balance his ends, ways and means while preventing the other side from doing so. Most important in this equation are the ways: to employ means without a way will lead to disaster, and whereas the ends and the means may be given, it is the general who must decide or devise the ways. Sun Tzu says in this respect:

> In war, then, let your great object be victory, not lengthy campaigns. Thus it may be known that the leader of armies is the arbiter of the people's fate, the man on whom it depends whether the nation shall be in peace or peril.

and:

> the highest form of generalship is to baulk the enemy's plans; the next best is to prevent the junction of the enemy's forces; the next is to attack the enemy's army in the field; and the worst policy of all is to besiege walled towns and cities ... the skilful leader subdues the enemy's troops without any fighting; he captures their cities without laying siege to them; he overthrows their king-doms without lengthy operations in the field. With his forces intact he disputes the mastery of the empire.

Norman Dixon – hardly a sympathetic or dispassionate commentator – remarks: 'The ideal senior commander may be viewed as a device for receiving, processing and transmitting information in a way which will yield the maximum gain for the minimum cost.' But this is too simplistic, even for Napoleonic times. The general may have to fill a series of incompatible roles: politician, leader, manager, supply specialist, public relations man – as well as strategist, operational commander and tactician. The exercise of command by a general, therefore, is not to be confused with simple lea-dership, or information processing. Command encompasses three essential functions: leadership, control and management (of men and resources), and decision-making. These functions vary according to the size and complexity of an army, but must always be exercised. Command is, like sovereignty, indivisible. This applies, too, at each level – Napoleon remarked on this at an early stage in his career as a general when faced with a division of command of the Army of Italy between himself and Kellermann. Writing to the Directory in Paris in May 1746 he said: 'I am certain that one bad General is better than two good ones.' And if command is indivisible between commanders, it is also not possible to separate a commander's responsibilities from his authority over resources, and his accountability for the consequences of actions undertaken in his name. Experience shows that if these are separated, trouble always follows.

Leadership

First, then, let us examine leadership. Leadership is a feature of the moral component of an army's fighting power – that is, the motivation of a force, or why an army fights. It will be bound up with the spirit and motivation of the troops, their trust in the skill of their commander, and their own courage and experience. Leadership, in its pure sense, has been defined rather well by Field Marshal Montgomery as the will to dominate, together with the character which inspires confidence. A leader has got to learn to dominate the events which surround him; he must never allow these events to get the better of him. General Shan Hackett remarks on battle leadership in particular: 'Pressures in battle are high, and in battle, in consequence, the problems of leadership stand out in bold relief ... leadership [in] command means getting people to do things ... willingly.' The essential qualities of leadership, and of a leader, do not vary greatly in the doctrines of Western nations, nor do they vary much over time. In the British army, they are held to include courage, willpower, the ability to communicate ideas and beliefs, the human touch, professional expertise, loyalty – including the development of subordinates, and the willingness to accept responsibility. Some of these bear brief examination now.

The first quality of a leader, and inseparable from military leadership at any level, is courage – both physical and moral courage. War is supremely dangerous and competitive, as Clausewitz reminds us: 'Primarily the element in which the operations of war are carried out is danger; but which is the first in danger? Courage.' Therefore, the greatest moral strength in war is gained by those with the greatest courage. The general can never be, in J. F. C. Fuller's words, just 'a prompter in the wings, but a key actor in the drama. He must experience danger.' This is because: 'War is, or anyhow should be, an heroic undertaking; for without heroism it can be no more than an animal conflict.' Fuller goes on to say that:

> The personality of the general is indispensable. He is the head, he is the all, of an army. It was not before the Carthaginian soldiers that Rome trembled, but before Hannibal. It was not the Macedonian phalanx that penetrated to India, but Alexander. It was not the French Army which reached the Weser and the Inn, it was Turenne.

Marshal de Saxe, whom Napoleon studied, says that 'the first quality a General should possess is courage, without which all others are of little value'. If the general is brave, therefore, and seen to be brave, he will influence the troops. They will trust his decisions even if it means hardship. Shared experience, especially where it involves hardship, danger, and the loss of comrades can be a powerful bond that will engender deep feelings of mutual trust and affection. However, no amount of experience can instil courage, because it is an instinctive quality – more of which later – and one which different people have in different amounts. It is, moreover, a finite resource which continued exposure to danger will erode: it is easy for anyone to be brave for a short time, but for a leader, what is most wearing is that he must be brave *all the time*. He also needs a great reserve of moral courage to take the hard decisions that will result in death and mutilation. There is no doubt that Napoleon was physically brave – 'death overtakes the coward, but never the brave until his hour has come', he said, and examples of his courage will be cited from Arcola to Lutzen. Nor did he have any difficulty with decisions which would lead to the death of thousands. Indeed, he was almost indifferent to individual suffering: 'What are the deaths of a million men to me?' he is quoted as saying. It is astonishing that his troops forgave this: success was, perhaps, more important in those days than compassion.

The ability to impose his will on his subordinates and on the enemy is without doubt one of the great, indeed absolute, requirements of generalship, and something which marked Napoleon throughout his career. Sun Tzu says:

> When the general is weak and without authority; when his orders are not clear and distinct; when there are no fixed duties assigned to officers and men, and the ranks are formed in a slovenly, haphazard manner, the result is utter disorganisation ... the general is the bulwark of the state: if the bulwark be strong at all points, the state will be strong; if the bulwark is defective, the state will be weak.

A strong will may itself be a sub-set of courage, since it leads to the exploitation of chance, the calculation of risk, rapid and accurate decision-making and the acceptance of responsibility. Clausewitz says that the strong will limits 'the agonies of doubt and the perils of hesitation when the motives for action are inadequate'. It is, therefore, not merely insight and emotion, but a force which gives direction. Good health and physical fitness are the building blocks of willpower, and they are also the physical foundations of moral strength and authority. This is so because, unless the general is capable of standing physical hardship, he cannot share it, and unless he shares this with his command, he loses moral authority.

The lower down the ladder of command one goes, then generally, the more that command and leadership are synonymous. This correspondence of command and leadership results from two things: the primacy of the mission or task, and the lack of delegated authority. The primacy of the mission at low levels means that the whole team at company level is in close contact with the enemy throughout the duration of that mission, and the primary task of the commander is to show the physical and moral example required to accomplish that mission in the face of extreme danger. It also means that the team has neither the ability to plan and conduct simultaneously, nor the means to consider any problem beyond the range of the contact battle, because of the lack of ability to see or shoot beyond it. There comes a point therefore – somewhere around the level of battalion command – above which command ceases to be primarily leadership driven, and is balanced by the other two elements. That is not to say that leadership ever disappears as an essential attribute of command.

But if command and leadership are synonymous at lower levels, what distinguishes the sort of leadership required by a general? The first thing is the sort of moral courage already mentioned. It is worthy of note that modern assessments of moral courage and character are frequently bound up with views of *morality*. In this context, there is a distinct connection between professional competence or fitness to command, and social (frequently sexual) behaviour. This connection is fuelled by the activities of the modern media. No such connection existed in Napoleon's day and any attempt to draw it would have been regarded as insane: *mores*, or customary standards of behaviour, are historically and culturally specific. One can say that if such standards had been applied then, neither Wellington nor Nelson, two of the main actors in Napoleon's downfall, would have got very far. What *was* important in Napoleonic times, however, was honour.

Next, the general has the duty of fostering mutual trust and understanding among his subordinate commanders. This may well require him to take them into his confidence. This is counter to the need to deceive or mislead the enemy and, often, commanders are not good at striking the balance between the two.

The degree to which a general shows leadership in his character, as opposed to the degree to which it has been grown during his training, may well be significant. How instinctive is his ability to lead? Are leaders really born? Logic would seem to indicate that although leaders may indeed be grown from seed as it were, the instinctive or born leader will be the more successful, as his powers of leadership, being instinctive, are deeply ingrained and more likely to survive stress. But 'instinct' is a word frequently misused. One view of instinct is that of an irrational and compelling motivational force: in this view, every instinct is accompanied by an emotion. Some recent genetic research, however, argues that the Darwinian view that behaviour is determined by our genes, and can thus be predicted, may be true. This is still controversial, and subject to research, but interesting when applied to a subject like Napoleon. An inheritance-based model of behaviour postulates that no amount of environmental or social engineering, no amount of appealing to the better nature of the criminal, for example, can change human nature. Matt Ridley, for example, suggests that 'The notion that animal behaviour is in the genes once troubled biologists as much as it now troubles social scientists.' A person genetically disposed to violence will always be violent. That said, there is considerable variation in predisposition to violence over time, within any society, and this variation may be too great to be accounted for by gene-based evolution. However, according to such theories of gene-based evolution, instinct is a genetic endowment. In that case, someone like Napoleon was programmed by his genes to be a leader. He came of generations of military leaders: leadership was inescapable. Instinct may also, according to this model, compel men like Napoleon to succeed in competitive situations, of which war is the most extreme example. Thus, the born leader will instinctively lead in times of danger; the trained leader may not, because his inescapable genetic inheritance will compel him to do otherwise.

Environment may play a part in the role of instinctive behaviour because, as human society became more organized, more urban, and more 'civilized', instinct may have been repressed in the interests of an orderly and law-abiding society. Field Marshal Slim threw light on this when he said: 'A man becomes a gentleman only by overcoming his instincts.' But warfare is inherently uncivilized, disorderly, chaotic – and ultimately competitive. It is not unreasonable to suggest, therefore, that the martial instincts – be they aggressive or defensive – of anyone to whom warfare has become the norm, like Napoleon, will come to the fore. This goes for followership, or aggression, or self-preservation, as well as for leadership. In the case of Napoleon, not only did he come from a family in which generations of leadership were an accomplished fact but also, as time went on, these instincts were reinforced during more than twenty years of fighting – and fighting wars in which, both in the early years of the Revolution, and also in the later period when Napoleon himself rather than France had become the target of a united Europe, the penalties of failure would have been catastrophic.

Decision-Making

Next, let us turn to decision-making. Decision-making is, by definition, a cognitive process, whether conscious or unconscious. The conscious method is through process; the unconscious is intuitive. Some people are strong at one, and some at the other. Rarely are people good at both, and when forced to do the one they are least good at – usually when this requires an intuitive leap with little help at hand – problems ensue. This is probably what provoked Norman Dixon to remark, rather unfairly, that 'the apparent intellectual failings of some military commanders are due not to lack of intelligence but to their feelings'. Making a decision in war takes courage, perhaps above all else, and enough has already been said on that subject.

For a commander like Napoleon who, as will be seen, rarely consulted allies or clients, and who surrounded himself with mediocrities who stood in no danger of becoming rivals, decision-making was bound to be largely an individual, and therefore intuitive, process and for this reason must be explored. Norman Dixon suggested a model for this, in which information is received by the individual and dealt with on two levels by the brain: at the first level, the information is stored in the memory, and at the second level, it contributes directly to the decision-making process. Memory, in turn, then contributes to the decision-making process by suggesting goals, options, probabilities of success, and pay-offs. Before proceeding further, however, some examination of what intuition is and how it operates is required.

Intuition is, essentially, the ability to arrive at decisions or conclusions without explicit or conscious processes of reasoned thinking. In the military sphere, intuition is still regarded as important and its incidence can be defined as the sum of a person's (or a group's) intelligence and experience. It is particularly relevant in a senior commander faced with complex, challenging and fast-moving situations, in which there is no time for a formal analytical process of review. When correctly engaged, it counters the tendency of generals – and their staffs – to quest for certainty in what is an essentially uncertain environment. Intuition, because it engages the sub-conscious, works quickly, giving, as Clausewitz remarked, 'the quick recognition of a truth that the mind would ordinarily miss or would per-ceive only after long study and reflection'. It can be of particular value where a commander is faced with a mass of similar-seeming information, and the requirement to make a fast decision. In this respect it is the converse of staff processes. This is not to suggest that process should be excluded. It has a role: that of proving or disproving what the commander thinks intuitively; or of filling in detail in complex problems. Ideally, it should be done ahead of battle as the basis of a plan, and to establish the intentions of an enemy, the resources required, timelines, decision points and their conditions, control measures, and so on. In doing this, process performs the valuable function of minimizing risk – and thus gives a commander more freedom later when intuition will have to take over. John Masters, who served as both formation commander and staff officer in Burma during the Second World War, reflected on this very subject of the interaction of commander and staff, of intuition and process. Although he did not use the same language, he is clearly expressing a similar view, one which had been developed in war:

> Staff work . . . can be learned by civilians, for only a quick and accurate mind and a retentive memory are needed. A commander can do with less of these attributes, but he must add a quality easy to recognise but hard to define – a strength of character, a determination with no obstinacy in it . . . The higher he stands the more he needs, too, another quality which cannot be taught by any quick means but is either there, by a stroke of genetic chance, or, more usually, is deposited cell by cell in the subconscious during the long years of study and practice. It is this quality that tells a commander, instantly and without cerebration, whether a plan is inherently sound or unsound. It is this that enables him to receive the advice of specialists and experts, and reach the proper decision.

This is the general as virtuoso, not simply as competent professional: the possessor of what in Napoleonic times would have been called genius.

If military selection has worked, and patronage has not exerted too powerful an influence, then a commander may often be the person with the greatest experience and, if not the highest intelligence in his command, then at least he may be in the 1st XI. His intuition should, therefore, be highly developed and can be supplemented by that of a team of senior advisers or subordinates, such as constitutes the tactical HQ of a modern formation. Norman Dixon suggests that: 'Given the hazards which attend attempts to make a rational decision, it might be thought that decisions arrived at jointly ... would have rather more chance of being sound.' There are dangers here, however. First, group decision-making encourages a diffusion of responsibility. In a military organization, and especially one in wartime, responsibility lies with the chain of command and not with the staff, as has already been pointed out. Second, although the engagement of a group might safeguard against an irrational decision by a commander whose intuitive powers have been diminished by outside pressures such as stress, boredom or emotional reactions, or by using templated solutions to problems on the basis of experience, the hierarchical nature of military structures can induce conformity in subordinates. Strong moral courage is often needed to challenge a superior, especially one who may hold the key to an officer's or soldier's future career progression. Napoleon seems to have recognized the dangers in group decision-making. He reserved this to himself, and himself alone, from the beginning of his military life – and he never departed from it.

One noteworthy aspect of generals with well-developed intuition is that their timing is excellent, as is their ability to recognize a change in the situation. Moreover, those who are not intuitive will be more likely, therefore, to suffer cognitive dissonance: that is, the inability to cope with information, knowledge or beliefs which conflict with a decision already made and thus recognize that a situation has changed, that a plan or course of action may no longer be valid. This sort of decision-making in changing circumstances, and the flow of information required to support it, raises the question of which position will best enable the general in battle to do the three essential things that a general must do to properly exercise his command: find out what is going on, communicate his intentions to his subordinates, and keep in contact with the staff so that they can solve problems. This question of where to place himself is a familiar one to any general, faced with the choice of whether to command forward, or to stay back, for command and control in a war is a question of communications in relation to time, so that decisions can be made that will control the course of events.

Throughout the execution of an operation, therefore, the general must constantly be in a position to receive the best available information, review the situation, and make fresh estimates in the light of events, changing the plan as required – since, as any soldier knows, no plan survives contact with the enemy intact. Clarity of thought, decision and action are essential – and in war-fighting, so is speed. Only thus will risks be calculated and the initiative be maintained. The general's intuitive process will be continuous, and the experienced general will, in a sense, feed it by positioning himself at the right place – and thereby develop an intuitive sense of where to be, when, so completing the circle. The dilemma is, should the general come forward to the troops to share the dangers and be at the decisive point? Or should he stand back at a place where information flow converges? Much, of course, depends on the level at which command is being exercised, but it was a particular issue in the days before radio, telephone or telegraph, when a general's ability to exercise command was limited to what he could see, or what could be brought to him by horsemen. In general terms, therefore, the nearer the front he was, the less the general could command. Given the ranges of weapons and the size of forces engaged, this was a limitation – but not a serious one at this point. Only when armies reached the size of those engaged from about 1806 onwards did this factor start to come into play.

Control and Management

Next, a very brief word on control. In the exercise of command, this is generally delegated to the staff, which plays a complementary role to the commander. Napoleon needed a good staff well employed, and took pains to assemble it – if not to develop and train it. Napoleon also understood clearly, and expected his subordinates also to understand, that the staff has no command responsibility – although it has duties. It has no responsibilities because staff officers (unless specified by the general) have no powers of decision or command: they implement previously agreed control measures, such as timings, routes, boundaries, fire-control measures and so on, in order to carry out the general's plan. The plan belongs to the general – not the staff. He will have led its development; he must lead its implementation. Therefore the general alone holds responsibility, and the staff must be absolutely clear on which decisions must be referred to him, and him alone; on which decisions can be taken by subordinates; on which must be referred to a superior authority; and on which are really decisions relating to control measures and can be taken by the appropriate staff officer. If generals do not obey this philosophy, then the personal factor in command is lost, and the staff system takes over. This is not to say that staff action should be regarded as somehow unsavoury. In the race to generate superior tempo, discussed elsewhere, it is the general who will contribute to success by a timely decision, and the staff which will implement that decision. The competition with the enemy can only be won by the correct engagement of both, especially in the preparation of a major campaign. Sun Tzu remarked on this, saying that:

> The General who wins a battle makes many calculations in his temple before the battle is fought. The general who loses a battle makes but few calculations beforehand. Thus do calculations lead to victory.

The staff will also, by churning through the many tedious but necessary calculations required to control an army, reduce the many uncertainties facing a commander's decision-making process. This is bound up with the general's function as manager of men and materiel, much of which, because of its complexity, has to be delegated to the staff. A management system there must be, and one that encompasses all the needs of an army: personnel management and documentation, training, intelligence gathering and processing, food supply, sanitation and drinking water, medical care, the maintenance of vehicles, weapons, animals, military justice and discipline, to name but a few. This will be explored further in Chapter VII.

The staff also gives the general time for reflection, so that he need not worry about minutiae. Frederick the Great, whom Napoleon greatly admired, wisely asked 'What is the good of experience if you do not reflect?' To return to the earlier discussion about the role of intuition, an illustration of how this interacts with the calculations of the staff may be useful. The American Civil War General Nathan Bedford Forrest believed that the core of success for a general, whether on the battlefield, campaign, or in strategic contests, lay in the maxim 'Get there first with the most'. By this he meant that it was necessary to manoeuvre so as to be in a position of advantage, from which force could be threatened or applied. The implicit question here is: Where is *there*? Determining the answer lies partly in the situational awareness and calculations of the staff, and partly in the general's intuition – plus the need to distract, deceive or dislocate* the enemy while getting there. Alternatively, or in addition, an enemy can be faced with an insoluble dilemma, such as that posed to Napoleon's lieutenants in Spain by the allied use of both regular forces and irregulars.

Conclusions

The weaker or more incompetent an enemy, the easier the business of generalship becomes; the converse is also true. Napoleon's successes show this to a marked degree: he easily crushed or overawed Spain, Denmark, the Netherlands, Switzerland and the smaller German and Italian states. He fared less well with the big players like Austria, Russia and the British Empire. When he did succeed, he did so at the cost of a great deal of blood and treasure. That he succeeded at all is due to the relative incompetence of the generals opposed to him, and the amazing inability of his opponents to analyse his system of strategic, operational and tactical manoeuvre. Even Wellington, who showed in the campaign of Vitoria that he had understood Napoleon's concepts, was caught out in 1815 by his expectation that Napoleon would try to cut him off from the sea, when to do so would push him and Blücher closer together. All evidence must have suggested that Napoleon would do the exact opposite – try to divide the allied armies in order to defeat them piecemeal.

Whole books can – indeed have – been written on the subject of generalship and the above is only a glancing blow at the target, but one that will be supplemented in the various chapters that follow. Command for a modern general is complicated beyond its counterpart in Napoleon's day,

---

* In military terms, dislocation is achieved through security and active deception, and makes an enemy direct his forces to a place of our choosing, rather than his.

and beyond the requirements of so-called conventional war. In a modern theatre of operations, the general may be dealing with war-fighting, counter-insurgency, counter-terrorism, peace-keeping, humanitarian relief, and the reform of local institutions simultaneously, within the same battle-space. Military factors may well be less important than economics, politics, or social needs, and the successful completion of one part of the campaign may obstruct the execution of its later stages. Any British officer involved in rebuilding the infrastructure of the former Yugoslavia, or Afghanistan, or Iraq after it had been comprehensively bombed by our own and our allies' air forces, or anyone involved in trying to re-raise the Iraqi army after its disbandment, will recognize this truth immediately. The legal and media factors of modern war also mean that a fourth essential function must be added to the modern general's skills. As well as finding out what is going on, communicating with his staff to solve problems, and communicating his intentions to his subordinates, he must also be prepared to explain his actions to his own people, to the enemy, and to the uncommitted.

It might be argued that because of the sort of complexity encountered in modern conflict, intuitive decision-making in the Napoleonic mode is not possible: that the general is faced with so many facets of a campaign, that he will be forced to rely on some formal process of evaluation in order to be able to make rational decisions. I believe, however, that the converse is true, especially if one accepts the contention that war and conflict are not rational. The general who surrenders himself wholly to process, or who allows himself to be deluged by the massive amounts of data available from modern command systems, and who abandons intuition, becomes the prisoner of that process and predictability. Defeating an agile insurgent or terrorist, or dealing with a complex dispute in a peace support operation, requires a clear head and the ability to see the essentials. At the same time, the general must remain open to information that contradicts received opinion, and encourage a questioning ethos among the staff.

Moreover, to deny the place of instinctive leadership or of intuitive decision-making is to rely wholly on technology and process – or pure reasoning. To do this in a competitive activity like war, where survival is at stake, is not only against nature, but dangerous. Instincts and intuitive judgements will always intrude on pure reasoning, and it is this that produces, among other things, unpredictability. It also produces the willingness to take risk, based on partial information, in the interests of out-manoeuvring an enemy in the uncertain field of conflict. Thus, in any contest between two opponents, one of whom relies heavily on process and technology, and one who relies on human ingenuity, the latter is more likely to triumph if all other things are equal.

This is the dynamic now being played out in Iraq and Afghanistan – but which Napoleon would have recognized from the experience of the Spanish guerrilla war. In Spain, as in any insurgent war, or any conflict in which there is a weaker side confronting a more powerful adversary, the result will be what has now become known as 'asymmetric' war. But fundamentally, what is often called insurgent, or guerrilla, warfare is a form of fighting that can be employed by any belligerent in any type of war; all warfare is, to a great extent, asymmetric, as each side seeks to pit its strengths against an opponent's weaknesses. The Napoleonic battle system is quite plainly in that tradition. As Professor Sir Lawrence Freedman has said:

> Adversaries will pick alternative strategies reflecting those the weak have consistently adopted against the strong: concentrating on imposing pain rather than winning battles; gaining time rather than moving to closure; targeting the enemy's domestic political base as much as his forward military capabilities; relying on his intolerance of casualties and his weaker stake in the resolution of the conflict.

That is not to say that some of these complications – especially counter-insurgency and dealing with the needs of the civilian population in con-quered territory – were not apparent in Napoleon's day: they were. They were dealt with, however, at a generally higher level than now, and they were managed without the immediacy of modern communications and the glare of the media. When we assess Napoleon as a general, then, it is important to stress once again that we do so according to the standards and expectations of *his* time – not ours.

And what of leadership? The modern general's area of responsibility may be huge, the troops dispersed and co-located with non-military bodies. They are likely to come from more than one nation, and more than one culture. In such a situation, the first challenge of leadership is to gain the trust, confidence and respect of the troops, and instil discipline. The results of a failure to instil discipline have been seen in Iraq in episodes such as Abu Gharayb and Haditha. Morale must be maintained, whether in the head-quarters or in remote detachments. Communication by the general remains, as ever, vital. The considerations of multi-nationality may require a general to be something of a diplomat; he will not have Napoleon's degree of dominance over his allies and their military contingents. National caveats, and different military cultures and political considerations at home will all bear on the mission; these factors test professional competence as much as any challenge in any major war in history. But these challenges, although considerable, are no different in kind in Iraq or Afghanistan than anything that faced Napoleon on the battlefield. Nor is courage at any less of a premium: in physical terms, battle is battle, and it is no easier to face enemy fire in Afghanistan than it was at Austerlitz or Waterloo. In some cases it can be harder, for modern insurgents – especially Islamic ones – do not deal with captives on the basis of Western values, or even of those practices which held good before the Geneva Conventions were framed. Surrender is, therefore, not an option, as it was to Napoleon and his contemporaries in most cases – the Spanish guerrillas and Russian Cossacks being noted exceptions. In irregular warfare, whether in Europe in 1812, or in Iraq and Afghanstan today, every fight tends to be a fight to the finish. In terms of moral courage, the sorts of decisions facing a general have not diminished. There is little or nothing, therefore, that changes the contention that the born leader, able instinctively to act in times of danger, is still needed.

II

Napoleon as Strategist

Strategy in the Napoleonic Age

Modern theories tend to separate strategy in its broadest sense – grand strategy as it is called – from military strategy. The former can be defined very simply as the attainment of national or alliance objectives using all such ways and means as are available, appropriate and legal. It is about a state's external political objectives, its relations with other powers, and the coupling of security issues with the organization of the state in all its facets, to ensure that its objectives can be met either through its own exertions or else through alliance. The latter is the implementation, in the light of available resources, of the military aspects of a political decision to make war. Field Marshal Alanbrooke defined it thus:

> to determine the aim, which should be political: to derive from that aim a series of military objectives to be achieved: to assess these objectives as to the military requirements they create, and the pre-conditions which the achievement of each is likely to necessitate: to measure available and potential resources against the requirements and to chart from this process a coherent pattern of priorities and a rational course of action.

But there is a circular aspect to this, since although the decision to make war is a political one, no government will take such a course without having the means to do so. Military strategy is, therefore, as Professor John Childs points out, a fundamental component in reaching the decision to go to war. Soldiers such as Turenne, Condé and Vauban informed the political and decision-making of Louis XIV, alongside his civilian ministers. By 1805, Napoleon combined the functions of head of state with those of supreme warlord, as had, for example, William III of England and Tsar Alexander I of Russia. It is difficult, therefore, to be too rigid with these modern definitions. Moreover, the world is a more complex place now: the industrial and technological revolutions of the nineteenth and twentieth centuries have broadened both the bases of war and the means of conducting it. However, it is true to say that by 1805, the notion of strategy was at least recognizably modern. As early as 1777, Joly de Maizeroy had defined it in his *Théories de la Guerre* thus:

Strategy ... combines time, places, means, various interests and considers all
... The former [i.e. tactics] reduces easily to firm rules, because it is entirely
geometrical like fortification; the latter [i.e. strategy] appears very much less
susceptible of it, because it is related to an infinity of circumstances, physical,
political and moral, which are never the same and which pertain entirely to
genius.

The notion of strategic objectives being achieved through means as
diverse as diplomacy, economic power, information warfare and military
power is not too far from this line of thought. Moreover, the requirements
of a successful strategic concept have not changed, and can be held to
include popular will and support; political resolve, nationally and collec-
tively; alliance or coalition unity of command and effort where this is
applicable; timely and appropriate force generation and deployment; a
secure base of operations; and, when operating away from home, the support, or at least compliance, of the local population and authorities.

The Archduke Charles distinguished military strategy and tactics by
saying that:

Strategy is the science of war: it produces the overall plans and it assumes
responsibility for the general course of military enterprises. It is, strictly, the
science of the commander-in-chief. Tactics is the art of war: it teaches the way
in which major military projects should be put into execution. Every formation
commander must possess this art.

Napoleon, like Carnot, cemented this separation of strategy from mere
grand tactics by exploiting the potential of mass armies, and by altering the
eighteenth-century notions of the relationship between movement and
firepower. Clausewitz, scarred as he was by the experience of Napoleonic
war, stressed the importance of the moral qualities of a nation and the
relationship between government, people and army. Even so, one must
continue to distinguish those areas in which Napoleonic notions of strategy
differ from those of today because of the absence of two factors: the full
impact of the Industrial Revolution, and the provision of military power in
peacetime as part of national political and economic systems. Some caution
is needed, however, because as Jomini pointed out in his work *The Art of
War*, technology may change, but principles seldom do. This is because of
the nature of war as competition, and because of the enduring nature of the
human condition already discussed:

new inventions ... seem to threaten a great revolution in army organisation,
armament and tactics. Strategy alone will remain unaltered, with its principles

Europe Under Napoleon, 1810

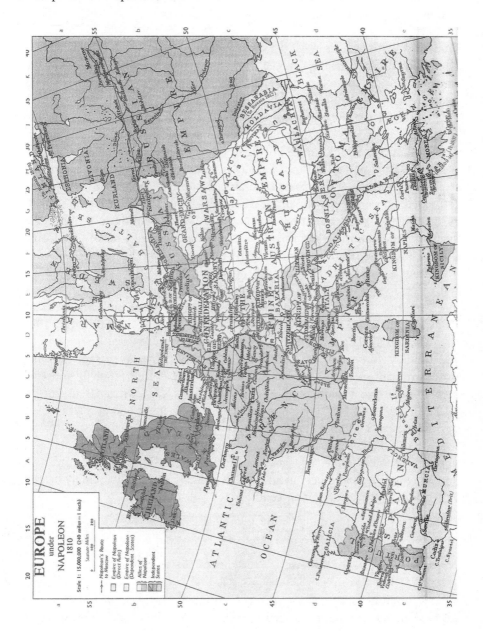

Source: Muir's Historical Atlas, 1974.

the same as under the Scipios ... since they are independent of the nature of arms.

One must further distinguish the sort of strategy practised by Napoleon, his allies and some of his opponents, from that of his implacable enemies the English. Britain, because of its worldwide empire, economic base, and strategic reach – through naval power – was arguably the only major power able to conduct strategy through means other than military power. In 1813 alone, Britain was able to subsidize her allies in Europe to the tune of almost £7.5 million: £2.486 million to Portugal, £1.335 million to Sweden, £1 million to Russia, £700,000 to Austria, £666,000 to Prussia, £877,000 to Spain and £440,000 to Sicily. The power of financial subsidy should not be under-estimated: it was the vast financial resources of the British Empire, as much as anything, which underpinned the allied will to continue the struggle against Napoleon. This, combined with its naval power, more than com-pensated for the relatively small size of Britain's army during the period.

Although Napoleon had demonstrated, as early as the beginning of the Italian campaign in 1796, that he had an excellent grasp of French strategy and its requirements, he was not in this position. Despite building excellent ships, his navy was never able to challenge the British – certainly not after the defeat of Trafalgar. On land, Revolutionary and Imperial France had to use military force, not in addition to the other instruments of national power, but in order to access them. Military power for Napoleon must be seen therefore *as* diplomacy, not merely in the Clausewitzian sense of an addition to it. As John Terraine remarked: 'The huge energy of the man permeated everything: its particular outlet was war, its sanction, victory.' So it seemed during the years of victory in Europe, from Marengo in 1800, to Ulm and Austerlitz in 1805, Jena in 1806, Friedland in 1807, Spain in 1808, and Wagram in 1809. Every great power in Europe was convincingly beaten in battle, whether alone or in coalition.

Napoleon's Strategic System

After 1791, war as the export of revolutionary ideology, as much as for expansion, was inevitable for any French regime. The reckless optimism of 1792 resulting from the ideals of Liberty, Equality and Fraternity was bound to cause upheavals and struggles against the old order throughout Europe, and the agency of this upheaval was the zeal and energy of the French people. Clausewitz remarked on this by saying that

NAPOLEON AS STRATEGIST   23

Clearly the tremendous effects of the French Revolution abroad were caused not so much by new military methods and concepts as by radical changes in policies and administration, by the character of government, altered conditions of the French people, and the like.

Napoleon himself said at the time of the Peace of Amiens: 'Between old monarchies and a young republic the spirit of hostility must always exist. In the present state of affairs, every peace treaty means no more than a brief armistice.' This, despite the fact that he was, as is usual with dictators, invariably claiming to be pursuing peace. On St Helena he portrayed this in grossly propagandist terms, claiming to be the father of a united Europe, but in fact, the only peace to which Napoleonic strategy was aimed was a peace dictated wholly and solely by the conqueror.

The Committee of Public Safety, the Directory, and then Napoleon himself, all built up barriers of territory beyond the so-called 'natural' frontiers of France, in order to ensure the security of the homeland and the Revolution. Alan Forrest remarks that as early as 1797, the whole French economy was geared to war, and domestic ambitions were predicated on military success. In time, French power was pushed out to the Oder, the Vistula, Warsaw, Madrid, Naples, and Moscow. By 1807, the original 83 *départements* of France had increased to 130. Thus, wars which began to safeguard the Revolution went on to be the means of exporting it, and later of consolidating the Napoleonic Empire and the legitimacy of its ruler. Revolutionary zeal was, during this process, almost inevitably replaced by more recognizable forms of diplomacy and power projection. Competition for trade and colonies overseas emphasized this process.

Wars were followed by treaties, or dynastic marriage, or the imposition of client rulers, but Napoleon was never able to convert former enemies into allies, except in the case of small, wholly dependent states such as Denmark and Saxony. Treaties of alliance produced subjects, like the Confederation of the Rhine or Holland, or restive satellites like Prussia. All were tolerated only as a source of men, money and materiel for further wars prompted by hatred of the only enemy never to submit to French power: England. By 1811, Napoleon was aiming not just at a stable limit to his empire in Europe through peace with Britain, but total domination of the world: his empire would have no limits. The hostility of the old monarchies, and especially of Britain, forced him to keep expanding until no opponents were left. In 1811 he remarked that 'in five years, I shall be master of the world: there only remains Russia, but I shall crush her.' Napoleon and his system existed only through greater and greater success, as the means to a favourable and lasting settlement; that is, one that saw Napoleon and his empire in control of the international system.

However, once the ideas of the French Revolution had taken hold in conquered territory, there was no guarantee that they could be controlled. One by-product was the growth of nationalism in Germany, Italy and Poland, which from 1812 onwards was to be part of Napoleon's undoing. His empire was, it seems, built on very shaky foundations.

Whenever war appeared likely – and in most cases Napoleon was attacked by others, albeit as a result of gross provocation – Napoleon would at once commence detailed research and planning, studying the relevant geography, history, climate and culture. Next would come detailed calculations in order to minimize chance and risk. Sun Tzu would have approved greatly of his dictum that 'Military science consists in calculating all the chances accurately in the first place, and then giving accident exactly, almost mathematically, its place'. Once hostilities existed between France and another power, Napoleon's foremost strategic objective was to destroy the enemy's army in battle, and thus break his opponent's will to resist. He would use the shortest and most brutal ways and means available to this end, and all else was secondary. Berthèzne quotes him as saying: 'I see only one thing, namely the enemy's main body. I try to crush it, confident that secondary matters will then settle themselves.' In this, he is clearly following the precepts of one of his heroes, Frederick the Great, in that 'it is battles that decide the fate of a state'. In his *Maximes* he writes of 'a careful balancing of means and results': a tailoring of all available military and political power to the requirements of his objective, with no distraction from the business of destroying the enemies' means to resist. Warfare for Napoleon had, therefore, to be a strategic offensive, in order to gain and maintain the initiative: 'Make war offensively,' he wrote. 'It is the sole means to become a great captain.'

The instrument of Napoleonic strategy was therefore the army. Even as late as 1813 it was in the general organization of his army and of his staff that Napoleon enjoyed his greatest advantage over his opponents. Building on previous experimental organizations employed in particular by Marshal de Saxe, the French army had instituted an all-arms divisional structure in 1796, and in 1804, his armies swollen by conscription, Napoleon created corps, each of up to five divisions. At that time there were ten of these corps, including the Guard, the reserve, and the cavalry. By 1812, there were 17, including allies. Each corps was in effect a miniature army organized to the task and the assessed abilities of its commander, normally a marshal. A corps would contain varying quantities of infantry, cavalry, artillery, engineers and bridging, with integral supply and medical units. The size of the corps could vary enormously, sometimes amounting to between one third and one half of the army. This will be discussed further when Napoleon's mastery of the operational art is examined.

Conscription was the means of generating the strategic mass that would carry out this work of destruction. Conscription began as a one-off act of necessity in the *levée en masse* of August 1793. From its inception as an annual process in 1799 until April 1815 there were 32 levies on native-born Frenchmen, as a result of which around two million men passed through the ranks of the army. This is without the clients and allies discussed in a separate chapter. No other policy intruded the Napoleonic state so force-fully into the lives of people or the fabric of states, for it was imposed throughout the Empire and the client states during the entire period of Napoleonic rule. Certainly, no other policy engendered so much hatred. It was, without doubt, a central issue of the Napoleonic strategic system, and as such, a continuous problem for mayors and heads of departments who were obliged to enforce it – not to mention a devastating imposition for the hundreds of thousands – if not millions – of families touched by it. Not surprisingly, the scale of avoidance – either legally through buying sub-stitutes, or illegally through desertion – was massive, especially in the annexed territories, and the policy was only maintained through heavy-handed enforcement. Napoleon himself had no interest in people's opinions or feelings: he was merely concerned to see that the system worked smoothly.

To achieve the concert of an army of ten corps or more, to direct and control such an army, to frame and transmit orders, and to gather intelli-gence and provide supplies, required an apparatus of command and control more advanced than anything previously attempted. Here was a classic demonstration of the correct relationship between doctrine and organiza-tion: Napoleon had decided what kind of wars he was going to fight; his organization would reflect that style of fighting. Napoleon was, as both Emperor and Commander in Chief, responsible to no one, called no councils of war and was able, on the basis of a general plan of operations, to direct campaigns as well as to issue orders for specific engagements. His headquarters was, therefore, geared entirely to Napoleon personally – not to the commander, regardless of who that might be.

Orders were issued through the staff which, by 1805, was fully organized and headed by Berthier, the Army Chief of Staff. No document left the headquarters nor was received by it unless it was properly logged. Its doings were recorded scrupulously in its war diaries and records of correspon-dence. Every corps had to submit a daily situation report, supplemented by the reports of Napoleon's own aides – usually general officers. In June 1813, for example, Napoleon instructed Lebrun to report to him on Oudinot's corps:

You will report to me on the status of his infantry, artillery, train, magazines and hospitals and also on his intelligence gathering in his corps area. In a word, you will report anything that could be of interest to me.

The problem, of course, was that the staff had no devolved responsibility, since everything was decided by Napoleon. He failed to develop his staff officers, just as he failed to develop his subordinate commanders, of which more will be said in the chapter dealing with Napoleon's personal qualities and character as a general. He was quite explicit about this, writing after Dresden: 'In my situation, no plan is acceptable in which I am not personally at the centre.'

The headquarters itself consisted of three principal branches. First, *le petit quartier général*, or Napoleon's personal headquarters. This can approximately be related to a modern tactical command centre, with the proviso that this one included many senior officers and was where Napoleon conducted his own planning. It contained three elements: the Statistical Bureau, responsible for strategic intelligence through agents, spies and missions abroad; the Secretariat or the Emperor's cabinet; and the Survey Department, responsible for providing Napoleon with the best available maps. Next came *le quartier général du major-général* – the General Staff under Berthier, responsible for tactical intelligence, the issue of orders, the provision of information on the state of the army, and all other matters of routine staff work. In many ways it was a larger replica of Napoleon's own personal headquarters. Berthier had three assistants: his own chief of staff who oversaw the processing of staff work and internal coordination; the Quartermaster of the army, responsible for camps, cantonments and marches; and the Director of the Topographical Department. Third, there was *le quartier general de l'intendant,* the Administrative Bureau or headquarters of the Quartermaster General, responsible for all matters of supply, and the hospitals and medical services. Its functions will be discussed in Chapter VII. In addition, there were the staffs of the commanders of the Artillery, Engineers, Military Police, and the Topographical Bureau. Below these came corps staffs which, although smaller, mirrored the functions of the army staff. This system of staff organization is still the basis of most army staffs today, and indeed is still described as the 'Napoleonic' model. However, there was then no staff college, and no system of supplying trained officers for the staff. In addition, there were arrangements for Napoleon's travel in close proximity to the enemy, which are outlined in Chapter V.

Early Essays

Let us see how well this strategic approach stood up. In Italy, Napoleon had, without doubt, shown a sound understanding of French strategic require-ments on the continental land mass of Europe. But what of matters more widely? The Revolutionary and Napoleonic Wars rapidly developed, like the Seven Years War, into a global conflict. Early in his career, Napoleon recognized that Britain was an irreconcilable enemy, and that a war between France and Britain would be a war of survival: only one of these two opponents would survive intact. As early as February 1798, he wrote to the Directory outlining three possible courses of action: make peace (difficult but not impossible given the right terms); invade (impracticable given the lack of French sea power); or adopt an indirect approach by threatening the chief instrument of British power – trade with the East. This, like much of what Napoleon did, had been in the minds of successive French adminis-trations for 50 years; it could be done, Napoleon believed, by dominating the trade routes through the Levant and possibly by restoring commu-nications with Tippoo Sahib, the French client in Mysore. By 1798 there was also the added impetus of replacing lost French colonies in the West Indies. On paper, such a strategy looked well and led to the expedition to Egypt, Lebanon and Syria. On land, Napoleon certainly made a good start once his forces had arrived in Egypt; however, he over-extended himself with the expedition to Acre. He was never able to make good his losses in men and materiel from the time of the battle of the Nile onwards, since strategic communications with France were severed by British naval power. Despite having realized that this naval power would frustrate any direct challenge to England through invasion, the fact that this same naval power, from its bases in the Mediterranean, would likewise frustrate his schemes in the East, seems to have been missed in his calculations. It was a lesson he did not forget.

Once it became clear that the expedition to the East was unlikely to succeed, Napoleon did what he was to do again in the future: he abandoned the army and rushed home to consolidate his position. One has to admire his nerve; if it had been the unique conditions of post-revolutionary France that had allowed Napoleon to become a general in the first place, it must be said that only those same conditions made it possible for him to escape disgrace and probably execution after this episode. Instead, he was able to exploit the chaotic situation and advance himself to First Consul and then to Emperor, combining in himself the powers of military commander and head of state. Thereafter, as we have already seen, French power was dominant on the continent of Europe. But the inexorable hostility of one inveterate foe, the English, caused him to make his first and greatest strategic miscalculation.

The Continental System

The Continental System, which came to its fullness under Napoleon, had begun as early as 1793. That it developed as it did, however, was the result of Napoleon's inability to carry through the invasion and conquest of Britain. After this, the system was really the only method for him to attack the British. In the aftermath of the collapse of the Peace of Amiens, French client states and allies, such as Spain and Naples, were obliged to adopt the embryonic system, and so too was Prussia after the formation of the Franco-Prussian alliance in February 1806. The closure of the Prussian coast to British trade brought in a state of war with Britain and a blockade of Prussian ports by the Royal Navy in April and May 1806. Furthermore, the articles which established the Confederation of the Rhine in July 1806 forbade all states in the confederation from trading with Britain.

It was not until alliance with Prussia had turned into war, and then war into conquest, that the Continental System was codified in the Berlin Decrees. In these decrees, which had monumental consequences for the Napoleonic state and its clients, Napoleon laid down the doctrine that it was the failure completely to exclude English influence which had led to the continuation of war since, as Napoleon wrote to the Emperor of Austria after his victory at Marengo in June 1800:

> The recent campaign is sufficient proof that it is not France which threatens the balance of power. Every day shows it is England – England, who has so monopolized world commerce and the empire of the seas that she can withstand single-handed the united fleets of Russia, Denmark, Sweden, France, Spain and Holland.

And again later:

> a great number of the Cabinets of Europe are sooner or later influenced by England: and without a solid peace with that Power, our people cannot enjoy the benefits which are ... the unique object of our life.

To bring about this solid peace, Napoleon proposed putting the British Isles in a state of exclusion. He was quite clear that in doing so, he was accepting war to the end: either Britain would be brought down or his empire would be destroyed – there was no possibility of compromise – and in this light, the attitudes of both the British government and Napoleon towards the Congress of Prague in 1813 and the Frankfurt proposals of 1814 are completely understandable. Napoleon knew well that the British national debt was enormous: by 1812 it had reached £500 million, and by comparison, it did not approach the same figure again until the First World War. Only the export trade could service this kind of debt and thus maintain Britain's ability to sustain war.

The important articles of the Berlin Decrees were first, that the British Isles were placed in a state of blockade; second, that all commerce and all correspondence were interdicted; and third, in Article 5, that all merchandise belonging to Britain, or coming from its factories and from its colonies, was forbidden. Article 10 stated that the decree would be communicated to Spain, Naples, Holland, Etruria and the other French allies and, although this was not stated, they would be obliged to consent to it. To underscore this last message, Napoleon immediately ordered Marshal Mortier to occupy the Hanseatic ports of Hamburg, Bremen and Lübeck, and to impose a land blockade on the estuaries of the Elbe and Weser rivers.

The years 1806 to 1812 were years of enormous economic strain for all the belligerent powers, and all Napoleon's diplomatic and military efforts were directed towards perfecting the system. The client states and allies, which as well as those already mentioned included the Confederation of the Rhine, the Grand Duchy of Warsaw and Denmark, had no choice but to accept the system; other states were coerced into it by military defeat. By the time of the invasion of Russia, only Turkey, Sicily and Portugal were officially outside it. Not that the client states or reluctant allies were at all in favour of the system – quite the reverse. Louis Bonaparte, King of Holland, for example, tried to gain exemption from it, but received the reply that:

> it is the only way to strike at England, and to force her to make peace. Without doubt it will cause harm to Holland and France: but it is worth while to suffer for a time and to have an advantageous peace.

Only two months later, however, Napoleon was again writing to Louis: 'I am informed that commerce between Holland and England has never been more active.'

Where the system worked, and Napoleon kept out British trade, Europe suffered, for the Continental System was not a blockade of Great Britain by France: the French navy was incapable of attempting this. Nor was it a blockade of the French Empire by Britain, for the British government freely issued licences for trading with Europe. The Continental System was a blockade of the French Empire by itself.

The Milan Decrees in 1807 further extended the system by increasing the pressure on neutral nations – but incidentally did little harm to Britain. This

decree stated that any ship of any nation which submitted to search by the
Royal Navy, or which paid any British dues, would be seized on entering a
French port. The decrees, followed by the further decrees of St Cloud and
Trianon in 1810, created the commercial borders of the French Empire,
keeping British goods out, but with the intention of letting French industry
and commerce fill the gap. This completely Franco-centric system even went
so far as to exclude manufactured goods from industrial areas within the
Empire when they competed with French manufacturers. Michael Broers
cites the example of the Grand Duchy of Berg, in which the resulting job
losses were dramatic: some 10,000 by 1810 – a contributing factor to the
revolts which broke out in the Confederation of the Rhine in January 1813.

. The Continental System really only worked where the French dominated
all the coasts. France and Italy were relatively secure, but Spain, Portugal,
Holland, Belgium and the Baltic were never properly committed. This state
of affairs was largely behind the incorporation of Holland into France in
1810, followed by northern Hanover and part of Westphalia in 1811. Even so
it almost worked, albeit indirectly, as America was more closely embroiled
in the affairs of Europe. But the extension of the system by the annexation
of the north-German littoral was bound to offend the Tsar, who was already
on bad terms with Napoleon over the matter of the proposed marriage of
the Grand Duchess Anna. The annexed territory included the Baltic port of
Lübeck, but also included the possessions of the Duke of Oldenburg, a
cousin of the Tsar, which had been guaranteed by the Franco-Russian
Treaty of Tilsit. Thus the annexations, aimed directly at control of the
Baltic, directly threatened Russian interests and violated treaty obligations.

Tsar Alexander had, as a result of the Treaty of Tilsit, joined the Continental System, but he had never excluded neutral shipping, which of
course carried British trade. At Leipzig fair in 1810, for example, 700 wagon-
loads of British goods were up for sale, all of which had come in through
Russia. In the same year, 1,200 ships under neutral flags discharged British
goods in Russian ports. Russia, in need of the money which customs dues
provided, was not about to end this situation. Tilsit had also bound the Tsar
to force Sweden to join the system and the Tsar had done so, by war. In
1809, the Swedes had joined the system and had forfeited Finland to the
Tsar. But after this war, the Swedes had continued to trade freely with
Britain and indeed, the more closely Napoleon controlled the north-
German coast and Denmark, the more the Swedes benefited from British
trade, both in Sweden proper and in Pomerania. This arrangement continued to prosper, despite a formal state of war between Sweden and Britain,
and despite the election of Bernadotte as Crown Prince of Sweden in 1810.
Indeed, Napoleon, by neither encouraging nor forbidding Bernadotte to

accept the title, seems to have accelerated Bernadotte's assimilation into Swedish life and the development of close relations between the Tsar and the Crown Prince.

Thus, the Continental System, perhaps because it was never in operation for long, succeeded only in setting most of Europe against Napoleon. But given that only one-third of Britain's trade was with Europe, while two-thirds was with the rest of the world, it was the indirect effect of the system which most nearly brought disaster to Britain, and which was to bring her into conflict with America.

In response to the Continental System, the British tried to do two things: first, to keep open the seas so that any neutral nation, especially America, could trade with them. This the Royal Navy generally succeeded in doing, despite the best efforts of French privateers – French privateers took 500 British ships per year on average between 1793 and 1815, while by 1811, some 4,000 former French ships flew the British flag. Second, they aimed to penalize any neutral state which adhered to the system. The mechanism for achieving the latter was the Orders-in-Council, issued in response to the Berlin Decrees from January 1807. The first order stated that:

> No vessel shall be permitted to trade from one port to another, both of which ports shall belong to or be in the possession of France or her allies, or shall be so far under their control, as that British vessels may not freely trade thereat.

Subsequent orders and the system of licences increased the pressure on both neutrals and states within the Continental System to defy Napoleon, and thus British goods continued to reach Europe in neutral ships, which were further encouraged by relaxation of the British navigation acts. As time went on, the licence system became a vital measure for keeping Wellington's Peninsular Army fed, chiefly on American grain.

In America, controls imposed by both France and Britain were bitterly resented, although it is doubtful if either President Jefferson, or his successor Madison, realized that the Berlin Decrees had brought in a total war. In 1807, Jefferson introduced an embargo act which prohibited US trade with all foreign nations. This act did far more harm than good, was widely ignored, and was replaced by the Non-Intercourse Act 1809, which prohibited trade with either France or Britain until each dropped their blockade decrees. This Act was intended to force both belligerents to abandon their controls, but again it did more harm to the US than to France or Britain. Napoleon's response was the Decree of Rambouillet, by which all US shipping entering French ports or found on the high seas was subject to seizure. In 1810, Congress repealed the Act, but offered to either belligerent power which respected neutral rights, the reward of refusing trade with the other.

Napoleon's next response was that the Milan Decrees would be revoked on the understanding that so would the Orders-in-Council, and in November 1810, Madison gave London three months to repeal the orders. Receiving no satisfactory response, he re-imposed the Embargo Act. Thus Napoleon, who had no intention whatsoever of weakening his system, hoodwinked the US and pushed her further towards war with Britain. Certainly, given the trade figures already described, the most dangerous situation for England was a successful Continental System and a disruption of US trade, and this is exactly what Napoleon achieved in 1811.

The results for the British economy were dramatic. Lancashire was deprived of raw cotton, and goods began to pile up at ports. British exports to the US fell from £111 million per year to £2 million, and the government found itself forced to pay for the vital American grain in gold rather than in goods. Weekly wages for workers fell by two-thirds, and in industrial Lancashire, a fifth of the population was thrown on to the rates by unemployment as the mills were forced to close. Worse still, food prices rose 87 per cent above their pre-war levels because of a bad harvest and the need to import grain from Italy, Poland, and even France – which Napoleon permitted in order to accelerate the drain on his rival's exchequer.

By late 1811 there were riots in Nottinghamshire, Staffordshire, Lancashire and Yorkshire, which required the diversion of troops from the Peninsula: the situation was critical, for a militant rebellion in England now would certainly have handed victory to Napoleon. But in fact, relief was already in sight. The Embargo and Non-Intercourse Acts had been hugely unpopular in America, especially in New England, and were widely ignored by the mercantile community, who were happy to continue to use British licences. In this they were encouraged by the British themselves, who after 1812 continued to trade with New England while blockading southern ports from the Gulf Coast to Long Island, thus increasing national divisions and anti-war sentiment in New England.

But Britain's real saviour was the Tsar. His famous Ukase of December 1810, which in effect gave preferential treatment to US shipping and thereby opened the door to British trade, effectively spelled the death of the Continental System. Napoleon's invasion of Russia in 1812 accelerated the process by opening the ports of Russia and Sweden to British ships as well: by the spring of 1813, British exports were at their highest level for years. Total exports were valued at £118 million for the year 1812–13, while taxation yielded £68 million, or five times the pre-war figure. Thus Britain, with a population of only 18 million, was in a position to subsidize the armies of the Sixth Coalition which would at last bring Napoleon down.

Spain

Napoleon's second great strategic miscalculation was again in part due to the hostility of Britain, but in part to a combination of more complex factors. Spain, a once powerful country which for centuries had been France's rival, was now to become a vassal. In so doing, Napoleon managed to trigger first the popular revolt in Spain (see Chapter VI), and then the British intervention in Portugal. The events of early 1808, culminating in the Convention of Cintra, had freed Portugal from the French and allowed the country to be used as a base of operations against the French in Spain itself. This had begun with Sir John Moore's autumn campaign of 1808, but it had been allocated wholly inadequate forces by the British government, and had failed. Once Napoleon himself had driven the British off, he departed the country, never to return, leaving the campaign in the hands of a series of subordinates. In 1809 the French, commanded by Marshal Soult, had once more invaded Portugal, only to be driven out by Wellington, who had then invaded Spain. During 1810 the French attempted to consolidate their position in the Peninsula but the following year, after emerging from the lines of Torres Vedras, Wellington had at last succeeded in clearing Portugal of the French for good.

The year 1812 proved as much a turning point in Spain as elsewhere. At the beginning of the year, Wellington had successfully stormed the fortresses of Badajoz and Cuidad Rodrigo and then, on 22 July, he defeated Marmont at Salamanca. But the French were not beaten yet. Marmont and Soult were able to concentrate against the allies, repulse them at Burgos, and in November, push them back with loss into Portugal, in a retreat which almost rivalled the retreat to Corunna in its severity. Thus, at the end of the year, the French military command still felt relatively in control as far as the British were concerned – at least on land. But after four years of hard campaigning, what had they to show for their pains? The frontier fortresses were in allied hands; Spain south of the Tagus had been lost; 20,000 prisoners had been shipped off to England in the last year alone – men desperately needed in Europe. General Foy wrote that

> Lord Wellington has retired unconquered ... having restored the Spaniards the country south of the Tagus, and made us destroy our magazines, our

fortifications – in a word all that we have gained by our conquest, and all that could assure the maintenance of it.

In the longer term too, all was far from well. First, the army in Spain had already been heavily milked of manpower for the Russian campaign. As the campaigning season of 1813 approached, the army would again be plundered, both of formed units and cadres of veterans as Napoleon desperately strove to rebuild his army in Central Europe. Second, the British exercised absolute control over the seas, so that all communications had to be across land. This laid them open to the third difficulty, the Spanish guerrilla war, discussed in Chapter VI.

Napoleon's continued insistence on trying to command the Spanish theatre by remote control – especially given the guerrilla-infested communications – did little to help his brother, the puppet King Joseph, and this was made worse by the Emperor's consistent under-estimation of both the guerrillas and of Wellington. This was probably brought about by the fact that with the departure of Marshals Soult, Souham and Marmont for the Central European theatre, there were few generals on the French side capable of manoeuvring a corps, let alone an army. Suchet could manoeuvre a corps, and Clausel had also proved his ability in 1812, but certainly such a task was far beyond the capacity of Joseph Bonaparte, as Napoleon well knew. However, in early 1813, the Emperor insisted that Joseph should make a demonstration towards Portugal in order to tie down the allies, a proposal which Joseph greeted with some heat:

> How am I to make a demonstration towards Portugal? to do so I must in the first instance concentrate the troops which is impossible owing to want of victuals. And what is the use of it, if I make such a demonstration? Wellington will not be deceived, for he knows that the whole Army is engaged in the north and that I have had to send large drafts to the Emperor.

Thus, as the 1813 campaigning season drew on, the French army of 198,000 men was dispersed throughout Spain, and Joseph could assemble at most 32,000 infantry, 9,000 cavalry and 100 guns without depleting his anti-guerrilla operations. This at a time when he knew that the allies had been reinforced and could be expected to move at any time. Thus came the stunning defeat at Vitoria, the battles in the Pyrenees and at Sorauren, and the loss of Spain. It was followed in 1814 by the invasion of France itself on two fronts. Even as this was being prepared, Napoleon tried to fire one last strategic shot at the unity of his allies: the Treaty of Valençay. After his return to Paris following the defeat of Leipzig, he took up the idea of releasing the imprisoned Ferdinand VII and restoring him to the Spanish throne; Joseph was contemptuously thrust aside. In return, he wanted a treaty favourable to France, which would release the 100,000 veteran troops on the Spanish border in order to stem the main allied invasion that he knew would come over the Rhine. To secure this, Napoleon was willing to evacuate his remaining fortresses in Catalonia and Valencia, and release Ferdinand. In return, he demanded no less than the withdrawal of Spain from the Sixth Coalition, a free pardon for all *Afrancescados*, and the eviction of foreign troops from Spain. Thus, Spain would cease to be a base for allied operations.

On paper this seemed an excellent scheme, but Napoleon failed to realize that Ferdinand would agree to anything in order to gain his release but, such was his detestation for Napoleon, with no intention of keeping his promises. Napoleon gambled heavily on Spanish hostility to the English, but entirely misunderstood the intense anti-French feelings that had been aroused by his annexations, and reprisals against guerrilla activity. How he could have believed that such a treaty was possible shows how his grasp of reality had slipped: Ferdinand in prison understood the situation better than Napoleon. Believing that the Treaty would be ratified by the Spanish *Cortes*, he drew off troops from the Spanish frontier, especially cavalry and artillery, which rendered it incapable of resisting effectively when the treaty was abrogated, and Spanish divisions formed part of the allied army that invaded southern France.

In Spain, Napoleon made a fatal strategic miscalculation which, combined with the Russian campaign and the Continental System, brought him down. He committed acts so insulting and so treacherous that he drove Spain into the arms of her ancient enemy, England. 'The whole affair', as he later remarked on St Helena, 'was too immoral'. The course of the war in Russia and later in Central Europe could well have been substantially altered by the addition of the 200,000 French and client troops tied down in Spain.

America

Although this may not have been his intention, it was the effect of Napoleon's Continental System on world trade that turned an essentially European series of wars into a world war. A key factor in its making was the role of America and its relations with France. From the late eighteenth century onwards, Americans for the most part regarded France with affection for her support in the Revolutionary War, and this received concrete expression in the Franco-American alliance of February 1778. The beginning of the Revolution in France, therefore, caused much satisfaction in many quarters of the United States. But the Terror showed such an unacceptable face to the USA that after the declaration of war by France against Great Britain in 1793, the USA continued to trade with both belligerent nations. Indeed on 19 November 1794, the USA and Britain went so far as to sign a treaty of friendship, commerce and navigation. This caused so much discord between the USA and France that in July 1798, Congress passed an act declaring the US government free of all treaty obligations towards France, and even began preparations for war. In France, the Directory rapidly realized that matters had got out of control and resolved to regain American goodwill. The US government was therefore invited to send commissioners to France to negotiate a new treaty. By the time the commissioners actually arrived in Paris, the Coup of *Brumaire* had made Bonaparte First Consul – although Talleyrand remained in control of foreign affairs. Napoleon at once demonstrated his personal interest in the treaty negotiations by appointing his brother Joseph as one of the French commissioners, and the result was a significant diplomatic success. The Convention of Paris, concluded in September 1800, declared friendship and peace between the two countries, while leaving the question of the Franco-American treaty of 1778 to a future round of negotiations.

The real significance of this convention lay in its provision for free trade and a lowering of tariff barriers, since even in 1800, Britain was piling up a large war debt which could only be serviced by exports of manufactured goods. Since nearly one-third of this export trade was to the USA, any reduction of it must assist France. At the same time, Bonaparte was engaged in the negotiations with London which led to the Peace of Amiens, and in concluding the second, secret, Treaty of San Ildefonso with Spain. By this latter treaty, France agreed to obtain Tuscany for the Duke of Parma – brother-in-law to King Charles IV of Spain – in return for which the Spanish government agreed to cede the territory of Louisiana to France, an arrangement which was subsequently confirmed in the Treaty of Luneville in February 1801.

Louisiana was costing Spain over $340 million per year to maintain and, combined with some alarm at US territorial ambitions, this proved a powerful spur on the Spanish to give up the territory. This vast territory had been French until 40 years previously, and it seems likely that Napoleon dreamed of replacing the lost Canadian New France of the eighteenth century with another, linking the islands of the Caribbean – Martinique, St Lucia, Guadeloupe, Haiti and Hispaniola – to the Mississippi valley and thence into the centre of North America, thus creating a French-speaking new world which would overshadow Spain, Britain and the USA. But France could hardly take possession of the territory while still at war with Britain,

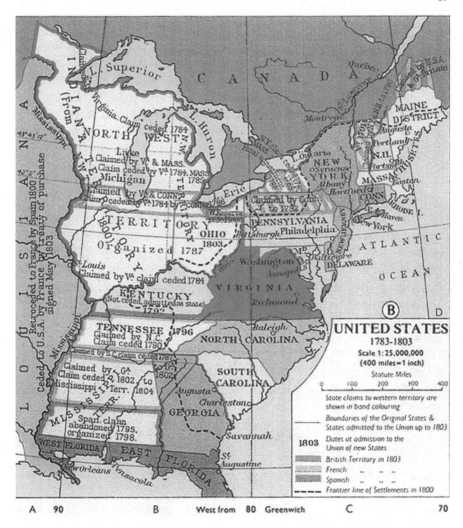

THE LOUISIANA PURCHASE
Source: *Muir's Historical Atlas* (London, 1974)

for to do so would only invite the British to seize it, and thus the Peace of
Amiens provided the opportunity for Napoleon to form General Victor's
expeditionary force to secure the territory. Clearly, however, the Spanish
government had second thoughts soon after the agreement and tried to
delay the actual handover until Napoleon had promised never to cede the
territory to a third power. The Spanish governor remained in post, and in

October 1802, Napoleon abolished the right of US citizens to trade through New Orleans.

This move, coming on top of the news of the cession, which in itself seemed to President Jefferson to renew the prospect of confrontation and conflict with France, pushed Jefferson to seek the purchase of the territory. In January 1803 he sent James Monroe as Minister Extraordinary and Plenipotentiary to Paris, authorizing him to open negotiations for the purchase of the east bank of the Mississippi River and the island of New Orleans, which would give the US a secure frontier and an outlet for trade. Negotiations had actually been initiated by Livingstone, the regular US Minister in Paris, prior to Monroe's arrival; Talleyrand was unwilling to negotiate, but Napoleon, when approached, probably prompted by the likely renewal of war with Britain and the need for money, was willing to sell the whole territory.

When Monroe arrived, the matter was soon arranged. A treaty of cession was signed on 30 April 1803 which transferred Louisiana to the USA, binding the US to pay 60 million francs ($15 million), with interest. Spain had at this point no choice but to agree, but the deal was certainly one of the many causes of bitterness between France and Spain which would later erupt into open war. As it was, in November 1803, the French commissioner, Laussat, at last received possession of Louisiana from the Spanish authorities, and immediately notified the American commissioners who were waiting at Fort Adams. On 20 December 1803, New Orleans became an American city, and the size of the USA doubled.

Russia

The mistake of invading and occupying Spain, combined with the invasion of Russia in 1812 was the biggest single factor in the downfall of Napoleon and his empire. At Tilsit, France had been the dominant player, largely dictating terms to Prussia and Russia. But, in the intervening years, the balance of advantage had swung towards Russia, at the same time as tensions increased. The Continental System was one such tension; others included Russian ambitions in the Balkans, the fate of Poland, the nomination of Bernadotte as Crown Prince of Sweden (despite how things later turned out), and the French annexation of the cities of the Hanseatic League. By 1811, Napoleon was firmly convinced that Tsar Alexander meant to fight, but he discounted the warnings of the size of the problem, asserting as usual that military defeat would bring the Tsar to his senses. The Tsar took a different view, believing that, as had happened in Spain, defeat on the battlefield did not necessarily translate into surrender or national sub-jugation. Saddam Hussein seems to have made the same calculation in Kuwait 200 years on. A similar asymmetry was at work in force generation. Napoleon demanded 40,000 troops from Austria and 20,000 from Prussia, as well as contingents from his clients and allies: of the 611,000 men in the *Grande Armée* of 1812, only 213,000 can be accounted as French. However, the Russians could more than match this by freeing up troops after the peace treaty with Turkey in May 1812, and the Swedish alliance in March which had followed the French seizure of Swedish Pomerania.

Once the invasion was launched, Napoleon was unable to force decisive engagement before Smolensk in mid-August. The army was already tired and the sickness rate high. The attempted manoeuvre of Smolensk came to nothing and the battle, although a tactical success, achieved little but more casualties. True, Napoleon captured one of the great symbolic cities of holy Russia, but the Russian armies had disengaged successfully.

The big question remains, why did Napoleon not stop at Smolensk? There is evidence that he considered doing just that. There were con-siderable advantages in doing so: the troops could be rested and re-supplied; the line of communication could be secured and Poland consolidated as an ally; and an early start could be made on the campaigning season of 1813, with only 280 miles to cover to reach Moscow. On the other hand, the Russians would be given more time to prepare, and bring up troops from Finland and the Turkish frontier. They could evacuate the towns, and raze the countryside – with all that meant for the French system of forage. A prolonged period around Smolensk would in any case mean instituting a formal system of supply, since living off the land would rapidly exhaust available food. Even at this early stage in the campaign, the massive failure of Napoleonic logistics was apparent. Despite unprecedented preparations, the supply of 600,000 men in a hostile country, over vast distances, proved impossible. Herds of cattle were too slow, living off the land meant star-vation, supply depots were too few and too small, and horse-drawn traffic over a few bad roads could not feed the troops nor service the depots. The Tsar could even mount a counter-attack, and maybe subvert the Austrians and Prussians. In addition to this, Napoleon needed a speedy conclusion to the war in order to force the Russians back into the Continental System before the odds began to tell against him in the field. It seems, therefore, that Napoleon's instincts as a soldier overcame his intuitive judgement as a statesman. But having made his decision, he found almost the exact same strategic dilemma confronting him at Moscow, in the aftermath of Bor-odino: should he now remain in Moscow, withdraw to Smolensk, or march

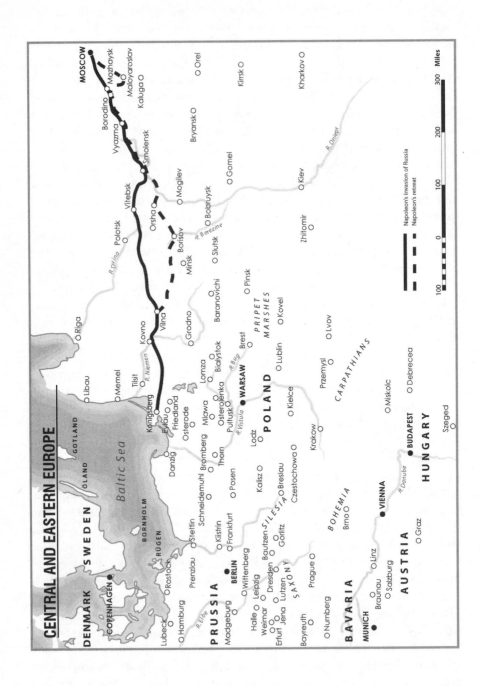

CENTRAL AND EASTERN EUROPE

Napoleon's invasion of Russia
Napoleon's retreat

Miles
100   0   100   200   300

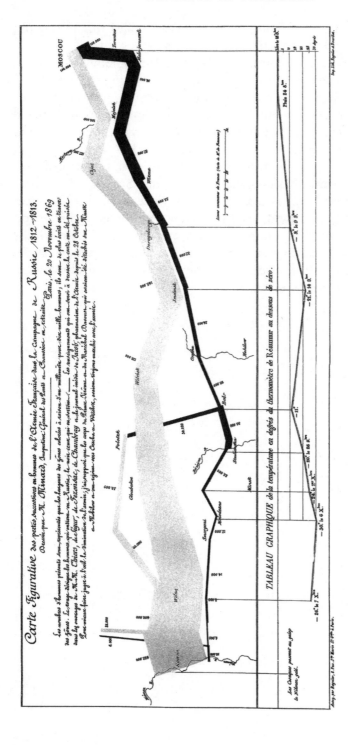

Napoleon's March to Moscow The War of 1812

This classic of Charles Joseph Minard (1781–1870), the French engineer, shows the terrible fate of Napoleon's army in Russia. Described by E. J. Marey as seeming to defy the pen of the historian by its brutal eloquence, this combination of data map and time-series, drawn in 1861, portrays the devastating losses suffered in Napoleon's Russian campaign of 1812. Beginning at the left on the Polish-Russian border near the Niemen River, the thick band shows the size of the army (422,000 men) as it invaded Russia in June 1812. The width of the band indicates the size of the army at each place on the map. In September, the army reached Moscow, which was by then sacked and deserted, with 100,000 men. The path of Napoleon's retreat from Moscow is depicted by the darker, lower band, which is linked to a temperature

scale and dates at the bottom of the chart. It was a bitterly cold winter, and many froze on the march out of Russia. As the graphic shows, the crossing of the Berezina River was a disaster, and the army finally struggled back into Poland with only 10,000 men remaining. Also shown are the movements of auxiliary troops, as they sought to protect the rear and the flank of the advancing army. Minard's graphic tells a rich, coherent story with its multivariate data, far more enlightening than just a single number bouncing along over time. Six variables are plotted: the size of the army, its location on a two-dimensional surface, direction of the army's movement, and temperature on various dates during the retreat from Moscow. It may well be the best statistical graphic ever drawn.

Edward R. Tufte, *The Visual Display of Quantitative Information*   Graphics Press Box 430 Cheshire, Connecticut 06410

Charles Joseph Minard

Figure 1 Napoleon's March to Moscow. The War of 1812

on St Petersburg? The calculations seem to have revealed that to stay put was to rot, and to advance meant death in the snow.

The disaster in Russia had a massive impact on French military potential: the Empire lost 570,000 men, 200,000 horses and 1,050 guns and, while the guns could be replaced, the men and horses were in increasingly short supply. More important was the effect on morale, for the defeat shattered the myth of Napoleonic invincibility and kindled the moves that resulted in the Sixth Coalition. In the final years of his reign, Napoleon might win battlefield victories again and again, but after Russia, and combined with the effects of the Spanish Ulcer and the Continental System, he was irrevocably set on the road to St Helena. There is no better example of the great truth that if strategy is flawed, then no matter how brilliant the tactical manoeuvres, no matter how inspired the operational art, failure will be inevitable. The American Revolutionary War was a recent example at the time, clear for all to see, and so no-one can now be accused of sitting in judgement with the benefit of hindsight.

III

Napoleon as Coalition General

Alliance and Coalition

Napoleon is more usually cited as a general who, with a unified command, opposed a series of coalitions, rather than as a coalition commander himself. Because of his supreme position at the centre of French power, he faced none of the difficulties with which, for example, Wellington, or Prince Charles of Schwarzenberg were so familiar and, as has been noted in Chapter II, he embodied in himself the positions of head of state and commander-in-chief. Napoleon called no councils of war, consulted no peers, had no need to placate any opinion – public or political. But coalitions vary according to circumstance, and the position of France in the Napoleonic coalition was so dominating that it was closer to the position of the Soviet Union in the Warsaw Pact, or to the USA in the Iraq or Afghanistan coalitions today, than to any member of the six coalitions that faced him (seven if the Waterloo campaign is considered separately). But it cannot be denied that, from 1806 at least, and certainly during the Russian campaign of 1812, Napoleon's armies were heavily reliant on manpower supplied by allies, client states or annexed territories.

This situation is a classic illustration of the fact, more difficult to determine among the Central European allies at that time, that coalitions are rarely a partnership of equals: power tends to lie with the strongest member, which will inevitably determine the effectiveness – politically as well as militarily – of the coalition. The diplomat, writer and diarist Harold Nicolson remarked on this, saying: 'The basis of any alliance, or coalition, is an agreement between two or more sovereign states to subordinate their separate interests to a single purpose.' Before proceeding further, therefore, it is necessary to highlight some key differences between established alliances, and coalitions. Alliances are often formed in peace-time against a readily definable, strategic threat, in order to provide long-term collective security for their members. Because of their long-term nature, alliances tend to produce political and military structures for consultation, liaison, command and control which, over time, become as well established as those of a single nation. Military contributions tend to reflect the economic power of alliance members, but the mutual trust and co-operation which develops over time can overcome any tensions that differences in burden-sharing brings. This can be offset, however, by the fact that the legal basis which alliances usually have in the form of a treaty means that every member, no matter how large or small its contributions, has an equal say in policy, and this can produce turgid and over-rigid decision-making mechanisms and, at worst, stagnation. Coalitions are by contrast, short term, born of the moment. The individual members may be very diverse in political structure, economic power and culture, but they have been brought together by a single unifying threat or a common goal. Military contributions are inevitably based on more short-term considerations, and the resulting structures for decision making, command and control are ad hoc and provisional. Coalitions drift together, forming around the nucleus of opposition and increasing with the spur of success; they also drift apart, since without the ties of treaty, national interest will re-assert itself once the common threat is gone. Success is arguably the biggest challenge to a coalition.

The difference between the Napoleonic model of coalition and the six that faced France throughout the Revolutionary and Napoleonic Wars was an important one: Napoleon retained sole command of his coalition, called no councils of war but rather issued decrees; he consulted no clients or allies, but merely informed them of his demands for troops or supplies. In October 1809, for example, he wrote to Count Wrede, commanding the Bavarian army, chiding him for the failure to suppress the rebellion in the Tyrol:

> tell me whether the Bavarians want to win my good or bad opinion. When troops are demoralized, it is for their commanders and officers to restore their morale, or die in the attempt.

In December of the same year he wrote to his brother the King of Holland, announcing the annexation of the kingdom to France, on the grounds that his brother had attempted to pursue an independent policy:

> I had hoped that, schooled in my policy, you would realize that Holland, once conquered by my peoples, must rely, for its independence, upon their generosity; that with no resources, no allies and no army, Holland could and inevitably would be conquered ... that your policy must therefore be the same as mine, and that Holland was bound by treaty to France. I therefore hoped that, in placing on the Dutch throne a prince of my own blood, I had found the happy mean which harmonized the interests of the two states, and united them in a common policy, and a common hatred of England.

Not for him were the difficult processes of compromise, consultation, and subordination of separate interest to an overriding common purpose faced by his opponents.

Napoleon himself seems to have believed, as Clausewitz later pointed out, that when faced by a coalition, several enemy centres of gravity – that is, that part of the enemy's power which if destroyed or neutralized will bring about his downfall – can be reduced to one by striking at the principal coalition partner. By this means, the vital concept of allied unity, which in a coalition may be the centre of gravity rather than any physical aspect, may be shattered. This explains his determination over the years to destroy England – the financial driving power of his enemies – by the Continental System, and his focus on the land power of Austria, and later Russia. In August 1805, he wrote to Talleyrand from the Camp at Boulogne, on the need to deal with Austria on land, having been unable to strike at England through an amphibious invasion:

> The more I reflect on the European situation, the more I see the urgency of taking decisive action. The fact is, I have nothing to hope for from the Austrian explanations ... This winter, under the title of an armed neutrality, she will sign her subsidy treaty, and her act of coalition; and in April I shall find 100,000 Russians in Poland, paid for – horses, guns, and all – by England, besides 15 to 20,000 English at Malta, and 15,000 Russians at Corfu. Then things will be in a pretty pass.

In October 1806 he wrote to Rochefoucauld, his ambassador at the Austrian Court, on the need to secure Austria as an ally, and thus neutralize the power of any continental coalition against him:

> I am too strong and well-situated to be afraid of anyone: all the same, the enormous efforts I have made are a burden on my subjects. I must have one of the three powers – Russia, Prussia or Austria – for an ally.

The allies were, conversely, in no doubt that Napoleon himself represented the centre of gravity of French power, as was proved by the way his clients fell away after his defeat at Leipzig, and by the allied declaration of war against Napoleon himself rather than France after the return from Elba.

French Clients and Allies

As we have seen, Napoleon's wars began in order to guarantee the frontiers which the Revolution had won: essentially the Rhine, the Alps and the Pyrenees, the so-called 'natural frontiers' of France. It was soon apparent, however, that these frontiers did not in themselves guarantee security and needed to be extended through the creation of buffer states. These, in turn, had to be defended, especially against the enmity of the British and their coalition-forming activities, and thus was born the system of client states and allies. Clearly, neither France nor Britain was capable of defeating the other without the extensive help of allies, except perhaps by a long and ruinous war of attrition. Apart from the territories physically annexed to France, these client states took two forms: first, satellite kingdoms and second, allies. The satellite kingdoms had usually begun as liberated territory under the Directory, and were transformed into kingdoms by the imposition of members of Napoleon's own family as crowned heads: Holland, Spain, Westphalia, Italy and Naples. From these, Napoleon drew military manpower and obtained income. Italy, the most successful of the kingdoms, supplied a total of 142,000 conscripts and 44,000 volunteers over the years, and its contribution in 1813 alone was 36,000 conscripts for an army which numbered 90,000 men, of whom 10,000 were in Spain and 28,000 in Central Europe. Westphalia, the creation of which marked the consolidation of the inner Empire, did even better. In 1813 the Westphalian army was 27,000 strong and the country also supported 30,000 French troops, making it the largest *per capita* supplier of manpower of all the satellite kingdoms and probably the most effective, as its troops served in every theatre of operations. By contrast, Naples produced an army of only 11,000, of whom only 2,000 were Neapolitans and the rest Germans, Frenchmen, Corsicans, Italians and North Africans. Spain, by contrast, was poor ground. Spanish brigades served in the French Army of Spain and in the Baltic, but the French army in the Peninsula was never less than 190,000 strong and very French: Spain probably cost France 300,000 casualties and around one billion francs over the years 1808–13, rather than contributing to the exchequer.

After the satellite kingdoms came the allies, of which the most numerous and military significant were in Germany. But there were others: Switzerland is worthy of mention since the Act of Mediation following the end of the French occupation and creation of the Helvetic Republic in 1803 made it more a satellite than an ally, with Napoleon as the Moderator of the Federation. The Act guaranteed Swiss integrity, in return for a contribution of 16,000 Swiss recruited directly into the French army. After the battle of Leipzig, the Swiss declared neutrality, but did not withdraw their subjects from the French armies. Although its parliament elected Bernadotte as Crown Prince, Sweden, never became a satellite kingdom. Its determined independence and disregard of the Continental System following Napoleon's refusal to back Swedish claims on Norway led to the French occupation of Swedish Pomerania in January 1812. This, in turn, brought Sweden into alliance with Russia, in return for the promise of assistance with the annexation of Norway. The Danes, who then ruled Norway, were in alliance with Napoleon, having been obliged to join the Continental System by the treaty of Tilsit, but they had been driven firmly into Napoleon's court by the British naval attack, and seizure of the Danish fleet in 1807, which made control over Norway almost impossible against Swedish rivalry.

The Confederation of the Rhine

Traditional French policy in Germany under the Bourbons had been to support the medium-sized German states like Baden, Württemberg, Saxony and Bavaria, as well as the Electors and Prince-Bishops of Mainz, Cologne and Wurzburg. This policy was aimed at the maintenance of French influence on both banks of the Rhine, but Bonaparte's early pursuit of an alliance with Prussia risked the support of the Catholic states, until his Treaty of Ratisbon re-shaped the political map of Germany (see Chapter IX). This treaty enlarged not only Prussia, but also Württemberg, Baden and Bavaria, consolidated many fragmentary land holdings, halved the number of smaller states and, as a result, reduced the influence of Austria. Its work was completed by the creation of the Confederation of the Rhine, which was entirely Napoleon's creature, and which united the small and medium-sized German states in an alliance which was protected by, and was dependent on, the French Empire. Thus, not only was Austrian influence reduced, but so too was that of Prussia.

The first move towards the confederation was the Franco-Bavarian treaty of August 1805, under which Bavaria agreed to contribute 20,000 troops in return for Napoleon's promise to 'seize all occasions which present themselves to augment the power and splendour of the House of Bavaria and to procure for its Parliament the enhancement ("*arrondissement*") and consistency of which they are capable'.

This treaty was followed by an alliance with Baden in September 1805, which produced 3,000 troops, and with Württemberg in October, which produced another 8,000 troops in return for a guarantee of independence and integrity. This treaty also supported the position of the Elector against his own parliament, should it fail to ratify the treaty. In addition, Sigismund Freiherr von Reizenstein, the Baden minister of state, proposed the creation of a security zone between Austria and France, in which Brixen, Trent and South Tyrol would be ceded to Italy; North Tyrol, Swabia and Upper

Austria to Bavaria, Wurzburg and Württemberg. This plan was partly carried out by Napoleon in the Treaty of Pressburg in December 1805, and this treaty, which also severed the ties between his clients and the old Holy Roman Empire of the German Nation, created the conditions for the Confederation to take shape. The Act of Confederation was signed in July 1806, the confederating states being Bavaria, Württemberg, Dahlberg, Baden, Berg, Hesse-Darmstadt, Nassau-Usingen, Nassau-Weilburg, Hohenzollern-Hechingen, Hohenzollern-Sigmaringen, Salm-Salm, Salm-Kirburg, Isenburg-Birstein, Arenberg, Liechtenstein and Leyen. These were later joined by Wurzburg, Saxony and the five Saxon duchies; Lippe-Schaumberg and Lippe-Detmold; the three Anhalt duchies; Waldeck; Schwarzburg-Rodelstadt and Schwarzburg Sonderhausen; the four principalities of Reuss; Mecklenburg-Strelitz and Mecklenburg-Schwerin; the Grand Duchy of Oldenburg; and the City of Frankfurt am Main. The Kingdom of Westphalia was declared a member as soon as it came into being. The treaty of confederation brought the Holy Roman Empire to an end and established a new *diet*, or assembly, in Frankfurt am Main, of which Napoleon was appointed Protector. The treaty also made a further reshaping of the map, and suppressed many of the smaller states: in the end, half the total number of states in Germany disappeared.

For Napoleon, the crucial article of the treaty was number 12, which laid down that:

> There shall be between the French Empire and the Confederate States of the Rhine, collectively and separately, an alliance in virtue of which every Continental war which one of the Contracting Parties shall have to sustain shall immediately become common to all the others.

Article 38 stated the number of troops that the confederates would supply: France would provide 200,000, Bavaria 30,000, Westphalia 12,500, for example, and then down to the smaller states which were to find 4,000 each. Thus, the confederation was partly a new security zone on the Rhine frontier, and partly a source of manpower – it made the *Befreiungskreig* of 1813 as much a German civil war as a war of liberation. Its creation ensured that the power of Prussia would have to be broken, and that war with Great Britain would continue, since Britain would never agree to French control over the great European river estuaries and ports. Indirectly, therefore, the Confederation led to the extension of the Continental System into Spain and Portugal. Because of this, the armies of Britain, Russia and Prussia would meet one day in Paris.

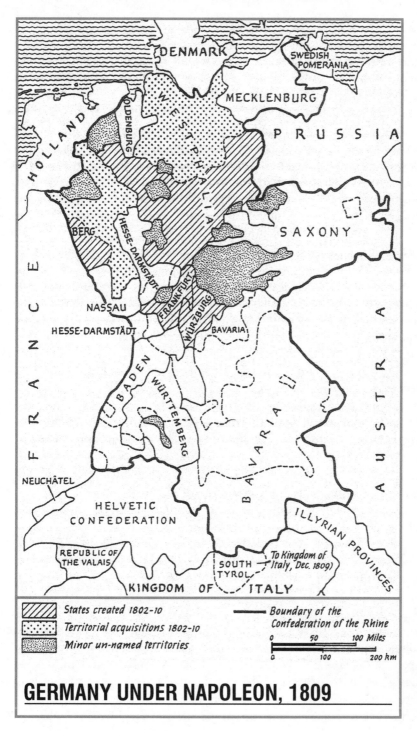

States created 1802-10
Territorial acquisitions 1802-10
Minor un-named territories

Boundary of the
Confederation of the Rhine

0   50   100 Miles
0   100   200 km

GERMANY UNDER NAPOLEON, 1809

Poland

If the creation of Westphalia as a satellite marked the consolidation of Napoleon's inner empire, the creation of the Grand Duchy of Warsaw marked the emergence of a greater empire. This state, built on the bedrock of Polish nationalism and the prejudices of the Polish aristocracy, rather than on the ideals of the *Code Napoléon*, was ruled *in absentia* by Napoleon's ally and figurehead, Frederick Augustus, King of Saxony. In practice, however, Napoleon himself retained direct control of the country. The creation of the Grand Duchy in 1807 was a political chimera: it fired up Polish hopes for the re-creation of their country, but in reality it was merely a tool of Napoleon's diplomacy, designed as a compromise with Russia – since its territory was formed mostly at the expense of Prussia – while at the same time drawing the Poles firmly into Napoleon's camp. But just as the creation of the Confederation of the Rhine guaranteed Prussian resistance, so the creation of the Grand Duchy of Warsaw was bound to offend Russia. In 1809, after Wagram, the Grand Duchy was enlarged by the addition of Austrian Galicia (see Chapter V), and at this point, the Tsar demanded a guarantee that Poland would never be revived as a kingdom. He never received any such assurance, but Napoleon never went further in the opposite direction, issuing only vague statements to the Poles in 1812, to the effect that he was embarking on a second Polish war. This, of course, raised the ambitions and expectations of the Poles, who contributed 90,000 troops to the Russian expedition, the remnants of which were still fighting in Central Europe right up to the end of 1813. The total Polish contribution to the *Grande Armée* over a six-year period was some 200,000 out of a population of 2.5 million, and therefore no other satellite or ally gave its support so strongly to Napoleon but, as Broers points out, 'The Grand Duchy was a living monument to the contradictions in the Napoleonic state system.'

Conscription, Coercion and Multinationality in the *Grande Armée*

Just as Britain financed and assembled the various European coalitions, so too Napoleon gathered his clients. As more and more territories were brought under the direct control of the Empire after 1809 – Dalmatia, the Papal States, Holland, Hanover, Northern Westphalia and the Hanseatic cities – largely to strengthen the Continental System, so this trend became more marked. So what, in coalition terms, did this system of alliances produce? A detailed look at the composition of Napoleon's armies in 1812 and 1813 provides some startling answers. In both years, the French armies in Spain, including those in Catalonia, numbered about 200,000 men, of whom approximately 20,000 – 10 per cent – were allies. These were Italians, Germans and Spanish.

The real degree of reliance on the clients and allies comes with an examination of the Central European army. In 1812, the *Grande Armée* for the invasion of Russia totalled 611,000, of whom 213,000, or one-third, were French. The remaining two-thirds consisted of 30,000 Austrians and 20,000 Prussians in two distinct national corps; 27,000 Italians and Croats; 5,000 Neapolitans; 17,000 Westphalians; 9,000 Swiss; 90,000 Poles – including the whole of the V Corps – and Lithuanians; 100,000 other Germans; and 100,000 from the annexed territories. In 1813, the army numbered between 230,000 and 280,000 at any one time, of which between 75,000 and 125,000 were certainly French – but this includes large numbers of Dutch, Catalonians, Illyrians, Belgians and northern Germans from the annexed territories. The remainder consisted of 8,000 Westphalians; 28,000 Italians; 12,000 Danes; and 9,000 Bavarians, as well as a separate Bavarian army of over 20,000 under Wrede; 13,000 Neapolitans; 15,000 Poles; 15,000 Saxons; 10,500 Wurttembergers; 7,000 from Baden; and 4,300 other Germans. Only one-third or less of the army can truly be said to have been French. To support these figures, a comparison of the various sources cited shows the corps structure of the *Grande Armée* in 1812 to have contained subordinate formations of nationalities as shown in the Appendix on p.207. In addition, the Dutch, Swiss, Belgian, Spanish, many Germans, and even Portuguese, were spread out as individuals throughout the corps. The Appendix does not include the Danish auxiliary corps under Prince Frederick William of Hesse which co-operated with Davout's XIII Corps, and was separate from the *Grande Armée*, nor the Bavarian army.

These enormous figures make it impossible to believe that Napoleon could have fought either campaign with a truly French army. They also dispel any doubts about the huge importance of the Spanish war in keeping such large numbers of wholly French troops tied down. Not that all were completely trustworthy: in 1812, the Austrians, Saxons, Bavarians and Poles had a national command; all others were divided into regimental, brigade or divisional groupings and assigned to multinational corps commanded by French generals. By 1813, only the Bavarian army under Count Wrede was allowed a truly independent role, as no doubt Napoleon was very mindful of the defection of the Austrians and Prussians in Russia, which had been achieved despite the attempts at integration. He was right to do so, given the example of the Saxon and other German contingents at Leipzig, and the Bavarians soon afterwards: thus, even in a coalition like Napoleon's, there is truth in the idea of allied unity as the centre of gravity of a coalition army. The method by which these vast armies were raised was conscription, discussed in Chapter II. Conscription, although unpopular, was the price of territorial gain for the client states, and a spur to reform, since without effective administrative structures and policing, the demands of the armies could not be satisfied, and some form of independence thereby guaranteed.

This is a parallel with Wellington's rule for integrating Portuguese brigades into British infantry divisions. Where Wellington's practice and Napoleon's part company is in adversity. Wellington always used his best British troops to cover a withdrawal, but in Central Europe, as the campaign of 1813 drew to its close, the client contingents were frequently used, cynically, as rearguards. Thus at Leipzig, the bulk of Macdonald's troops on the final day were Poles, Italians and Germans. And in the north, the Danes were faced with conducting a delaying action against odds of five-to-one around Hamburg until they separated themselves from Davout before the battle of Bornhoeven, and then concluded the Treaty of Kiel in January 1814. The casualty figures for 1813–14 bear this out: 21,000 out of 28,000 Italians; 5,500 out of 9,000 Bavarians; 9,000 out of 15,000 Poles.

Conclusions

The achievement of strategic unity of purpose has to be seen as a vital ingredient in the success of coalition war at any time. It was not easily achieved, but when one compares the results of the coerced contributions from Prussia and Austria in Napoleon's invasion of Russia in 1812, with the combination of nations joined in free will against him a year later, one significant factor emerges – the willingness to take losses. In 1812, Prussia and Austria were quite unprepared to suffer for the French cause, yet in 1813, both were willing to suffer huge casualties. Conversely, as the campaigns of 1813 progressed, Napoleon's coalition gradually fell apart as his German and Italian clients realized that he was losing – thus the defections during and after Leipzig.

But even when unity of purpose is achieved, coalitions remain a partnership of unequals. The Napoleonic coalition is an excellent illustration of this characteristic, since it was absolutely dominated by the French. Strategic and operational plans were directed entirely towards the expansion of Napoleon's own interest and the clients and allies – German and Italian states, Denmark and Switzerland – or annexed territories like Holland, became more and more merely a source of troops and money. Thus, power in coalition warfare lies with the strongest member, and the effectiveness of the coalition will be determined by that member. Logically therefore, in a partnership of unequals, Napoleon was right – the dominant member becomes the centre of gravity, especially since, as Clausewitz reminds us, 'War is ... an act of force to compel our enemy to do our will'. Compliance by weaker members of a coalition will naturally follow the subjugation of the strongest, and following this logic to its rather brutal conclusion, it seems that smaller partners will generally have to accept a coalition plan dictated by the most powerful member, or leave if they have the luxury of doing so.

Napoleon also believed, as Clausewitz later stated, that when faced with a coalition, several centres of gravity can be reduced to one by striking at the principal coalition partner. By this means, the vital concept of allied unity – which in a coalition may actually be the centre of gravity rather than any physical aspect – may be shattered. This explains Napoleon's determination over the years to destroy England by the Continental System. It may also partly explain his defeat in 1813, since on several occasions Napoleon set his sights on particular pieces of territory, rather than on the business of delivering a knockout blow against either the Russian or Austrian armies. His enemies clearly profited by this mistake, and the converse is also true: the allies of the Sixth Coalition were in no doubt that Napoleon himself represented the centre of gravity of his empire and indeed, once he had been defeated at Leipzig, his clients began to desert.

Clausewitz also addressed the mechanics of strategic direction from his experience of having fought against Napoleon, saying that:

> The first, the supreme, the most far-reaching act of judgement that the statesman and commander have to make is to establish ... the kind of war on which they are embarking: neither mistaking it for, nor trying to turn it into, something which is alien to its nature, This is the first of all strategic questions and the most comprehensive.

Clausewitz believed this to be true of all war, but he implies that in coalition war it is vital that the political nature of any coalition is determined at the strategic level, and its aims made clear to its military commanders. Equally, generals have a duty to explain clearly the realities of the military situation to their political masters. Military objectives may not be identical with political ends, especially at the operational level of war, although they may lead directly or indirectly to their achievement, but the constraints imposed by a partnership of unequals can limit military freedom of action. In the Napoleonic Empire, this military/political interface was artificially compressed. Napoleon represented the supreme authority in both civil and military affairs, which is an abnormal situation, as the case of his opponents shows. In the Sixth Coalition, for example, Wittgenstein, then Barclay de Tolly, and finally Prince Charles of Schwarzenberg were appointed to supreme military command, but the personal presence of the allied monarchs on the battlefield inevitably led to a blurring of responsibilities and an interference in operational detail which, with the advent of real-time communications, has become all too familiar to modern generals.

For Napoleon, coalition war was a vicious circle of necessity. The extension of the Empire flowed from the nationalism unleashed by the Revolution, which he then tried to harness as a French-led pan-European super state. On St Helena, he presented this in highly propagandist terms:

> There are in Europe more than thirty million French, fifteen million Spanish, fifteen million Italians, thirty million Germans. I would have wished to make each of these peoples a single united body ... Europe thus divided into nationalities freely formed and free internally, peace between states would have become easier: the United States of Europe would have become a possibility.

What Napoleon really aimed to create was not a free association of nations, but an empire directed from Paris. From 1809 onwards this looked increasingly fragile as resistance to the French state grew in Italy, Spain and Germany. In Westphalia, for example, revolts broke out in 1811 following the Spanish example. The further the scheme was extended, fuelled by the need to make the Continental System watertight, the larger were the military forces required, both to defend the existing territory and to extend it. This need, combined with the huge losses in Spain, in Central Europe, and later in Russia, wore down the ability of France herself to supply manpower for the armies, to the extent that reliance on the annexed territories, clients and allies had to increase. The price of greater reliance was increased security guarantees, thus completing the circle. So, if Napoleon had succeeded in sustaining his empire after 1813, it must be certain that, like his *Grande Armée*, it would before long have become an organization that was two-thirds foreign.

IV

Campaigning – Napoleon and the Operational Art

Campaigning

Modern doctrine describes the operational level of war as the vital link, or gearing, between military strategic objectives and the tactical employment of forces in battles and engagements. It is the level at which campaigns and major operations are planned, sustained, sequenced and directed. 'It is', says the British army's doctrine publication *Operations*:

> the responsibility of the operational level commander to determine the campaign plan required to achieve the desired military strategic end-state within the designated theatre of operations.

In this, it draws heavily on the writings of Napoleon's contemporary, Baron Jomini, and on Soviet theorists such as Marshal Mikhail Tukhachevskii, and A. A. Svechin – who tells us that 'tactics make the steps from which operational leaps are assembled; strategy points the path'. In the years following the Second World War, operational art lay largely dormant in the West, submerged under the Central European General Deployment Plan, until reinvigorated in the US by the emergence of the doctrine of Air-Land battle in the late 1980s, and the writings of Edward Luttwak in particular. In the British army, the late Field Marshal Sir Nigel Bagnall is widely, and rightly, regarded as the father of its re-birth.

Explicit in the business of campaigning is the military defeat of an enemy, which is defined by the British Army as 'diminishing the effectiveness of the enemy to the extent that he is either unable to participate in combat or at least cannot fulfil his intentions'. This is a notion that Napoleon understood completely, as will be discussed further. It also encapsulates both the physical destruction of an enemy's ability to prosecute war, and the destruction of his will to fight. The latter is often more efficient, if more indirect, for as Napoleon himself remarked, 'More battles are decided by loss of hope, than by loss of blood'. Its ways are pre-emption, dislocation, and disruption; its means include firepower, superior force ratios, superior tempo, simultaneous action, and surprise.

Thus, the business of the operational level and its commander is campaigning. A campaign can be defined very simply as a set of military operations planned and conducted to achieve a strategic objective, within a given time and geographical area. In modern terms, it will normally involve lines of operation for maritime, land and air forces, and may also include economic warfare and, in complex emergencies, the reconstruction of essential infrastructure, security sector reform, and the establishment of governance. Thus, a campaign is set within the context of operational art: it is not just grand tactics, or strategy writ small. The general engaged in campaigning must, therefore, satisfy himself on a number of key questions at the outset of his planning, and these have not changed much since Napoleon's day, despite the alteration in circumstances. Which military conditions must be attained to achieve strategic and operational objectives? What sequence of actions is most likely to produce these conditions? How should military resources be applied to best accomplish that sequence of actions? Are the associated risks acceptable?

Clausewitz points out two key concepts for the operational general. First, the principle of culmination – that is, the point at which one side starts winning and the other starts losing, either offensively or defensively. Second, the notion of the decisive act, or the decisive operation – that which causes an enemy to culminate. War is seldom so straightforward as to permit one single decisive act, usually what is decisive is a combination of several actions. But herein lies the very essence of generalship at the operational level: determining those things that are going to be decisive, and then bringing those circumstances to pass. Thus, sequencing events through a series of decisive points is a key part of planning, as is deciding on simultaneous actions and effects to overwhelm an enemy.

Invariably, what is going to be decisive will have a direct relationship to the centre of gravity of an opponent – that this, the aspect of the enemy's power or capability which if destroyed or neutralized will bring about his collapse. This must be attacked through its critical vulnerabilities, while one's own centre of gravity must be protected from attack. The general must, therefore, be aware of both centres of gravity: those characteristics, capabilities, or localities from which a nation, an alliance, a military force or even a loose confederation like Al-Qua'eda derives its freedom of action, its moral and physical strength, or its will to fight. In Napoleonic terms this was usually something physical, such as the enemy army, or his capital city. However, it can be a group of people or a person – for the French, it was indeed probably Napoleon himself – a resource, natural or industrial; or even something intangible like the will to resist.

The Napoleonic Campaigning System

Would Napoleon have understood this notion of the operational level? Certainly. Although military theory at the time spoke only of strategy and tactics, the campaign was a well-understood idea, as was the concept of operational manoeuvre, usually referred to as 'Grand Tactics'. The very concept of centre of gravity stems from interpretations of the Napoleonic system by theorists such as Clausewitz and Jomini. In explaining what constituted defeat, Clausewitz said that the centre of gravity was 'the hub of all power and movement, on which everything depends ... the point at which all our energies should be directed.' He identified the centre of gravity as typically being the enemy's army, later acknowledging that it could also include 'the capital ... the army of [an enemy's] protector ... community of interest ... the personalities of the leaders and public opinion'. Clausewitz, therefore, used the term as part of an argument to support the sort of decisive, Napoleonic, strength against strength, attritional encounter which he had so often witnessed.

Modern notions focus on the idea of critical vulnerabilities, and pitting strength against weakness – of manoeuvre. Napoleon had a good understanding of this, although when possessed of overwhelming strength, as he often was, attrition rather than manoeuvre was a perfectly respectable method of fighting. Jomini, who had fought both for and against Napoleon, talks for example of the need to direct 'the mass of one's forces successively on to the decisive points in the theatre of war – as far as possible against the communications of the enemy without disrupting one's own'. Here he probably had in mind the autumn campaign of 1813, in which the allies sought as far as possible to avoid pitched battles with Napoleon himself – who had invariably bested them – concentrating instead on his subordinates and his rear areas. Napoleon was equally clear that his army must have only a single line of operations, with a clearly defined target. But it was quite usual for Napoleon to insist that the French army should always move in such a way as to place itself on the flanks and rear of the enemy, and that the army should strive to turn an enemy's exposed flank and so cut him off from his capital, his allies and his supplies.

For Napoleon, the centre of gravity at the operational level was almost invariably the enemy's army, and the most fundamental, decisive act in achieving his strategic objectives was its destruction in battle by the fastest means available. When faced with a coalition, as he often was, the centre of gravity was the strongest member of that coalition and its army, without whom the rest would fall away as the vital unity of the coalition was shattered. As he himself said: 'It is upon the field of battle that the fate of

fortresses and empires is decided.' By this means he would break the
enemy's will to resist so that all else – the conquest of territory in particular
– would follow, as a result of what Frederick the Great had called 'the
bloody decision'. 'I see only one thing', Napoleon declared in 1797, 'namely
the enemy's main body. I try to crush it, confident that secondary matters
will then settle themselves.' Not for him the tedious business of siege warfare
which had characterized much of eighteenth-century operations.

From this basic idea flowed a series of principles, set out in his *Maximes*,
in which one can recognize several of the modern principles of war. These,
carefully thought out, give the lie to Napoleon's oft-quoted remark that 'Je
n'ai jamais eu un plan d'operations'. A glance at the voluminous published
correspondence of the Emperor underlines this. First came offensive action:
'Make war offensively, it is the sole means,' Napoleon said. Offensive action
has already been cited as one of the keys to seizing and maintaining the
initiative, and this he combined with security and deception to produce his
general rule that 'the whole business of war is a well reasoned and circumspect defensive, followed by a rapid and audacious attack'. This attack
would often involve simultaneous actions: dispersed moves and battlefield
concentration; through pinning one enemy force by attritional attack while
drawing off reserves; by moving other forces into a position from where an
attack could be threatened; then by exploiting any weakness produced by a
massive combination of artillery fire, infantry attack, and cavalry
exploitation.

But Napoleon's reference to the defensive is important: not that Napoleon ever wished to fight a defensive battle, but rather to ensure that he
could mount a well-balanced attack from a secure centre of operations, with
his communications well established. In this, as in most things, Napoleon's
planning was very thorough, as has been remarked on during the examination of his strategic capability. In his correspondence he noted that

> I am accustomed to thinking out what I shall do three or four months in
> advance, and I base my calculations on the worst conceivable situation ...
> Nothing in war is attained except by calculation. During a campaign, whatever
> is not profoundly considered in all its detail is without results ... chance alone
> can never bring success.

This sort of calculation would usually throw up the need for several alternative or contingency plans – what in modern terminology are termed
'branches', which was in fact the term used by his teacher Bourcet, from
whom he drew this notion.

Second, speed and mobility were features of all Napoleon's campaigns.
His troops used to say that 'the Emperor has discovered a new way of

waging war – he uses our legs instead of our bayonets'. This may have been true at the operational level on certain occasions, but it was not true where battles were concerned, as will be discussed later. In 1805, for example, Napoleon moved 210,000 men from the Rhine to the Danube, and then part of the force on to Ulm, in only 17 days. In the same campaign, Davout's III Corps marched 140 kilometres in 48 hours – still a pretty respectable performance.* Speed, therefore, along with offensive action, good security provided by extensive cavalry screens, and the deceiving effects of dispersal, were the chief means of producing operational surprise, and time and again he did surprise his enemies.

Napoleon's insistence on rapid movement highlights his obsession with time and space: 'Space we can recover, lost time never'; 'I may lose a battle, but I shall never lose a minute.' Despite what has been said about rapid marching, it must be stressed that Napoleon only occasionally gained time from demanding superhuman efforts of marching from his troops – this was, after all, uneconomical since the losses through straggling were always huge. More usually, he gained time from very careful selection of routes, and meticulous movement planning, expecting only a modest 15 to 18 kilometres a day for marching troops. The ultimate reason for this insistence on rapidity was concentration of force: the assembly of the greatest number of men at the correct time and place to achieve a favourable battle situation. In Napoleonic terms, such assembly or concentration meant the placing of his major formations within marching distance of the intended place of battle: in other words, when conducting a campaign, Napoleon sought to initiate it with a combination of different axes of advance, and conclude it with a general, and decisive, engagement.

This assembly of troops was achieved after approach marches in which dispersion was the rule, since dispersion made use of more routes and was therefore quicker, and increased security. Moreover, dispersal in the approach was seen as a means of inducing an enemy to disperse *his* army, thus laying the enemy open to a rapid French re-concentration against one part of the enemy's scattered forces. Deception was, therefore, of central importance in achieving surprise. Napoleon's enemies had to be kept in a state of uncertainty, which could not be achieved by mere secrecy.

Dispersion was, too, an operational necessity: in order to impose decisive defeat upon an enemy with a massive force at his disposal – like Austria or

---

* The British 1st Armoured Division, for example, with its 10,000 vehicles and 33,000 men at war establishment, plans to move at an average of 20 kilometres in the hour rather than Davout's 3 kilometres in the hour, but it requires time for halts and rest, and for the major business of refuelling. In addition, its column length is so great that almost 48 hours would have to be added to any travel time to allow for the time taken for this column to pass along its route. More will be said of this in Chapter VII.

Russia – it was necessary for Napoleon to commit forces of greater or equal strength. This, in itself, demanded the extension of the army's front. From this it becomes obvious that dispersal was also a logistical necessity, and this will be discussed later. A notable example of the process was the Ulm campaign in 1805. Napoleon's army front extended for 200 kilometres during the period 20 to 30 September as he began the move from Boulogne. It was steadily reduced as the army approached his enemy, so that by 3 October it was less than 100 kilometres, and on the day before the encirclement of General Mack's force, it was only seventy kilometres.

Thus, by achieving a carefully phased concentration after a period of dispersion, as at Ulm or Jena, Napoleon managed to reconcile the principle of concentration of force with the sometimes contradictory requirements of security and deception, in order to produce the greatest possible number of troops at the time and place of his choosing. This reconciliation of the advantages and disadvantages of mass and dispersal, and the fusing of these two contradictory elements into a single operation of war, was Napoleon's greatest contribution to the art of war at the operational level, and marked him, despite his many near disasters, as a master of the art of campaigning, but it is no easy matter, as Edward Luttwak points out in his description of the conscious use of paradox in war:

> As for secrecy and deception, the two classic agencies of surprise that often set the stage for manoeuvre, they too exact some cost of their own. Secrecy is often recommended to those who practise war as if it were costless, but an enemy can rarely be denied all knowledge of an impending action without some sacrifice of valuable preparations ... every limit on the assembly and preliminary approach of the combat forces will leave them less well arrayed and less well positioned than they might have been.

Napoleon's late seventeenth and eighteenth-century forebears had often distinguished rigidly between manoeuvre and giving battle: in Turenne's time, for example, the operational art – or strategy as it was then called – demanded an evasion of general engagements. The notable exception to this was Frederick the Great, from whom Napoleon drew so much inspiration. Napoleon, with his sights always fixed on the opportunity for a decisive battle, mobilized the entire resources of the state and then combined marching, fighting and pursuing into one process. Before the Russian campaign took such a terrible toll of trained soldiers, horses and capable subordinates, he would often try to concentrate actually on the projected field of battle in the face of the enemy, such as at Ulm. Later in his career he was obliged, as at Bautzen, to concentrate short of the battlefield and out of contact with the enemy. This does not affect the central theme of the interplay between campaign and battle: the decisive engagement was the crown of the campaign.

Of course, the converse of concentration of force is economy of effort. Napoleon never neglected this. He would always calculate with the greatest care just how many resources were required for a particular operation: 'a careful balancing of means and results'. Unnecessary waste of manpower and materiel had to be avoided – which is not the same as engaging in attrition under favourable circumstances – as had the construction of elaborate systems in the rear areas, and detaching troops to secondary objectives which could wait their turn: 'Breaking windows with golden guineas', as he called it. So, having selected one particular aim, everything else was secondary. In the campaign of 1806, for example, Napoleon wrote to his brother of his intention of leaving his entire left flank from Bamberg to the Rhine uncovered 'so as to have almost 200,000 men united on a single battlefield': economy of effort on a grand scale indeed.

Operational Manoeuvre 1 – The Central Position

Despite his careful study of the enemy, ground, weather and general conditions – recognizing that no two campaigns are ever the same – Napoleon was content throughout his career to use only three basic operational manoeuvres. No one manoeuvre was necessarily exclusive of the other two: Napoleon could combine features of all three into a single campaign. The first of these is usually known as 'the strategy of the central position'. This manoeuvre was adopted when, as was often the case, Napoleon was faced by a coalition. The manoeuvre was designed to separate the various enemy forces and destroy them by producing local superiority in a series of strikes against scattered adversaries, rather than one great crushing blow. The French army would be divided into two wings, each of two or three corps, under a designated army commander. A central reserve would be maintained under Napoleon's control.

Next, after the usual careful reconnaissance and study, the Emperor would select an enemy inter-army boundary or weak spot. A massive attack would then be mounted to seize and occupy this area in strength, establishing it as a centre of operations. One wing of the army would then march to and make contact with the closest enemy force in a pinning action while the reserve manoeuvred to out-flank it. Meanwhile, the other wing would act as a corps of observation to contain, harry, and if possible defeat other enemy forces. With one part of the enemy force seen off, Napoleon would detach one portion of the pinning force to conduct a pursuit and then

Figure 2

The Manoeuvre of the Central Position (1)
The Break-in

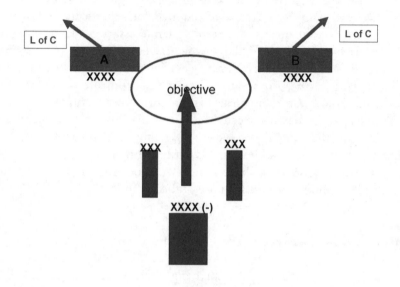

The Manoeuvre of the Central Position (2)
Separating the Enemy

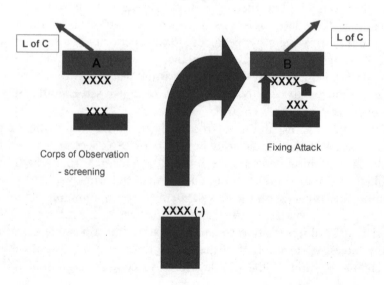

The Manoeuvre of the Central Position (3)
Completion

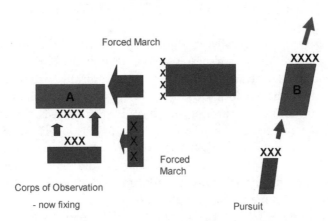

repeat the operation against the remaining enemy force. This was a risky business, as exemplified by its best-known example, the Waterloo Campaign.

When Napoleon reassumed control of the French state, no state of actual war existed between France and the allies: Napoleon himself was treated as a criminal, and there was no immediate military move into France. There were those on the allied side who considered that, faced with overwhelming odds, Napoleon would have no choice but to adopt a strategic and operational defensive. They little understood their opponent, despite 20 years of war. Even with his back to the wall, it was not in Napoleon's nature to fight defensive battles. Moreover, he realized that the only chance of avoiding a second Leipzig was to destroy the various allied armies before they could unite. Weighing the odds, his best chance seemed to be an operational defensive in the east and south to keep the Austrians and Russians at bay – they would in any case take some time to appear – while mounting an operational offensive against the Anglo-Dutch and Prussian armies in the north. This offered several attractive additional advantages. First, it would punish the Prussians for their duplicity in 1812 – the Convention of Tauroggen was neither forgiven nor forgotten. Second, it allowed him to pose his strength against the allies' weakest formations. Third, it would destroy the army of his inveterate foes, the British. With defeat, they might be induced to sue for peace and without English money, no coalition could long stand against him. It could be argued, therefore, that Napoleon saw his enemies' strategic centre of gravity as in London. Finally, the Netherlands and Belgium had for 20 years been part of France, and

Bonapartist sympathies were strong. An attack northwards might recover lost territory, which would help Napoleon's prestige, as well as increasing his military potential in terms of recruits, horses, supplies and industrial capacity.

Looking more specifically at allied dispositions in the Low Countries, there were additional weaknesses to be exploited. The Prussians were centred round Namur, with their line of communication running eastwards into Germany. The Anglo-Dutch army was centred round Brussels, with its line of communication running north and west towards the coast. Wellington had remained in the west for two main reasons. First, he wished to keep a close eye on his Dutch-Belgian troops, whose loyalty he also saw as questionable. This made both the field army and the frontier fortresses vulnerable. Second, he felt that if Napoleon did attack, he would use the strategy of envelopment, marching round the allied right flank and cutting communications with the sea. In fact, Napoleon had discounted envelopment, since it would achieve what he sought to avoid – it would push the Anglo-Dutch and Prussians together. Instead, Napoleon had his eye on the gap between Wellington and Blücher, a gap through which ran the Spanish Road: the great paved highway from Charleroi to Brussels. His intention, therefore, was to employ the strategy of the central position: mask Wellington, defeat Blücher, then turn and destroy Wellington. He wrote to Ney: 'I have adopted for this campaign the following general principle, to divide my army into two wings and a reserve. The Guard shall form the reserve and I shall bring it into action on either wing just as the actual circumstances may dictate. Also, according to circumstances, I shall draw troops from either wing to strengthen my reserve.'

His operational plan, in accordance with the envelopment strategy, was simple. Marshal Ney would, with the corps of Marshals Reille and Drouet D'Erlon, and some cavalry, seize the crossroads at Quatre Bras, south of Brussels, and hold it with a portion of his force, thus masking Wellington. He himself, with two corps and two cavalry corps, would attack the Prussians frontally at Ligny in order to fix them. Reille's main body would then execute a tactical envelopment manoeuvre against the Prussian right flank, and draw off the Prussian reserves. Once Blücher had been induced to weaken his centre, the battle would be decided by the devastating fire of massed artillery and a simultaneous attack by the Guard and the cavalry, reinforced by the corps of D'Erlon which was to march to join the Emperor once Quatre Bras was secure. With the Prussians beaten, Napoleon could then turn his entire army against Wellington.

Having determined his plan, Napoleon moved with his customary rapidity. After concentrating the army in conditions of great secrecy and security, he crossed the Sambre River at Charleroi early on 15 June. A feint in the direction of Mons made Wellington hesitate for a day, still worried about his right flank. Thereafter, however, almost nothing went according to plan. Ney failed to understand his master's intention, and became decisively engaged with Wellington at Quatre Bras, achieving no more than a drawn encounter, but with the result that D'Erlon spent the day marching and counter-marching between Quatre Bras and Ligny, trying to fulfil Napoleon's orders but being summoned back by Ney. In consequence, the Prussians, although badly mauled, escaped destruction. Blücher was able to withdraw northwards, maintaining communication with Wellington and shadowed by a large detached corps under Grouchy, which again was never brought into combat and thus improved the force ratios against Napoleon. Poor weather, and poor battle tactics by Napoleon at Waterloo meant that Wellington was able to hold on long enough for Blücher's force to execute its own enveloping manoeuvre against the French right wing at Plancenoit. Napoleon was caught in his own trap, forced to weaken his own centre and reserves, so that his final grand attack failed and the rout of his army followed.

Operational Manoeuvre 2 – The Envelopment

The second basic manoeuvre was known as 'the strategy of envelopment' (*la manoeuvre sur le derrières*). In this manoeuvre, once the enemy's main army had been identified, a pinning or fixing action would be undertaken by part of Napoleon's force, using a series of frontal feint attacks. Next, the rest of the army would be marched by the fastest possible covered route to the flanks or rear, where it would if possible occupy a natural barrier, such as a river line or mountain barrier, from which to isolate the enemy. The final stage would be an advance on to the enemy offering him the choice of fighting on Napoleon's terms, or surrendering. Thus, the enemy force would be destroyed by a combination of physical encirclement and psychological disruption. The Spring Campaign of 1813, culminating at Bautzen, should have been a supreme example of the strategy of envelopment. The flank attack was also, whenever possible, associated with the positioning of forces astride the enemy's line of retreat, which would turn an outflanking manoeuvre into a true turning manoeuvre. Bautzen was planned with this in mind, although the ineptitude of Ney prevented its execution, and thus a brief description of the Spring Campaign of 1813 may illuminate Napoleon's strategy of envelopment.

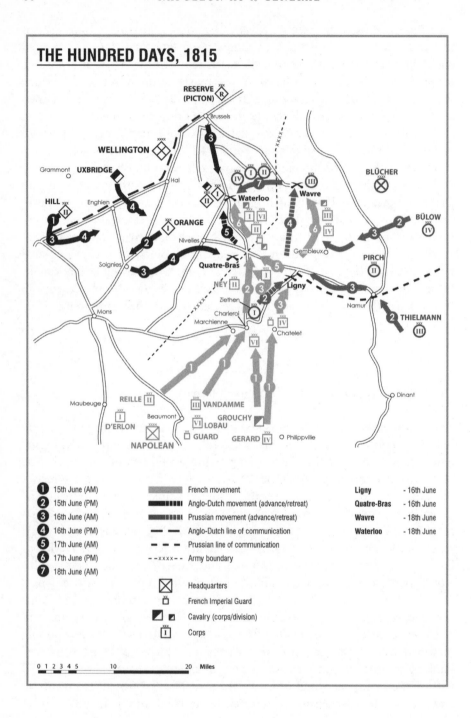

THE HUNDRED DAYS, 1815

RESERVE
(PICTON)

Brussels

WELLINGTON

Grammont   UXBRIDGE

BLÜCHER

Hal

Waterloo   Wavre

HILL   Enghien

BÜLOW

ORANGE

Nivelles

PIRCH

Soignies

Quatre-Bras

Ziethen   Ligny

NEY

Mons

THIELMANN

Charleroi
Marchienne   Chatelet

Namur

Dinant

REILLE   VANDAMME
Maubeuge

GROUCHY
Beaumont   LOBAU

D'ERLON   GUARD   GERARD   O Philippville

NAPOLEAN

❶	15th June (AM)		French movement		Ligny	- 16th June
❷	15th June (PM)		Anglo-Dutch movement (advance/retreat)		Quatre-Bras	- 16th June
❸	16th June (AM)		Prussian movement (advance/retreat)		Wavre	- 18th June
❹	16th June (PM)		Anglo-Dutch line of communication		Waterloo	- 18th June
❺	17th June (AM)		Prussian line of communication			
❻	17th June (PM)		Army boundary			
❼	18th June (AM)					

Headquarters

French Imperial Guard

Cavalry (corps/division)

Corps

0 1 2 3 4 5   10   20   Miles

On 1 May 1813 the French Army of the Elbe was ordered to complete its passage over the Saale and move on Leipzig in three columns, preceded by a strong advance guard. In the north, Lauriston's V Corps, Macdonald's XI Corps and the Guard would cross at Merseburg and move directly on Leipzig. In the centre, Ney's III Corps, followed by Marmont's I Corps, would cross at Weissenfels and head initially for Lutzen. Further south, Bertrand's IV Corps and Oudinot's XII Corps would cross near Naumberg and head north-east. Napoleon was aware of some kind of allied presence near Zwenkau but faulty reconnaissance, probably due to the inexperience of his cavalry, failed to reveal that at Zwenkau lay Wittgenstein's army of four Prussian corps, some 75,000 strong, supported by a further strong Russian corps in reserve. Napoleon, therefore, determined to retain the initiative by pushing on to occupy Leipzig, relying on Ney to protect his southern flank against this as yet unspecified threat.

Meanwhile, patrols of allied cavalry were busy, and in due course they reported to Wittgenstein that the main body of the French was pressing on towards Leipzig and that a weak flank guard was positioned in the area of Kaja. Another strong force was detected even further south, near Teuchern. The allied assessment was substantially correct. Wittgenstein decided, therefore, to annihilate this flank guard, being unaware of Ney's main body. His orders were for General Kleist's corps to hold Leipzig in the north, while General Miloradovich's Russian corps was to move forward towards Zeitz to block Bertrand. Meanwhile, the rest of the allied army, some 48,000 infantry, 24,000 cavalry and nearly 500 guns, was to press on and cut the main Lutzen-Weissenfels road before turning northwards to attack the flank and rear of the French main army. Thus, after a sequence of events which provides a salutary lesson in the necessity for high quality reconnaissance forces, the scene was set for a classic meeting engagement. This duly took place at Lutzen, where Gustavus Adolphus of Sweden had met his death. After a grinding struggle by Ney's corps to hold the allied attack for most of the day, the battle was decided by flanking attacks from both north and south, supported by the fire of a huge massed battery of artillery.

The victory was incomplete, for the allies made off in reasonable order, and the crippling shortage of French cavalry made pursuit almost impossible. Lutzen undoubtedly ended in a victory for Napoleon, who had showed his old flair and skill of improvisation which had been absent for some time. Lutzen not only gave Napoleon the initiative in 1813, but also, perhaps more importantly, it regained the reputation which he had lost in Russia. It had been dearly bought. The French lost 20,000 casualties, the allies lost 18,000, and in addition, they received a very severe shaking. True, the allies had caught Napoleon by surprise but the customary flexibility of

Figure 3

The Envelopment (1)
Fixing the Enemy

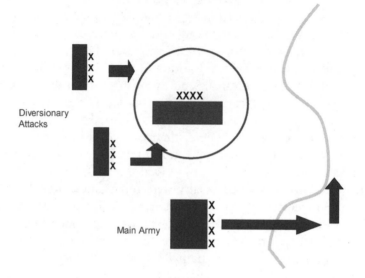

The Envelopment (2)
Manoeuvre Against the Rear

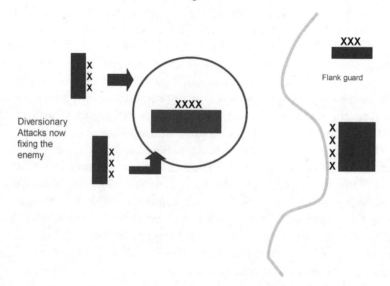

The Envelopment (3) - Destruction

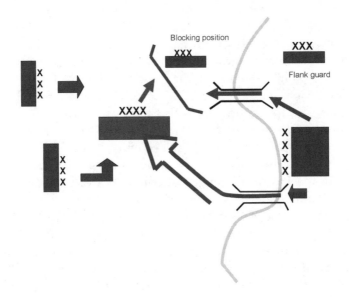

his dispositions – in three columns – had enabled him to react to the unexpected energetically and successfully. By applying the principles of concentration of force, speed and offensive action he had rapidly turned the tables on his enemies to seize back operational and tactical surprise.

The Napoleonic command system and his staff, weakened by losses as they were, were still clearly more than a match for the divided allies. Napoleon himself exercised undisputed command without any possibility of interference; Wittgenstein, on the other hand, faced the practical problems of a coalition commander at the tactical level: the need for consultation with the Prussians and the associated difficulties of language, different tactical doctrine and staff procedures, and interference from the Tsar, all affected his ability to conduct battle with the speed and flexibility of his opponent. On top of all that, Napoleon had once again shown that he could judge better than the allies the moment to launch reserves, and still understood better than they the vital necessity of supporting manoeuvre with firepower. His plan for battle, as worked out in the saddle and executed on the field, remains a classic blueprint for the conduct of a meeting engagement even today.

Soon after the battle of Lutzen, Napoleon's limited cavalry was fully occupied in trying to identify the movements of his enemies. Napoleon himself felt it most likely that they would retire towards the city of Bautzen in order to preserve their line of communications through Warsaw, while detaching part of their force to screen Berlin. His plan now, therefore, called for a large detached force of almost five corps to be formed under Ney's command, which was to cross the Elbe at Torgau and Wittenberg, take the Saxon Army into the VII Corps, and threaten Berlin. While Ney moved north, Napoleon himself would follow the allies through Dresden. By this means Napoleon hoped to detach the Prussians from the Russians and then destroy the two armies piecemeal. The focus on Berlin also reflects Napoleon's continuing preoccupation with an early intention of advancing to Danzig on the Prussian coast. Even allowing for Napoleon having a clear grasp of the difficulties of preserving allied unity, it is difficult to see why he was so obsessed with Berlin, unless it was to repay Frederick William's treachery in the Treaty of Kalisch. Either he had a very strong belief in the capture of Berlin as a decisive point in his attack on allied unity, or else he had put aside his own beliefs, disregarding the probability that by beating the allied army in battle, he would inevitably capture Berlin.

The allied main army withdrew to Bautzen, where a strong new position was surveyed and prepared by the Russian engineers. Napoleon followed up, throwing a bridge across the Elbe at Briesnitz just south of Dresden, and by the evening of 11 May Napoleon had 70,000 troops across the Elbe, and another 45,000 at Torgau. A short operational pause then followed, during which Napoleon decided to simplify his command arrangements to conform with his scheme for Ney's force. The Army of the Elbe and the Army of the Main, Napoleon's main army, were merged. Napoleon also used the pause to convert Dresden into his new centre of operations.

On 12 May Napoleon began a reconnaissance in force towards Bautzen in order to fix the allies, while Ney's army moved forward to concentrate at Luckau ready for a drive on Berlin. By 16 May, he ran the allies to ground at Bautzen. Napoleon, therefore, ordered three corps to fix the enemy while Oudinot's XII Corps worked around to the south of the allied position. Napoleon also sent word to Ney to be ready to march south with his own corps and Lauriston's V Corps, but Ney was also ordered to detach the II and VII Corps to continue the march on Berlin. Ney, however, failed to understand what was required of him, and in the end he marched south with all four corps. This was in many ways a sensible course of action, and had Ney concentrated this force, the outcome of Bautzen would have been substantially different. As it was, his two leading corps were separated by 24 hours' marching from the remainder. Ney never grasped the Emperor's intention, and it must be said that Napoleon's instructions were far from clear. What the Emperor actually intended was very simple: to fix the allies frontally, and then roll up their position from the north and rear. Ney's slowness and Napoleon's divergence from his own principles were, however, to rob him of a decisive victory and ruin this brilliantly simple plan. The battle of Bautzen would provide a strong contrast with Lutzen in three ways. First, Lutzen was fought on a confined battlefield, while Bautzen took place on an extended frontage of seven miles. Second, Lutzen was a meeting engagement where ground was nothing; Bautzen was a set piece battle fought on a selected position where ground was everything. Third Lutzen was won by manoeuvre, while Bautzen was – deliberately – to contain a strong element of attrition.

Bautzen was a two-day battle of great ferocity. Napoleon's plan called for his leading corps to pin the enemy frontally, a deliberately attritional attack designed to wear the allies down, forcing the allies to weaken the centre and then commit their reserves in order to block this move. Concurrent with Ney's move, the corps of Lauriston would move from the north deep into the allied rear, seize the village of Hochkirch, and block the withdrawal route. Then at the critical moment, the Guard and the corps of Bertrand, under Soult's command, would smash the allied centre north of Bautzen. Although the allies were well entrenched, and Napoleon's formations were tired, the French were at a numerical advantage throughout, and Napoleon was confident that if all went well, Bautzen would be a second Jena.

Bautzen should have been the perfect Napoleonic battle and the culmination of the Spring Campaign – but it was not. Its failings have as much to say on this as did the successes of Lutzen. First, the declining quality of the *Grande Armée* was becoming obvious. On the allied side, the Russians and Prussians showed determination and the desire for revenge, and their troops were gaining in experience all the time. Second, Napoleon's command and staff system were still good, but they had declined. Napoleon had aimed to concentrate actually on the battlefield rather than short of it, and the event showed that the system was no longer capable of executing his intentions. Ney is often held responsible for the failure of the plan, for his failure to cut the allied retreat allowed the allies to escape the trap, but part of the failure must lie in an over-centralized command which did nothing to educate subordinates or allow them initiative. The choice of Ney was equally flawed, as with a man so impetuous and so little given to analytical thought, there was every chance of a disaster. Third, the shortage of cavalry made it very difficult to form a reserve capable of conducting a pursuit. By contrast, the allied superiority in quality and numbers of mobile troops allowed them to form an effective rearguard, and thus break clean.

Throughout the next three days the allied withdrawal continued towards Schweidnitz in Silesia, followed up by the French. Both sides had lost the chance of any quick, decisive victory. When the Austrians, therefore,

proposed a ceasefire and the possibility, with their mediation, of a negotiated settlement, both sides were willing to accept. On 2 June a 36 hour
truce began, extended on 4 June, after a short conference, to 20 July. This
was again later extended to 10 August, with six days' notice to be given
before hostilities recommenced. Thus the Spring Campaign came to an
abrupt and somewhat unexpected close.

Operational Manoeuvre 3 – Penetration

The third manoeuvre may be very briefly described – the strategic pene-
tration. This was devised as an introduction to one of the other two
manoeuvres. It consisted simply of smashing through a defensive cordon to
seize some town or city as a centre of operations. The attack across the River
Niemen to Vilna in 1812 as a prelude to the separation of the Russian armies
of Barclay de Tolly and Prince Bagration is a good example of this
manoeuvre.

In preparation for his campaign in Russia, Napoleon made detailed
preparations following extensive study, for he did not underestimate either
the enemy or the environment. His calculations revealed that he would need
a field army of half a million men plus a secure line of communication: the
largest force he ever commanded on campaign, and which included, as
already noted in Chapter III, huge numbers of clients and allies. To conduct
the campaign, Napoleon formed a force in three echelons. The leading
echelon consisted of a group of three armies. The first of these was the main
army, commanded by Napoleon himself, consisting of around 250,000 men
– mostly native Frenchmen – in four corps and two cavalry corps. The
second and third armies, under Eugène de Beauharnais and Jerome Bonaparte, plus the two independent corps of MacDonald and Schwarzenberg,
consisted mainly of allies, and were to secure the flanks and rear of the main
army. Behind this huge spearhead was the second echelon, around 165,000
men in two corps and various allied formations, designed to act as battle
replacements for the main army. In the third echelon was Augereau's corps
of 60,000 men, mostly deployed in garrisons and fortresses. This huge army
was supported by a logistic organisation of 26 transport battalions, and it
must be remembered that as well as half a million men, the French army
included 200,000 animals and 25,000 vehicles of all types.

As had become his habit, Napoleon insisted on attending to most of the
detail of this venture himself, which meant that much was left undone.
There were vast problems of food supply, forage, ammunition, mobilization
of animals, the provision and training of sufficient leadership at all levels,

and the redeployment of troops from other theatres: enough friction to bring the army to a halt before ever the enemy or the weather took a hand.

In selecting his main avenue of approach into Russia, Napoleon considered the enemy, as the object of his problem, and two additional factors: weather and ground. His intelligence system had told him that the army of Field Marshal Mikhail Barclay de Tolly, 127,000 strong, was well spread out in a security cordon, while the armies of Prince Peter Bagration and Field Marshal Mikhail Kutusov were some way back into Russia. If he could smash through this cordon and seize Vilna, while drawing off Bagration to the south, he would be able first to split Tolly's army and destroy in detail such of it as mattered, then sever Russian communications back to St Petersburg, and then be able to turn on Bagration and destroy his army. For these reasons, as well as those of logistics and rear security, Napoleon selected the line from a concentration area around Kovno, through Vilna, to Vitebsk and Smolensk, as the main avenue of approach. To support it and draw Bagration off, Schwarzenberg's Austrians were to mount a deception operation suggesting a drive on Moscow south of the Pripet marshes. Once the main Russian field armies were destroyed, Napoleon would move on Moscow and complete the subjugation of his enemy. The invasion of Russia began on 22 June 1812.

The early part of the campaign did not, however, turn out as planned as Vilna had been designated as the main rendezvous for Bagration and the Tsar. On 1 July 1812, Napoleon issued orders to spring a gigantic trap, but as on so many other occasions, his subordinates mistook him or failed to comply with his orders, allowing the Russian army to escape. Vilna was duly occupied but the Russian operational plan – to avoid battle and gain time in exchange for space, drew the French ever deeper into Russia and ensured that by the time Smolensk was reached, exhaustion and over-extension provided only hard strategic choices for Napoleon.

Operational Manoeuvre 4 – The Battalion Square

The last of Napoleon's operational manoeuvres was the battalion square – the celebrated *battalion carrée*, which was partly operational manoeuvre and partly organizational tool. The army, preceded by a strong cavalry screen, would be divided into up to three columns each of two or three corps under a designated army commander. A central reserve, usually consisting of the Guard with possibly one other corps, reserve artillery and most of the heavy cavalry, was maintained under the Emperor's personal control. The columns would move on separate routes, the customary day's march away

Figure 4

Le Batallion Carrée

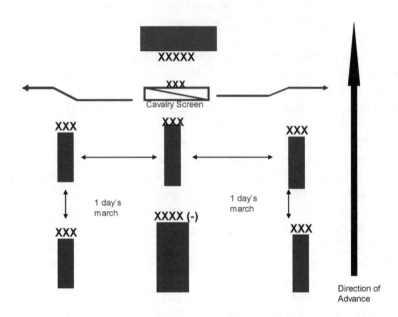

from each other, so that even if lateral communications were poor, the columns were fully capable of meeting and defeating, or at least pinning, any enemy force it met in a meeting engagement, while Napoleon man-oeuvred the rest of the army to destroy the enemy force from the flanks and rear. This disposition of forces would enable the army to meet an attack from any direction, even where Napoleon's knowledge of the enemy's location remained vague. Napoleon's mastery of all-round defence at operational level was never better illustrated than by the *battalion carrée*; its flexibility was admirably illustrated in the approach to Jena in 1806, and will be cited at more length in one of the three case studies which complete this book.

Army Organization

The *corps d'armée* organization which made these manoeuvres possible has been mentioned in Chapter II, and some further examination is now necessary. Like much of what Napoleon did, the *Grande Armée* was built on earlier foundations – in this case, the Revolutionary army of Carnot. At first, he intended the army to be around 200,000 men, divided into seven corps, each with a minimum of two divisions, a cavalry brigade, and organic artillery, engineers and supply troops. Over time, and with the aid of conscription and the absorption of client states, the army grew massively. By 1812, there were 611,000 men mobilized against Russia, with another 250,000 in Spain and the Mediterranean.

Nor did the corps remain of standard size. They were organized according to their tasks, and according to the abilities of their commander, and therefore varied considerably. They might have two, three, four or five divisions; a brigade or a division of cavalry, or sometimes no cavalry at all. But no matter what their size, because they were a well-balanced mix of infantry, guns, and cavalry, each corps was capable of fighting a superior enemy for some time and, as a basic principle, Napoleon would insist on corps being able to support each other. This meant keeping a maximum of a day's march apart – about or 15 to 18 kilometres as previously outlined. Thus an army corps could survive on its own for some time until other help arrived, as was well illustrated by Ney's Corps at Lutzen in the spring of 1813.

Perhaps of greater importance than even the corps was the creation by Napoleon of an artillery reserve of 12-pounder guns, almost a quarter of the army's guns in total; and the eight divisions of the heavy cavalry reserve, with their own horse artillery. These formations, held at the operational level under his personal command, along with the Imperial Guard, complemented the corps system. They could produce significant results at the point of greatest emphasis when a decision was required. After the Russian campaign, however, the army was always sadly lacking in cavalry, and this had a significant effect on Napoleon's ability to exploit any success he may have achieved.

The Imperial Guard completed the army. Originally no more than a reinforced regiment, in 1805 this corps numbered only 5,000 grenadiers, 2,000 cavalry and 24 guns. A little over a year later, it had grown to more than 12,000 men, and by 1812, more than 50,000. During its heyday, the corps had three distinct elements. First came the Old Guard. This was the heart of the force and comprised regiments of grenadiers, *chasseurs*, horse-grenadiers, light cavalry, dragoons, lancers and Mamelukes, as well as detachments of gunners, engineers, gendarmes and marines. A minimum of five years' service in two campaigns was required for entry, and selection and transfer into the Guard from the rest of the army went on continuously. Thus the Guard had the classic advantages and disadvantages of any *corps d'élite*: it gave the rest of the army something to which every man could aspire, but the constant creaming off of the best troops degraded the quality of standard infantry divisions, especially in NCOs. The creation of German *sturm batallionen* in late 1917 had much the same effect, as arguably did the creation of the *Waffen SS*.

In 1806, the Middle Guard was established, with regiments of fusiliers and *voltiguers*. Then in 1809 came the Young Guard, with regiments of *voltiguers* and *tirailleurs*. These were the cream of each class of new conscripts. To serve in the Guard was considered the ultimate privilege of any soldier's life, and it attracted considerable advantages in conditions of service: higher pay, more and better rations, and better equipment allowances. The men of the Guard were also frequently transported in carts rather than having to march, and were kept out of the line in battle until the critical moment. Thus, Napoleon always had a strong reserve of elite troops, owing special allegiance to him personally. It is not surprising, therefore, that he was unwilling to commit his favourite children to battle too often. But creaming off the best soldiers from his army, and then not using them, merely placed additional burdens on the standard divisions and probably increased the cost of winning battles still further.

Command Organization, Intelligence and Communications

With his army thus organized, Napoleon needed only to issue instructions through the staff for the movements of each corps as a whole, while the corps commander in turn dealt with the divisional commanders, they with the brigadiers, and so on. Although the corps were thus capable of independent action, they were very much tactical units, directed to the same higher purpose of the General at the operational level. But the important point was that the whole army was under unified command: gone were the old front armies of the Revolution. There was now only one French army, owing its allegiance to one man.

The general organization of the headquarters and its relationship to Napoleon has already been described in an earlier chapter. During a campaign, Napoleon would decide what tactical objectives were necessary to achieve the political object of his campaign and decide the sequence of action; allocating, in broad terms, resources, priorities and tasks, and earmarking reserves. The role of Berthier and the staff was to translate the Emperor's intentions and direction into detailed control measures – routes, boundaries, timings, allocation of subordinate formations, liaison, communications, billeting arrangements, supply, intelligence, and so on. Only by these means could a dispersed force be brought together at the right time and place. Control measures also reflected the necessity to balance the tasks allocated by Napoleon against the available manpower, firepower, and logistic support in order to work out the frontages of the advance and the depth of the march. These details required, then as now, foresight, steadfastness, promptness, and a clear understanding of the commander's intent. To do this, the staff had to be an efficient and flexible organization for control, in the hands of its chief.

The gathering and analysis of intelligence, referred to already in the chapter on strategy, was and is a key area in the direction of operational plans. The direction of intelligence is a command function, and the commander must, himself, clearly set out his critical information requirements, which will initially drive the allocation of resources in order to collect the information, and later lead the planning of the campaign. This is because of the blindingly obvious fact that intelligence is focused on the object of the general's problem – the enemy. The business of intelligence does not therefore stand alone, but is tightly woven into all operational planning and execution. In Napoleonic times, of course, there were no technical means available to gather intelligence: no intercept, no spy satellites, no drones or surveillance devices, just the Mark I eyeball. In all his campaigns, Napoleon had to put in place a thorough system and organization based on human intelligence, to supply him with information on the enemy's political situation, the territory over which the campaign would be fought, and the situation of the enemy army. In 1809, for example, he allocated 10,000 francs per month for espionage in Bavaria and Austria, in order to gain information on Austrian movements in Styria and Carinthia. A particularly well-documented example which illustrates Napoleon's intelligence operation is the organization set up for the invasion of Russia.

As early as 21 December 1811, Napoleon gave instructions for Baron Bignon to take charge of the secret police, 'with the duties of spying on the enemy army, translating intercepted letters and documents, collecting prisoners' reports etc.'. He was to secure the services of Poles – the Poles being well-disposed allies of the French – who could speak not only Polish, but also Russian and German like natives; these men should be soldiers who had seen some campaign service. These men should know Lithuania, Livonia, Courland, Podolia, Volhynia and the Ukraine. They would then be responsible for interviewing prisoners to extract information, and for running carefully selected agents, who would be well paid for their reports. In the meantime, other agents were to be sent immediately to report on the roads from St Petersburg to Vina, Riga, Memel, Kiev; the roads from Bucharest to St Petersburg, Moscow and Grodno; and the state of the fortifications of Riga, Dinaburg, Pinsk and Grodno. A budget of 12,000 francs per month was set aside for this work alone, and reports were to be sent daily by any means available.

At lower levels, the work of this department would be supplemented by the tactical intelligence provided by the light cavalry regiments of the army, corps and divisions whose chief task was reconnaissance, and indeed counter-reconnaissance against enemy cavalry. In Russia, this was especially necessary because of the enemy's use of Cossack, Bashkir and Kalmach irregular horse for harrying and raiding, as well as regular light cavalry.

Finally, there had to be a means of receiving and transmitting all this information from home, and to Napoleon's subordinates. At the strategic and operational levels, there were two principal methods of communication: the post and the semaphore. Sea communication was also used to communicate with overseas garrisons, but this was very vulnerable to interception by the Royal Navy. The post system, in which all secret correspondence was transmitted in cipher, relied on horsemen using pre-positioned relays of fresh horses at inns, fortresses and military headquarters. This system covered the whole of the Empire and, in general, worked efficiently. In some areas it was prone to interdiction – especially in Spain. The infamous 29th *Bulletin*, for example, was dispatched from Molodecho on the Polish frontier on 3 December 1812. It reached Paris a mere four days later; it is highly questionable whether a letter posted today in Poland would be received as quickly in France. However, because of guerrilla-infested roads, it did not reach Joseph Bonaparte in Madrid until 6 January 1813, a full month later. By contrast, Lord Liverpool had it in London via the smugglers' route on 21 December 1812.

The semaphore system was the second key element in Napoleon's communications. This had been established from 1792 onwards by the Chappe brothers, at a time when Revolutionary France needed fast and reliable information. The first line ran 190 kilometres from Lille to Paris. Later lines ran to Strasbourg, Mainz, Dunkirk, Brussels, Boulogne, Antwerp, Metz, and Lyon; to the French territories and garrisons in Italy at Milan, Venice and Mantua; and as far as the Spanish frontier. The system relied on towers in line of sight to each other, sending messages in code, using a mast with wooden arms which could be arranged in combinations, each depicting a character. The system was fast, allowing about three characters a minute to be transmitted by a well-trained crew. Soult, for example, signalled Napoleon from the Spanish frontier on 26 July 1813, and received a reply from Mainz on 1 August. A message could be sent to Venice in six hours, and Lille in one hour.

Thus at the strategic and operational levels, Napoleon could be reasonably sure that his intentions could be communicated, and that he in turn could receive good intelligence. Lower down, things were much less certain. In those days, long before the advent of radio, orders and dispatches were usually sent by mounted courier, usually with at least three sets going by different routes in case of interception. Confusion was usual, as when more than one set of orders was sent out, later sets often reached the recipient before the original dispatches. Once battle was joined, pre-arranged signals, such as cannon or rocket fire, were also used to co-ordinate the movement of bodies of troops. Napoleon's signal for the attack on the Prussians at Ligny in 1815, for example, was three cannon shots, repeated three times. At lower levels still, the drum, bugle, and trumpet signals – or at sea, flags – remained much as they had been since the early-seventeenth-century author Thomas Markham wrote that 'the drum is the voice of the commander'.

Conclusions

The most surprising thing about Napoleon's success at the operational level was that he got away with it for so long. What allowed him to do so was the sheer size and organizational strength of the *Grande Armée* itself. His battery of manoeuvres was after all, limited; and a thorough analysis of previous battles allied with good reconnaissance should have shown his enemies what he was about, and allowed them first to counter him and then to play back his own techniques against him. There were huge risks, for example, in marching divided, and against good quality opposition, he would have been punished. Armies that march divided risk being brought to battle divided, and therefore on unfavourable terms, but for most of his career, Napoleon was opposed by inferior generalship, or by coalitions with a divided command. As late as 1813, he was able to handle the Central European allies very severely with a set-piece envelopment at Bautzen, which was a re-run of several previous battles, yet the penny did not seem to drop. Even Wellington, who of all the allied generals seems most clearly to have understood Napoleon's methods, was hoodwinked in the campaign of the hundred days.

This is not to say that he did get away with it all the time. The campaign in Egypt and Syria was nothing short of a disaster. Russia was a debacle. His subordinates never succeeded in maintaining the initiative in Spain for long, and the Hundred Days ended in abdication and exile. Even during those campaigns which can be accounted successful, there were serious, sometimes near-disastrous, setbacks – for too often, the system of marching divided resulted in Napoleon being left waiting for some subordinate to arrive, while his troops withstood the devastation of close-quarter battle in the appalling conditions of the day. At Jena, for example, Bernadotte never arrived at all, and Davout, instead of clinching the day, met the Prussian main body by pure chance at Auerstadt, winning a battle against all the odds and receiving from Napoleon cruel jibes about his eyesight. At Marengo, the day was saved only by the arrival of Desaix, and at Eylau, by Ney. Ney failed to repeat this feat at Bautzen, allowing the allies to escape. In 1815, D'Erlon spent a day marching and counter-marching between Ligny and Quatre Bras, and at Waterloo, Grouchy never closed with the battlefield.

These potential disasters were as often as not averted by sheer bloody fighting at the tactical level, and this will be examined more closely in the next chapter. For this reason as well as others already outlined, the balance sheet favours Napoleon as an operational general. But once again it must be stressed that, there is no greater military truth than that if strategy is flawed, no matter how brilliant the tactical manoeuvres, no matter how inspired the operational art, failure will be inevitable.

V

Napoleon on the Battlefield

Battle

This chapter concerns Napoleon as a tactician, and examines both his use of battles and engagements as decisive acts, and the tactical methods he used to win them. In Napoleonic terms, 'tactics' was the study of the engagement, or the science of handling men, guns and horses in close contact with the enemy. This is not too dissimilar from modern definitions, which describe tactics as the art of disposing troops on the battlefield in close contact with the enemy, and the provision of direct logistic support, and the tactical level of war as being that at which actual physical combat takes place. Despite the changes in technology since Napoleon's day, it remains an art, not a science, since it remains a clash of wills, and of human ingenuity, rather than the mere application of force.

For Napoleon, there was an inescapable connection between the campaign and the battle: the campaign was constructed to achieve his strategic objectives, and was designed to bring the enemy to battle, a battle that would be the decisive act of any war. In this, he was being true to that essential requirement of generalship described in the opening chapter, even though he himself would not have expressed it in those precise terms – that of determining those things that are going to be decisive. The purpose of battle was not merely to defeat the enemy's army – the operational centre of gravity – but to destroy it and thus end any war at one stroke. Napoleon's contemporary, Jomini, who was at various times both subordinate and opponent, wrote of this, that the general must concentrate on the battlefield:

> the bulk of [his] force at the decisive point or against the section of the enemy line which one wishes to overwhelm, and ensuring that these forces are sent forward with vigour and concentration so as to produce a simultaneous result.

By destroying the opposing army, the enemy's strategic centre of gravity could be directly threatened: be it the capital city, or vital resources, or a key leader. The campaigns of Marengo, Ulm and Austerlitz, Jena, Eylau and Friedland are all illustrations of this principle in action. Thus, it must be apparent that while distinctions may be drawn between strategy, operational art and tactics using considerations of time, resources, or geography, strategy and operational art have by no means been suspended when battle is joined. Manoeuvring throughout the theatre of operations, and in the realm of diplomacy, continues not only before and after, but also during a battle. This is implicit in Clausewitz's celebrated but often misquoted and still more often misunderstood remark that

> We maintain ... that war is simply a continuation of political intercourse, with the addition of other means. We ... want to make it clear that war in itself does not suspend political intercourse or change it into something entirely different. In essentials that intercourse continues, irrespective of the means it employs.

The close connection between strategic objectives, operational manoeuvre and battle was underlined by Napoleon's own position as head of state, head of government and commander in chief: in such an unrivalled position, he could ensure the unbroken maintenance of the aim from the beginning to the end of a war – something that few others, even absolute rulers like Stalin, have been able to achieve. The same intelligence thus prepared the general strategic conditions and objectives, set the operational scenery, and joined the engagement. Today, the position of a commander at the strategic or operational levels is rather different. He may indeed assist in preparing the general conditions for engaging an enemy; he may exert influence on the course of battles by assigning resources, priorities, boundaries, rules of engagement and so on. But the execution of a battle – what Tukachevskii called 'the practical resolution of strategic measures' – will be entrusted to a subordinate combined arms commander.

Napoleon's Men

Although it is not intended here to descend into the minute detail of tactical battlefield movements, some understanding of what the different arms were capable of doing is important. This is not least because the training of the army to carry out these movements, or drills – since in Napoleonic times, tactics and drill were still inextricably intertwined – remains the responsibility of the general. The Duke of Wellington's dictum was universally applicable, and still holds good: that the first duty of an officer is 'so to train the men under his command that they may without question beat any force opposed to them in the field'.

Napoleon himself was originally an artillery officer, and the French artillery was therefore well equipped and its gunnery excellent. The calibres of the guns have been described in Chapter IV, but most important were 'the Emperor's beautiful daughters', the 12-pounder guns of the corps artillery, and the artillery reserve under his own command. The guns could fire ball at long range – about 1,000 yards being the maximum effective range – or canister for close work. Smaller-calibre guns accompanied the divisions or were formed into horse artillery batteries to accompany the cavalry. From 1806 onwards these guns were increasingly used in massed batteries designed to smash a hole in the enemy's line, which the infantry and cavalry could exploit. 'Missile weapons have now become the principal weapons,' Napoleon wrote; and later, 'It is with artillery that war is made.' He also remarked that 'it is necessary to have as much artillery as the enemy. Experience shows that it is necessary to have four guns for every thousand men.'

The heavy cavalry – cuirassiers, lancers, dragoons, horse grenadiers, carabineers and so on – were formed into regiments of at least two squadrons, a squadron being two troops each of around 40 horsemen. The task of the heavy cavalry was to break enemy infantry or cavalry formations by massed charges, and much emphasis was laid on the ability to re-form after a charge: this being the legacy of the lack of discipline of the cavalry of the Revolutionary period. The bulk of the heavies were usually held as reserve formations under Napoleon's command. The carabineers and horse grenadiers also acted as mounted infantry. The duties of the light cavalry – hussars, light dragoons, *chasseurs à cheval* – were scouting, pursuit, and rear area security. A cavalry brigade formed of all disciplines usually formed part of each corps. It was the arm of the *Grande Armée*, however, which never recovered its former expertise after the Russian campaign, not least because of the growing shortage of horses in Western Europe after 20 years of warfare.

As ever, it was Napoleon's infantry which bore the brunt of battle. Each soldier was armed with a smooth-bore musket, bayonet and sword, and carried 50 rounds of cartridge. The effective range of the musket was 100 yards and this, combined with the inaccuracy of the weapon and the thick smoke produced by black powder, meant that battle tactics were inevitably based on closely packed masses of men producing a high density of fire. By 1809, the infantry was formed into battalions of nine companies, with up to 140 men in each company, with three or four battalions forming a regiment. The standard battle formation for a company was in three ranks. The battalion could therefore form into line for either attack or defence, or square to repulse cavalry, or into column of divisions for attack. All infantry formations were trained to change formation rapidly, and in the face of the enemy. In column, a battalion would form up on a two-company frontage, about 50 yards across and with a depth of four companies in three ranks, 20 yards deep. A divisional attack formation would consist of at least 12 battalion columns formed in line, or staggered in what was known as an echelon. This mass of men was trained to march to within 100 yards of the enemy, fire a series of volleys, and then close with the bayonet. It was this formation which had developed from the unruly but fiercely aggressive tactics of the Revolutionary armies, and which it was felt best harnessed the *élan* of the French soldier – or steadied a mass of possibly shaky conscripts.

Napoleon himself favoured a formation known as mixed order – *l'ordre mixte* – as espoused by Guibert. In this formation, a regiment would form up with one battalion in line, and the other two in column on either flank. This formation was felt to give the best combination of firepower and shock action, and be the most flexible. The French infantry, although it bested all the great armies of Europe at one time or another, was the one part of the army which was never a match for the discipline of the British regulars, with their steady, accurate fire, and their habit of forming two ranks rather than three, in order to lap round attacking columns and pour fire into them from three sides.

One other discipline within the infantry should be mentioned: the light infantry. Within each battalion, the ninth company was a light company known as *voltigeurs*. At divisional level there was an additional battalion of light infantry known as *tirailleurs*. The officers and NCOs of these units often carried rifles rather than muskets, and their task was to move ahead of an attacking column, or screen a defensive position, forming a cloud of skirmishers. This cloud, or swarm, would both keep the enemy light troops away from the French main body, and also break the cohesion of an attacking force by picking off officers and NCOs, and forcing attacking units constantly to reform to fill gaps caused by casualties.

Napoleon as Battlefield Commander

Given the nature and ranges of weapons just described, and the size of armies of the period, Napoleon could generally expect to be in a position to observe and control any battle personally from one or two key positions of observation. The organization of his headquarters and staff has been outlined in Chapter II, but what of the arrangements for Napoleon's travel in close proximity to the enemy? For like a modern commander, Napoleon required the ability to separate himself and his tactical headquarters from the *impedimenta* of the main headquarters. With the Emperor were two aides, two duty officers, two interpreters, a page and a groom, Berthier or another senior staff officer, Caulincourt, Guyot and the duty marshal. About 400 metres behind came a group of staff officers and aides, and after another 400 metres, a group of Berthier's staff – all covered by an escort found by the cavalry of the Guard. These arrangements were most necessary, for Napoleon insisted on personal reconnaissance at every opportunity. They gave him the flexibility that any general needs to move rapidly, with a reasonable degree of protection, in order to exercise *command* at wherever the decisive point of a battle might be – but for limited periods. In doing so, he would reinforce his own intuitive powers of decision-making, by ensuring that his own awareness of the situation was as current as it could be. Meanwhile the main headquarters, which were much larger, kept *control* of the army. Napoleon could use this main headquarters for planning, or could return to it to rest and recuperate under the umbrella of its life-support, or could base himself there to command the battle in, for example, a dispersed situation where the flow of information most naturally coalesced in main headquarters through its communications network. This flexibility allowed Napoleon to do the three things, already mentioned, which any general must be able to do in order to fulfil his command functions: to find out what is going on, to communicate his intentions to his subordinates, and to maintain contact with the staff so that problems can be solved.

Close co-operation was relatively simple at that period, not only between corps, but between the various arms and services of the entire army. Napoleon himself, crucially, never allowed control of any battle to slip from his hand, except on a very few occasions. When he did so, the outcome was a bad one for the French, as Marengo almost proved, and Aspern-Essling and Waterloo certainly did. It is often said that Napoleon did not interest himself in tactics: this does not stand close examination. It is true that only rarely did he issue any detailed guidance on corps-level tactical employment, but it is also true that it was Napoleon who devised and issued the battle plans, and then directed the combined attacks of infantry, cavalry reserves, and massed batteries of guns. What a modern corps or divisional commander carries out on the battlefield today in conventional war within his own sphere of command, therefore, Napoleon himself performed on the entire field of battle. And there is no doubt that his personal presence was a huge force multiplier: wherever the dreaded cries of '*Vive l'Empereur!*' arose, French troops took heart, and their enemies despaired.

But what of Napoleon's tactics themselves? First, it should be understood that Napoleon rarely fought a truly defensive battle, even when he was strategically and operationally on the defensive. There are arguably only three occasions when he did so: Leipzig in 1813, and La Rothière and Arcis in 1814. Even then, he only did so as a last resort. The principle of offensive action was an imperative from the strategic level right down to the tactical.

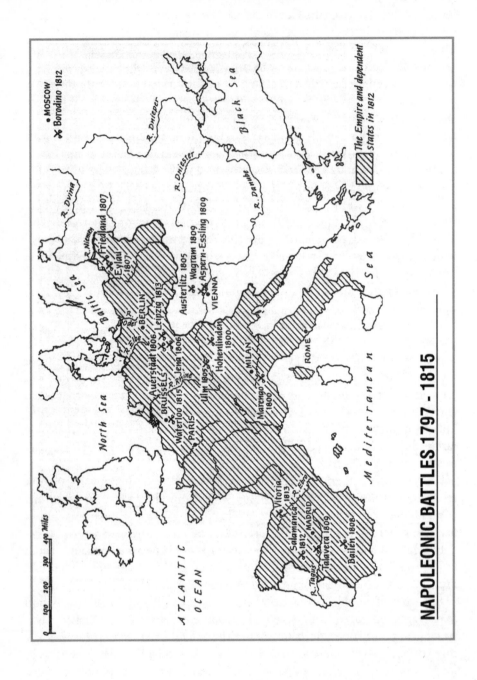

NAPOLEONIC BATTLES 1797 - 1815

When seeking contact with the enemy, therefore, if contact was made too late to achieve a decision that same day, Napoleon would often launch a short-term spoiling attack to deceive or confuse the enemy, and then hope to exploit the ensuing uncertainty early the following day. This was done as much as anything to seize or maintain the initiative. Paradoxically, however, although the French preferred the offensive, it was those opponents who maintained a solid defensive that caused them the most grief. The British in the Peninsula and at Waterloo are the most obvious example, but the same can be said for the Russians at Eylau and Borodino.

Napoleon was influenced by his studies as much in his tactical ideas as in his strategic and operational thinking. In particular, he followed the example of Frederick the Great, especially in his development of a battle system which would break the enemy's line, thus exposing him to a fatal stroke. This he sought to achieve by a variety of means: deception, diversion, or spoiling attacks to provoke an ill-considered counter-attack, as well as the more brutal expedient of tearing out a flank by physical assault.

The main Napoleonic battle drill varied from engagement to engagement, but the basic ingredients were the same. By 1815, Wellington could remark to Picton on the field of Waterloo, 'Well, they are coming on in the same old style.' And Picton could reply, 'Yes, and we'll just have to meet them, in the same old style.' A heavy artillery barrage would shake the enemy, then the swarm of skirmishers would dominate the ground between the opposing forces, while Napoleon and his subordinates studied the enemy's dispositions. Next, fixing or pinning attacks would be mounted by part of the army to engage the enemy frontally and reduce his freedom of action. While this was going on, either a whole corps or elements of the reserve, especially cavalry, would mount an enveloping attack from a flank, designed to draw off the enemy's reserves, or make him weaken his strongest positions. This was an important element in the Napoleonic battle system. 'It is by turning the enemy, by attacking his flank, that battles are won,' Napoleon said, and it is not surprising, therefore, that this technique featured in almost every important engagement he fought from Arcola to Dresden. It was as important for its psychological effect on the enemy as for its physical effect, and the chief target of this effect would be the enemy commander. The flank attack came in two variations. First, there was the turning movement, in which one or more corps would descend on the enemy from an unexpected direction as a result of an operational level manoeuvre, as was intended at Jena. This often produced what seemed to be two battles – what David Chandler called the double battle – even though in fact it was a single engagement. Second, there was always the possibility of a simple tactical flank attack by a corps, as with Soult at Bautzen.

If the flank attack succeeded in upsetting the enemy's equilibrium, then with his reserves drawn off and his rear threatened, the enemy might well break his line, and begin to retreat. At this point the final stroke would begin. The artillery of the reserve would be moved forward no more than 500 yards from the enemy, and would very rapidly blast a hole in the enemy line. Thus, either by dislocation or by fire, the enemy's line would be fractured and his position made vulnerable. Infantry columns would then attack, supported by the French cavalry and its horse artillery, which would try to force the enemy infantry into a square, making them yet more vulnerable to both artillery and infantry attack. If not immediately successful, these attacks could be repeated as necessary until the enemy was either driven from the field or thoroughly penetrated. Napoleon would accept huge casualties to achieve this situation. At this point either the Guard or the heavy cavalry reserve would finish the job. Success depended on near-perfect timing, and simultaneous action by several arms, but once the enemy line was broken, the battle was as good as won: when the system worked, therefore, it was devastating.

The Battle System (1): Friedland 1807

In the aftermath of the battle of Jena, Napoleon was faced with some important strategic and operational decisions.* True, he had beaten the Prussian army and occupied his capital, but the Prussian king refused to surrender. Moreover, Prussia's ally Russia was about to enter the lists. Strategically, Napoleon took steps rapidly to occupy the Prussian coast and extend the Continental System. He also made plans to secure a future client state by creating a puppet kingdom of Poland, to be known as the Grand Duchy of Warsaw, from peoples and territory to be seized from Prussia, Russia and Austria. Operationally, he created two additional corps, the IX, from Bavarian and Württemberg troops, which was placed under his brother Jérôme's command, and the X, from Poles, under Lefebvre. Then, both to keep the Russians at a distance and to mobilize Polish support, he detached a large force of three corps and a cavalry corps under Murat to occupy the line of the Vistula, east of Warsaw. These were the corps of Davout (III), Lannes (V) and Augereau (VII). Faced with this advance, the Russian advanced guard under General Count Levin Benigsen abandoned Warsaw and withdrew. Napoleon then moved the remainder of his army,

* The campaign of Jena-Auerstadt is dealt with as a case study in Chapter IX.

consisting of the corps of Bernadotte (I), Soult (IV), Ney (VI), and the Guard, forward into Poland, and followed up the Russian withdrawal.

A nasty battle was fought in rain and mud on 26 December 1806 at Pultusk. Napoleon claimed victory on the ground that he had been left in possession of the field, but it cost him 3,000 casualties and the goodwill of the army, which grumbled exceedingly at the weather and the season. Accordingly, the army went into winter quarters. As usual, staying in one place created logistic shortages. These were particularly severe for the corps of Ney, who in January 1807 pushed northwards into the more fertile territory of East Prussia. From this raid grew the battle of Eylau on 8 February 1807, a drawn contest, again fought in the worst sort of winter weather, and again resulting in severe casualties: it was, in fact, the bloodiest battle that Napoleon had fought up to that date.

In the weeks that followed, Napoleon took steps to reinforce and reorganize the army in East Prussia, and to reduce the Prussian fortresses of Danzig, Graudenz and Kolberg. With Danzig captured, Napoleon moved his line of communication from Berlin northwards, to make Danzig his advanced base and logistic hub. By early June, Benigsen's force had also been reinforced and refitted, and numbered 100,000 men. On 4 June, Benigsen took the offensive and pushed Ney's corps back over the Passarge River. A prompt counter-attack by the I, III, IV, V and VIII corps restored the situation.

The counter-attack also regained the operational and tactical initiative for Napoleon, who decided that in order to maintain it he would himself go on the offensive and drive the Russians out of East Prussia entirely. The army began to advance on 8 June, and on 10 June a hard battle was fought around the Russians' entrenched position at Heilsberg, in which Napoleon attacked the Russians frontally, with no attempt at finesse or manoeuvre. For his pains, he received a severe mauling, and lost over 10,000 men. He succeeded in obliging Benigsen to withdraw on the following day through manoeuvre, and thus remained in possession of the ground. Because of this, he again claimed a victory – but it did not feel like one to the army.

The Russians retreated towards the small town of Friedland, the lowest point at which they could cross the River Alle, before it flowed into the much larger Pregel. Napoleon had guessed that this was where the Russians would stand, and he therefore had two choices of approach to the Russian position: east of the river, or west. The western route was the shorter, and moreover would uncover the Russians' advanced base in Königsberg, garrisoned by a Prussian corps under General Anton von L'Estocq, where they had collected huge depots of stores. However, to approach Friedland from the west would serve to drive Benigsen back on his line of communication

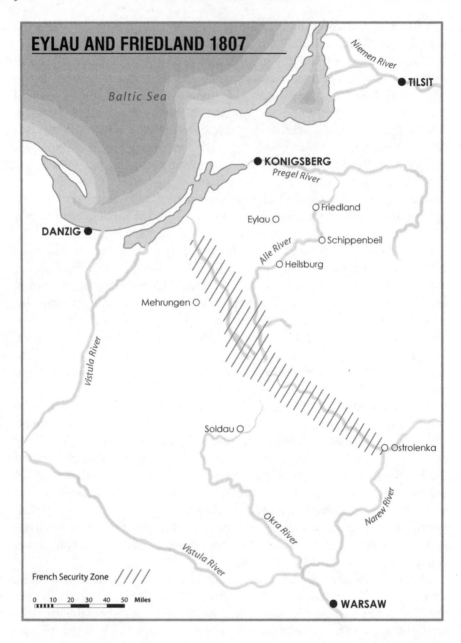

EYLAU AND FRIEDLAND 1807

through Riga, and Napoleon had neither the forces nor the logistic support to pursue him into Russia. The eastern approach, on the other hand, offered the chance to outflank Benigsen in true Napoleonic style, sever his communications, and drive him into the confined position of the Königsberg peninsula. It did, however, require long forced marches with an uncertain supply situation, and an exposed flank. Perhaps uncharacteristically, Napoleon opted for the western approach.

Napoleon's plan, as set out in a directive to his corps commanders early on 14 June, was that the left wing of the *Grande Armée* under Murat, consisting of the III Corps under Davout, and IV Corps under Soult, and part of the Cavalry Corps, would pursue L'Estocq northwards towards Königsberg. If possible, they were to seize the city by a *coup de main*. In doing this, he seriously weakened his main army for no good reason. L'Estocq's force was only 25,000 strong, whereas Napoleon was detaching around 60,000 men and, in doing so, he failed to achieve concentration of force at a time when he had determined on a decisive battle.

Lannes had, in fact, moved off ahead of the rest of the army, and had been identified by Benigsen, who realized that the corps was beyond the mutual support of the rest of Napoleon's army. At 9.00 p.m. on the night of 13 June, word came from Lannes that the Russians were indeed at Friedland in strength. But whether this was the main army or simply an advanced guard, was not clear. Napoleon sent word back to Lannes that he was to storm the place and, in the meantime, the other formations of the army would move up to support him. In fact, Benigsen fully intended to attack and destroy Lannes, and had three bridges built in order to move troops to the western side of the Alle. The first engagements of 14 June took place around the villages of Posthenen and Heinrichsdorf. Fortunately for Lannes, the Russian attacks were not pressed home in strength, for it was now clear that this was the Russian main army. Lannes knew his duty: to fix the larger enemy force, giving time for Napoleon to bring up the rest of the army.

Benigsen had drawn his 46,000 troops up to form a bridgehead on the western side of the Alle, forming a front across the eastward-bending loop of the river at Friedland. Six divisions were deployed in two lines, well supported by artillery, but the lines were divided by the Millstream, over which several plank bridges were hastily thrown. The lines were around four miles long. The Russian north flank was anchored on the Dambrau wood, held by a force of Cossack cavalry. The south was anchored on the Sortlach wood, which was garrisoned by 3,000 light troops. Command of the troops on the left was held by General Prince Peter Bagration and General Kologrivov, while the right was commanded by General Prince Andrei Gortshakov.

Napoleon had meanwhile ordered the rest of the army to move directly on Friedland in three columns, with Mortier's VIII Corps on the left, and Ney's VI Corps on the right. The Guard Corps and the I Corps under Victor, who had replaced the wounded Bernadotte, together formed the reserve and were to move on the centre route, which had been taken earlier by Lannes. Napoleon himself arrived at Friedland around midday: it was the seventh anniversary of Marengo and Napoleon, always superstitious, determined to do battle that day. He was still uncertain as to whether this was the whole of Benigsen's force, but he sent word nonetheless to Murat, expecting that he would be in possession of Königsberg, and ordering him to send Davout's corps and two regiments of heavy cavalry to Friedland, as the battle might roll over into the following day.

It was not until 4.00 p.m. that the French army had closed up to Benigsen's position in strength. Napoleon's personal reconnaissance of the position told him that Benigsen had constrained himself badly by packing so large a force into so small a bridgehead with his back to the river, and that his ability to manoeuvre was still further constrained by the Millstream. Moreover, the meandering course of the river meant that there were several high bluffs or spurs from which the Russian position could be enfiladed. The opportunity was, he felt, too good, and he scotched all talk of holding over the attack until the next day.

Once the Guard had come up, Napoleon disposed around 80,000 men – enough for a decisive result. His intention was to concentrate on that part of the Russian force to the south of the Millstream. These would be the target for the corps of Ney, who would be reinforced by Oudinot's division and Latour-Maubourg's dragoon division. The attack of Ney's corps would initiate the battle, and all available guns would fire in his support. Lannes' corps, reinforced with a cavalry division, would occupy the centre of the line, and Mortier the left; Mortier was given strict orders to hold fast, and act as the hinge on which the rest of the army would pivot from right to left. Two cavalry divisions under Generals Emmanuel Grouchy and Jean d'Espagnes were to be prepared to support Ney, and attack as soon as the Russians showed signs of retreating. The Guard and the corps of Victor, reinforced with a cavalry division, were maintained in reserve.

At 5.30 p.m. Napoleon gave the signal for the attack: three salvoes from 20 guns fired in rapid succession. Ney's troops advanced with the spire of Friedland church as their axis, much to the surprise of Benigsen, who had considered the day too far gone. He had, moreover, been in the process of issuing orders for a withdrawal, having realized the peril of his position. Seeing the attack develop, he at once cancelled the orders. As Ney's men advanced, Benigsen thought he saw the opportunity for a counter-move, and sent several regiments of Cossacks into a gap between the two leading French divisions. Latour-Maubourg's dragoons, however, blocked the attack, and the Cossacks drew off.

At this point, Napoleon ordered Victor's corps to move up behind Ney, whose men now came under extremely heavy Russian artillery fire from the far bank of the river. This was enough to halt Ney's men, and seeing this, Benigsen again ordered a cavalry attack on the French extreme left. The French troops began to waver, but the situation was saved by Victor's leading regiments, which caught the attacking cavalry in the flank. The horsemen turned tail and fled back into the Russian position, causing chaos as they did so. The confusion was exploited by the French artillery, and especially by the guns of Victor's corps, 36 12-pounders, which were brought into an enfilade position overlooking the Russian position. Advancing by bounds, the guns closed from 600 yards, to 300, to 150, and eventually to no more than 60 yards from the Russian infantry. Despite being well within musket range of their enemies, the devastating fire of this battery produced a horrific result on the crowded Russian formations, so that Ney, with characteristic bravery, was able to lead his men forward.

Benigsen did his best to relieve the pressure on his left by attacking the corps of Lannes and Mortier, but made no headway; indeed he only succeeded in fixing the larger part of his force. In increasing frustration, Benigsen tried once more to counter-attack Ney, this time with infantry. The attack was thrown back, and many of the Russian infantry perished in the river. Ney's corps pressed its advantage, and fought its way into the outskirts of Friedland. Benigsen then played his final card – an attack on Ney's corps by the Russian Imperial Guard. But this attack made no more progress than any of the others: a combination of artillery fire, musketry and the bayonet felled the Guardsmen in swathes. By 8.30 p.m., Ney was virtually in control of the town.

While Ney had pressed on, Lannes' corps had repulsed a series of infantry and cavalry attacks, and also advanced in the centre, while Mortier held firm on the left. Benigsen realized that he was faced with complete disaster if he did not at once break off the action and retire across the river. Three of his four bridges were down, but the one bridge and a ford opposite the village of Kloschenen were just sufficient: the eastern bank was lined with Russian batteries and, under their covering fire, with a rearguard formed by the Russian cavalry, the hapless Russian infantry was able to scramble to safety. This was the moment when Napoleon might have been expected to complete his victory by unleashing the heavy cavalry and the Guard – but it was not to be so. Perhaps he missed the presence of Murat, who would certainly have led such an attack, but whatever the reason, the moment was lost, and soon afterwards dusk began to gather.

As the Russians withdrew, the French kept up a pursuit of sorts until 11.00 p.m. Casualties had once again been enormous: the Russians lost at least 18,000 killed, wounded and captured out of 46,000 engaged, and abandoned 80 pieces of artillery. The French lost 8,000 out of 86,000, but since neither the Guard nor I Corps had been engaged, the losses were concentrated disproportionately in the V and VI Corps. The battle had been a striking tactical victory for Napoleon, of the sort that he had sought since Jena. But the Russian army had been able to get away, and the battle had not, therefore, been the ultimate destructive blow that Napoleon had planned. He was, however, jubilant, writing to Joséphine: 'My children have worthily celebrated the anniversary of Marengo. The battle of Friedland will be just as famous and as glorious for my people.'

The battle certainly proved operationally and strategically decisive, whatever its immediate tactical outcome. On 19 June Benigsen asked for an armistice, which Napoleon was glad to grant, since he now occupied all of Prussia, had no means of advancing into Russia, and was dependent on increasingly stretched communications. On 25 June, the celebrated meeting between Napoleon and Tsar Alexander took place on a raft in the River Nieman. Two weeks later, peace treaties were signed at Tilsit with the Russians and Prussians. The Grand Duchy of Warsaw became a reality; all Prussian territory west of the Elbe River was ceded to a new kingdom of Westphalia, to be ruled by Jérôme Bonaparte; and the Continental System was completed with the accession of Russia.

The Battle System (2): Wagram 1809

Wagram, fought on 5 and 6 July 1809, came only six weeks after Napoleon's defeat at Aspern-Essling, at the hands of Austria's most accomplished general, the Archduke Charles. On that occasion, Napoleon, having occupied the Austrian capital of Vienna, had attempted to cross the Danube as a preliminary to destroying the Archduke's army; however, his intelligence was hopelessly inadequate and he succeeded only in walking into a carefully-laid ambush. His losses of 44,000 were truly appalling, and in the aftermath his army suffered from shortages of food and fodder. Napoleon did, however, maintain possession of the island of Lobau in the Danube, which he intended to use as a launch pad for a renewed attempt at a crossing. In the aftermath of Aspern-Essling, he made a careful reconnaissance of the far bank from the island and from the home bank, and made his plans. While he did so, the Austrians made no attempt to exploit the initiative which they had gained.

In essence, Napoleon planned to deceive the Austrians by a feint at the site of an earlier pontoon crossing from the northern end of Lobau towards Essling. Once the Austrians were decisively engaged in this attack, the real crossing would take place from a smaller island three miles downstream of

Lobau, which he named the Ile Alexandre, after Berthier. Pontoon bridges were to be prepared in secret by the artillery – the arm responsible, in the French army, for bridging – and put in place between the home bank and the island immediately before the feint attack; a wooden bridge was then to be constructed from the island to the far side, using pile-driving. Huge quantities of stores were ferried to the island for this task, using barges manned by the Marines of the Guard.

Napoleon then proceeded to reorganize and re-fit the army ready for this battle. The first task was to rebuild the bridge from Lobau to the south bank of the Danube, which the Austrians had broken using barges during the battle of Aspern-Essling, so that he could evacuate his 10,000 wounded to the hospitals in Vienna. He also ordered up another corps, that of Marmont, from Dalmatia, for he knew that once the news of Aspern-Essling got out, he stood in grave danger of a revolt in Germany. A victory, therefore, was imperative. By the end of June he had assembled a force of 175,000 men in 25 infantry and ten cavalry divisions, supported by 544 guns. These were formed into ten corps commanded by Marshals Walther (the Guard), Massena (IV), Oudinot (II), Davout (III), Bernadotte (IX), Prince Eugène de Beauharnais (Army of Italy), Marmont (XI), Macdonald (XII), and Bessières (Reserve Cavalry). In addition, he had the corps of Lefebvre (VII) and Vandamme (VIII) providing flank and rear security, and the Bavarian division of General Count Wrede. All these troops except for Massena's men were evacuated to the south bank, but Massena's troops were put to work fortifying the island as a secure base for operations.

On the evening of 30 June, Napoleon launched his feint, and met almost no resistance. As a result, Massena was able to advance as far as the village of Aspern, and then erect a trestle bridge. However, the Archduke Charles was not to be gulled by Napoleon. His cavalry and outposts had established and maintained observation over the whole river, and he had drawn up his army of 130,000 men, supported by 400 guns, in a 12-mile semi-circle, on the north bank of the Danube, using a series of hills, spurs and the Russbach stream to anchor his position. Into this noose, Charles intended to draw Napoleon in a repeat of Aspern-Essling. The noose would be drawn tight when the one gap at the south-east extremity of his line was closed by the corps of his brother, the Archduke John, who had been ordered to march up from his position near Pressburg.

Napoleon was once again let down by his intelligence system, and had no inkling of the Austrian dispositions, but clearly felt confident in his preparations. The Austrians had, after all, made no moves to attack him and had concentrated on strengthening their positions. Indeed, it was only on 1 July that Charles realized that something was afoot, and the following day

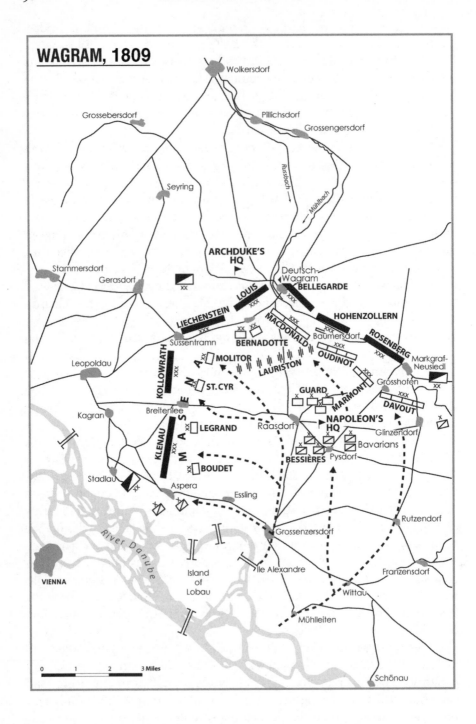

WAGRAM, 1809

Wolkersdorf

Grossebersdorf

Pillichsdorf

Grossengersdorf

Seyring

Russbach

Mühlbach

ARCHDUKE'S HQ

Stammersdorf

Deutsch-Wagram

Gerasdorf

BELLEGARDE

LOUIS

LIECHENSTEIN

HOHENZOLLERN

MACDONALD

ROSENBERG

Süssentramn

BERNADOTTE

Baumersdorf

Leopoldau

MOLITOR

OUDINOT

Markgraf-Neusiedl

LAURISTON

ST.CYR

Grosshofen

GUARD

DAVOUT

Kagran

Breitenlee

MARMONT

KLENAU

LEGRAND

Raasdorf

NAPOLEON'S HQ

Glinzendorf

Bavarians

MASENA

KOLLOWRATH

BOUDET

BESSIÈRES

Pysdorf

Stadlau

Aspera

Essling

Rutzendorf

Grossenzersdorf

Franzensdorf

River Danube

Island of Lobau

Ile Alexandre

Wittau

VIENNA

Mühlleiten

0   1   2   3 Miles

Schönau

he withdrew his army to its old positions, much less well fortified, in order to avoid being outflanked in the event of a French crossing in strength. On 2 July Napoleon issued orders for the main crossing, which was to take place in three echelons. First would be the corps of Davout, Oudinot and Massena. Second would be the corps of Eugène, Bernadotte, Marmont and Macdonald; the Guard; and Wrede's division. Third would be Bessières and his cavalry. At dusk on 4 July, covered by a heavy bombardment, the crossing commenced. A violent thunderstorm happened to break out as night fell, and the combination of weather, darkness and artillery effectively screened the assault, so that by dawn a strong bridgehead had been established, despite some confusion caused by Davout's corps crossing at the wrong point. Had the Austrians attacked at or before dawn, while the crossing was still under way, there would surely have been another French disaster. But they did not, and by any standards, this was a triumph of staff work: to have transported perhaps 150,000 men with their horses, guns and wagons across one of the great rivers of Europe, in darkness, during a single night, would almost certainly be beyond any modern army.

Having built up his force rapidly on the far bank, and thereby seized the initiative, Napoleon could then manoeuvre the army on the Danube plain, against the Austrian army. The morning was hot and sunny after the night's rain and it took until mid-afternoon for the French to close up to the Austrian main position, and until early evening to complete the crossing of the Guard and the reserve cavalry. The Archduke decided to remain on the defensive and not try to regain the initiative – not least because the corps of the Archduke John had not arrived. This left the Austrians vulnerable, as Napoleon had effectively secured a central position between the two parts of the Austrian army under the two Archdukes, Charles and John. Napoleon, therefore, had a free hand to unleash his battle plan. In accordance with his usual practice, he decided to launch a frontal attack straight away, before dark, against the Austrian entrenchments along the Russbach stream. Not surprisingly, perhaps, the attack failed: the orders did not reach all his subordinates in time for a simultaneous assault, so the attacks went in piecemeal, allowing the Austrians to concentrate their fire on each of the three attacking French corps – those of Massena, Oudinot, and Bernadotte – in turn. This they followed up with fierce counter-attacks, causing the Italian troops in the French army to break. They were only rallied by the bayonets of the Guard. Napoleon had no choice but to break off the action as darkness fell. On the first day, therefore, the honours were roughly even.

Napoleon certainly intended to renew the attack early the next day; however, it was the Austrians who attacked. Charles was inspired by the successful defence of the previous evening; he felt certain that his brother

John would appear in a short time, and he was confident that he could sweep the French back into the Danube. The first attack came on the French right, and Davout's corps was pushed back; the Austrians were only halted by massed artillery fire. Even so, the situation appeared grim: if the Austrians could advance along the Danube, then the French would be cut off from their bridges and line of communication. Napoleon was faced with the choice of moving his reserves to block the Austrian attack, which would take time, or launching his own attack on the Austrian centre and left around the village of Wagram. Characteristically, he adopted the latter, riskier, course.

Telling Massena to hold firm, and reinforcing him with guns, Napoleon ordered his Chief of Artillery, General Lauriston, to mass the 112 guns of the Guard and his reserve into a grand battery opposite the Austrian centre. Before he could launch his attack, news came in that Bernadotte had given way, and then, before Napoleon's own attack could get under way, two Austrian corps attacked Massena's extended French troops on the left of the French line. Massena's two flanking divisions, separated by nearly seven miles, were pushed back almost to the village of Essling. But Charles did not exploit his success, and Napoleon was given time to bring up reserves to block the attack.

Deciding against any further more complicated manoeuvres, Napoleon decided to repair the breaches in his line by offensive action. After a lengthy bombardment, the French heavy cavalry charged the now-shaken Austrian troops. This was enough to halt the Austrian attack in the centre, and give Napoleon the chance to re-form ready for a major assault. Davout's corps crossed the Russbach to the south of the village of Markgraf-Neusiedl and, after a bitter struggle, began to roll up the Austrian left wing. Napoleon could see the smoke of this battle, and thus mark its progress. He decided that, with the Austrian left under severe pressure, the moment had come for his *coup de grâce*. Supported by the grand battery, the corps of Macdonald and Oudinot moved forward, drawing punishing fire from the Austrian artillery. Macdonald's 8,000 men made contact with the main Austrian position, but could not penetrate it. Reduced to only 1,500 effectives, Macdonald called for help. Napoleon had to act rapidly, and he did. Orders were issued to Eugène, Wrede, and part of the Guard to move up and reinforce Macdonald, leaving Napoleon with only two regiments of the Guard uncommitted: should the Archduke John appear, all might well be lost. But at 4.00 p.m. Charles learned that his brother John's corps was still ten miles away: the plan to encircle the French army could not now work. Charles decided to cut his losses, and disengage. This he succeeded in doing – an extremely difficult manoeuvre, skilfully executed – and the Austrian army withdrew northwards in good order. Napoleon was unable to pursue, as his troops were exhausted by 16 hours of marching and heavy fighting in the July heat. Moreover, Napoleon still expected the Archduke John to appear, and did not wish to be caught in the flank. Napoleon had won, but the losses were enormous. Four hundred guns had been in action on both sides, at close range, as well as concentrated volleys of musketry. Best estimates are that the French lost 40,000 killed, wounded and prisoners – a quarter of the force engaged – including 40 general officers. Napoleon also lost 12 Eagles and 21 guns. The Austrians lost roughly the same number of casualties, plus ten Colours and 20 guns.

The Austrian army moved northwards into Moravia, followed next day by the French. There was a sharp battle at Znaim on 10 July, and on 11 July, the Emperor of Austria asked for an armistice. Napoleon was glad to offer one, for his communications were extended and his logistic situation was not solid. In his correspondence, Napoleon made somewhat exaggerated claims of the battle, writing to the Empress Joséphine on 7 July that 'The enemy is flying in disorder, and everything is proceeding according to plan'. In fact, the enemy army was still intact and under arms. As a battle, therefore, Wagram was not successful in destroying the Austrian army, but it inflicted so severe a mauling that the will of the Emperor to resist was broken. Three months of negotiations followed the armistice, which eventually resulted in a peace treaty being signed at Schönbrunn on 14 October – the third anniversary of Jena. Napoleon and his Polish and Bavarian allies gained some considerable areas of territory, including Dalmatia and parts of Croatia, and some three million citizens; the Austrians paid an indemnity of 85 million francs, and agreed to maintain the Continental System against the British. Finally, the Austrian army was limited to 150,000 men.

If not completely successful as an action in itself, Wagram nevertheless proves the connection between the strategic objective of a favourable peace with Austria, thus unhinging the coalition against Napoleon by defeating its strongest member; the Austrian will to fight as the strategic centre of gravity; the Austrian army as the operational centre of gravity (it was clearly not the enemy capital city, since this had been occupied and the war had continued); and battle as the tactical means of inflicting unacceptable damage.

Conclusions

If Napoleon was brilliant at the operational level, there was little glitter, and less subtlety on the battlefield. True, he produced a run of successes in his early years, leading up to the triumph of Jena-Auerstadt. Thereafter, however, for every victory, the truth is that there was a disaster or near disaster which had to be recovered. He won at Friedland, but only after the bitter winter battle of Eylau; Wagram recovered the near-disaster of Aspern-Essling at huge cost; and there was little to celebrate at Borodino. The flash of genius was again apparent at Lutzen, but Bautzen was a draw, and the success of Dresden was followed by Kulm, the Katzbach, and Leipzig. Ligny was an illusion, shattered by Quatre Bras and Waterloo. And in other theatres of war, like Spain and Portugal, where the dreaded cries of '*Vive l'Empereur!*' were absent, his subordinates were roundly and regularly thrashed – by 1813, at the hands of Spanish troops at that. And even though he did succeed in grinding down the armies of most of his European opponents at one time or another, his armies never succeeded in intimidating the British, whose use of the reverse slope to minimize the effects of artillery fire and surprise infantry attacks; and whose decimation of the attacking columns by devastating quantities of accurate musketry confounded the French time after time.

One common aspect of Napoleonic battles, regardless of the opposition, was the blood-letting. Because of his insistence on rapid marching to gain time, and because this enabled him, at Ulm, to outmanoeuvre an enemy and force a surrender without fighting – what Sun Tzu called the acme of success as a general – the myth grew up that, as old soldiers would repeat, 'the Emperor uses our legs instead of our bayonets'. Nothing in subsequent history shows this to be true. In battle after battle, the French conscripts would hold on in desperate combat, waiting for support from the rest of the army, which was marching divided. Then, when the greatest possible mass had been assembled, the day would be settled – either in victory or in a draw – by the crude application of force: massed artillery fire to blast holes in the enemy, and columns of infantry and cavalry pouring in. There is no subtlety here and, as the quality of the army declined as each campaign took its 30 or 40 per cent casualties – more, far more, in Russia, where out of almost 500,000 French and client troops (not including the Austrian and Prussian corps), only about 60,000 escaped – so its battlefield performance declined.

A key judgement for any general is to understand what his army is capable of doing, and what is beyond its abilities. Montgomery is scorned for his carefully prepared battles with their limited objectives, but in truth, he knew that his army was not capable of complex manoeuvre, especially against an enemy as accomplished as the Germans. In the early years, Napoleon's *Grande Armée* was the most capable battlefield force in the world, and Napoleon could, accordingly, demand feats of endurance, sacrifice, and complexity which were beyond those of his opponents. But the quality of its later performance declined with the quality of the troops, and indeed the quality of the marshalate, as casualties took their toll. After the Russian campaign, for example, Napoleon never tried to unite dispersed corps *on* the battlefield in the presence of the enemy during offensive operations – but rather short of it. He could no longer rely on a high-quality holding action to buy time for the assembly of his main army. As performance declined, so the cost of fighting rose still higher. Bautzen cost Napoleon more than 20,000 casualties – twice what his opponents lost. Despite Dresden, the French army then lost 150,000 men killed, wounded and prisoners between June and September 1813, without counting sick and stragglers. Leipzig cost him 70,000 killed, wounded, sick and captured, including 17 general officers. Waterloo was to cost him 47,000 in dead and wounded. As a percentage of the numbers engaged, these figures equal the very worst days on the Western Front and yet the generals of the Great War are vilified, while Napoleon's reputation still shines.

VI

Rear Area Security and Counter-Insurgency

Insurgency and Counter-Insurgency

One should never forget that Napoleon and his system were themselves the product of a successful insurgency, which had become a revolution, had succeeded, and had then proceeded to export itself by force of arms. It secured itself by military force, and would brook no counter-revolution, nor countenance any further attempts at insurgency in its domains. The severity with which the revolt in the Vendée 1793–6 was put down illustrates this well: the government in Paris saw treason and conspiracy in both the revolt, and in the inability of the new Republican army to crush it quickly. In the final 'Pacification' phase of subduing the revolt, anywhere between 40,000 and 250,000 people were massacred in the Vendée, out of an estimated population of 800,000. There were forced evacuations, and destruction of crops, forests and villages. The Republican government also reacted very badly to insurrections in its conquered or annexed territories, as will be shown in the concluding section of this chapter.

Of course, insurgency and counter-insurgency were not new in the Napoleonic age, although they would not have been described in those terms: revolts, uprisings and rebellions had been common since the time of the Roman Empire, as had the practice of states in putting them down – or being overthrown by them. In the two centuries before Napoleon there had been frequent examples: the Revolts of the Catalans and the Low Countries against the Spanish, the English Civil War, Tackay's slave rebellion in Jamaica in 1760, the revolt of the United Irishmen in 1798, the Prosser rebellion in America in 1800, and the American Revolutionary War are all examples of insurgency and counter-insurgency. These were generally rebellions which aimed either to throw off rule by another nation, or to change the nature of government; that is, the modification or seizure of the state by a group of non-state actors. States and their governments generally responded in the same way that authoritarian governments do today – the Russians in Chechnya, for example – by overwhelming military force aimed at forcing the insurgents to accept that which they sought to reject, or die. Insurgent forces, then as now, usually relied on dispersed tactical actions, loosely linked by ideology, and orchestrated into a sequence which eventually built to strategic significance. They would also have recognized Mao Tse-tung's doctrine of the insurgent as embedded in the popular support of contemporary society and people.

Modern notions of counter-insurgency in the West have viewed insurgency as a symptom of a political, social, economic or cultural problem – or a combination of such problems – and have, therefore, seen military force as sub-strategic; that is, it will be aimed at ameliorating a problem or dealing with symptoms, rather than addressing the root cause of the insurgency. The experience of the British and French in particular, in late colonial times, stressed the primacy of political and economic lines of operation to remove the causes of insurgency. Sir Gerald Templer summed this up in Malaya when he said that 'the shooting side of this business is only 25% of the trouble'. From the Briggs Plan onwards, the main effort has been to displace the influence of the insurgent from society, supplant insurgent support within the population, marginalize the insurgents themselves and deny their popular base. The people remain the prize in this contest to mobilize support for the cause. Repression may, therefore, diminish the capability of the insurgency, but frequently it fires its motivation. Victory is not just the military destruction of an insurgent network, but also the destruction of its political network, and the discrediting of its ideas among the population, to the point where the insurgency is no longer a threat – indeed, it has become an irrelevancy. In many cases, this has led the political structure of the insurgency to adopt a political programme and become part of the system it originally challenged, abandoning violence as not only irrelevant, but actually harmful to its cause. The IRA is the latest group to take this line in modern times.

Rear Area Security

The security of the rear areas of an army, and its lines of communication, will be affected by insurgency, and the result will be the diversion or dispersion of troops for security duties, as was the case with the French armies in Spain. Alternatively, the rear areas may need to be secured against the raiding of regular or irregular forces which penetrate or go around the main army, as happened to the *Grande Armée* in Russia, and during the campaign in Germany in 1813, when bodies of Cossack, Bashkir and Kalmach horsemen were used against the lines of communication. Throughout the autumn campaign of 1813, for example, French communications had been harried mercilessly by German partisans and flying columns of Cossacks and Bashkirs, whose activities were almost out of control. At Weissenfels on

12 September, a column under General Thielmann took 1,000 prisoners and 26 guns. Six days later, the same column took 200 prisoners in Mersebeck. At Altenburg on 28 September Thielmann again, with seven Cossack regiments and some *Freikorps*, drove out the French garrison and took another 1,000 prisoners.

This pattern was repeated throughout Germany, and the result, combined with battle losses, sickness and straggling was alarming. From the end of the Armistice of Pleiswitz to the end of September 1813, the French lost 150,000 men killed, wounded and taken prisoner in battles and small actions, plus another 50,000 sick and straggling. By October 1813, the supply situation of the *Grande Armée* in Germany had become so bad, and deteriorating roads and bad weather exacerbated by merciless Russian raiding, that its troops were reduced to only eight ounces of bread per day instead of 28, and had almost no meat. Napoleon was forced to turn his attention to this drastic situation. First, he ordered the move of large quantities of flour and other stores to Dresden by barge, the transfer of which was to be covered by the move of Marmont and Murat with their entire corps. Next, he set about pacifying the rear areas. General Lefebvre-Desnoettes' division was reinforced to a strength of 4,000 cavalry at Freiburg and 2,000 at Lorge. This force was ordered to clear the Cossacks from the west side of the Elbe, while a division of Victor's corps was also ordered to Freiburg; and the newly formed IX Corps of Marshal Augereau was ordered to march to Jena from Würzburg in order to keep open the crossings over the Saale. These measures worked, but represented a diversion of resources that Napoleon, especially with his chronic lack of cavalry, could ill afford.

The use of regular and irregular forces in this way by the allies in Central Europe, by the British and Spanish in the Peninsula, and indeed by the English and their native American allies in North America, is an interesting example of simultaneous effect at the operational level of war: if the French were to concentrate against the regular field army, which Napoleon of course always sought to do, they stood the chance of exposing their rear areas to raiding. If, on the other hand, Napoleon diverted troops to guarding dispersed depots, or convoys, or patrolling routes, then he weakened his field army and laid himself open to conventional defeat. Thus, the problem of the rear area had the potential to confront any general, unless possessed of a great wealth of resources, with a dilemma that he could not solve.

Case Study – Spain and the Guerrillas

Napoleon's interest in Spain dated from a series of treaties in 1800 which obliged Spain to subsidize French military operations, and which turned the Spanish army and navy into French puppets. The treaty of San Ildefonso created a kingdom in Etruria for the son-in-law of Charles IV of Spain, in return for which Spain ceded her territories in Louisiana to France, on condition that they would not be disposed of to any other party. This arrangement ended in disaster for Spain, with the Louisiana Purchase in 1803, which was a violation of the San Ildefonso treaty – but one that Spain could not prevent. The annexure of the Spanish navy merely brought about its destruction at Trafalgar, and the added insult of the loss of Spain's West Indian colonies.

These humiliations stirred up much anti-French feeling in Spain, but in 1806, Napoleon was at the height of his power and was in no mood to be defied. Anti-French demonstrations gave him the excuse to consolidate his grip over the whole of the Peninsula, and thus complete the Continental System, exclude the British, and dominate the Mediterranean. He sought to effect his desired strategic objectives by the Franco-Spanish campaign against Portugal in 1808. Having moved French troops into Spain for this, it was simple to engineer the 5 May 1808 Agreement, which caused Charles IV to abdicate in favour of Joseph Bonaparte. After that, it was only a short step to the imprisonment of Charles's heir, Ferdinand VII, at Valençay.

The consequence of Napoleon's actions was not at all what he had intended. He managed to trigger first the revolt in Spain, and then the British intervention in Portugal. From these grew the so-called Spanish Ulcer. For the Spanish, the revolt became a war of national liberation, fought by both the Spanish regular army, and by large regional bands of guerrillas. Some guerrilla bands were formed by regular troops acting as irregulars; conversely, over time, the most successful guerrilla bands – or more accurately *partidas* – became strong enough to act as regular troops. To drive the Spaniards to this pitch was quite an achievement on Napoleon's part, for there was no prolonged historic rivalry between France and Spain – indeed quite the reverse – and for ten of the 12 years before 1808 (1796–1801 and 1804–8), Spain had been at war with Britain and allied with France. Religious views of the English as heretics underscored national rivalries which had festered since the Armada, and above all the pride of the Spanish nation made co-operation with England very difficult. General Castaños remarked on this to his French prisoners after the battle of Baylen, saying, 'Do not let Napoleon persevere in aiming at a conquest which is unattainable. Do not let him force us into the arms of the English. They are hateful to us.'

Even so there were signs in 1810 and 1811 that French control was gaining ground in Spain, especially in Catalonia, and that the establishment of order and normal government was supported by local people. However, anti-French sentiment and support for the guerrilla war remained strong. As French raiding, requisitioning, and plundering increased in Spain, so did Spanish hostility. In December 1808 the Spanish Council of Regency legalized the guerrillas, and after Salamanca – a blow from which French prestige never recovered – the guerrillas were imbued with new confidence. The guerrillas, numbering some 16,000 in Biscay and Guipuscoa and 19,000 in Navarre, were able to surround and destroy isolated French garrisons, as they did at Tafalla; destroy bridges; ambush troops; raid supply convoys and depots; loot; kill; and burn, whenever a weakness was exposed. So bad was the menace that in order to keep the lines of communication open, every village along the main roads had to be garrisoned, every road had to be patrolled, every convoy and despatch rider had to be escorted. The French practice of carrying out reprisals only increased Spanish hatred, and no captured French soldier could expect mercy or quarter at the hands of the guerrillas. Writing to his brother Joseph as early as 1808, Napoleon said that:

In all my military life I have never come across anything so despicable as these Spanish bands ... take care you do not destroy the spirit of the army by refusing to allow retaliation upon the Spaniards. It is impossible to show consideration towards brigands who murder my wounded, and commit every kind of outrage.

It was because of this domination by the guerrillas that Napoleon's dispatches to his brother in early January did not reach Madrid until 16 February. The effect of the threat can be seen in a snapshot of the French armies in the Peninsula in March 1813. The Army of Portugal, under General Reille, with his headquarters in Salamanca, consisted of around 40,000 men in eight infantry divisions, a cavalry division and a division of dragoons. This army was deployed behind the Tormes and Esla rivers in order to watch the allied forces in northern Portugal and Spanish Galicia, but four of Reille's divisions had been diverted to assist the Army of the North in anti-guerrilla operations. The Army of the Centre under General Drouet D'Erlon numbered some 16,000 men and was given three tasks which were, to a great extent, contradictory: to cover Madrid; to connect the other armies by means of mobile columns; and to operate against the guerrillas in central Spain. The Army of Aragon and Catalonia, under General Suchet, was tasked with holding the line of communications back through Perpignan. Suchet had about 64,000 men in all, but the majority were tied down in garrisons and in routine anti-guerrilla protection tasks, leaving him only some 18,000 men readily available for mobile operations.

The French system of forage (see Chapter VII) also played into the guerrillas' hands, both in increasing French unpopularity and in presenting targets for ambush. But when Marmont in 1812 attempted to institute a commissariat and supply system, the internal security situation had deteriorated so badly that this too, with its reliance on established supply routes, became an easy target for the guerrillas. The guerrillas probably maintained a force of around 50,000 men under arms at any one time, and their activities cost the French around 145,000 casualties between 1808 and 1814. They were also responsible for the deaths of around 30,000 *Afrancescados*, or collaborators. The greatest military contribution of the guerrillas was in helping to present the French with that insoluble tactical dilemma through the interaction of regular and irregular forces. Wellington's great achievement in this respect was to persuade the guerrillas to take part in a concerted plan and then, during the course of 1813, to bring them gradually into the regular army.

Napoleon's Response to Insurgency

Modern notions of insurgency and its remedies were far in the future during the Napoleonic era, and one cannot therefore judge Napoleon's response by our standards. To understand his response, therefore, one must understand the context in which he operated, which was essentially that of the Enlightenment. It was this movement, whose leaders saw themselves as a courageous elite leading the world into the light of progress after a long period of irrationality, superstition and tyranny, that created the intellectual conditions for the American and French revolutions, the independence movements in South America, and the desire for freedom in Poland. The existing institutions of Church and State were all questioned and attacked by philosophers and writers such as Thomas Paine, David Hume, Jean-Jacques Rousseau and Adam Smith. What perhaps most exercised all the leading exponents of the Enlightenment was the question of what constituted the proper relationship between the citizen and the monarch, or the State. The idea that civilized society is a contract between the individual and the State was strongly pushed by Rousseau, Hume, and later Jefferson in the United States. Nationality, therefore, was more than preference.

The Enlightenment philosophers were also exercised by the contest between divine right and natural law as the basis for ordering society, and while it might be supposed that divine right would be used as the basis for absolutism, and natural law for more libertarian ideas, natural law in fact began as an abstraction of divine right: as Thomas Hobbes set out, God does not rule the universe arbitrarily, but through natural laws that he enacts on Earth. However, the framing of this idea had unintended consequences, for once it was used to uphold the position of monarchy, it could also be used to assert the rights of subjects, and if natural laws existed as duties or obligations, so too did natural rights.

What both theories had in common was an insistence on orderly society and properly functioning government. Although Thomas Paine dismissed monarchy and viewed all government as, at best, a necessary evil, even he proposed free public education and a minimum wage – measures which would have required the functioning of some machinery of government. Frederick the Great's enlightened despotism was based on the requirement for the power of the State to hold back the chaos and anarchy of war and rebellion. Adam Smith advocated government that was active in not only the economy, but also in public education, the law and judiciary, and in security. When the radical Whig Edmund Burke published his denunciation of the French Revolution in 1790, he was greeted with outrage by Paine, Jefferson and Fox. However, other Enlightenment politicians agreed with his view, which was that this was not a movement towards representative, constitutional government, but rather a violent rebellion against proper authority, disconnected from the complexities and realities of civilized society; it would, moreover, end in disaster.

The likely response of republican governments to insurgency during the period of the Enlightenment can thus be guessed, and a foretaste of what could be expected was given as early as 1786 in the infant United States of America. Shay's rebellion began as a reaction by small farmers angered at crushing taxes and debt. These farmers organized into a militia, and closed the courts. The leaders of the United States, despite the ideals espoused in the Declaration of Independence and the Constitution, were as firmly wedded to the need for property qualifications to support the franchise, to public order, and to rule by educated men of means, as their former colonial masters had been. Many were quick to represent the Shayites as levellers and incendiaries. General Henry Knox wrote to George Washington, saying that 'their [the Shayites] creed is that the property of the United States [having been freed from British tyranny] by the exertions of *all*, ought to be the common property of *all*'. That great advocate of revolution, Samuel Adams, was so disturbed by the rebellion that he called for the execution of those involved, saying that 'In monarchy, the crime of treason may admit of being pardoned or lightly punished, but the man who dares rebel against the laws of republic ought to suffer death.' Although untrue, this did the trick, and the rebellion was broken up by force. A more telling lesson, perhaps, was that, in exchange for amnesty, Shay's followers escaped hanging in return for a ban from holding elected office, voting, and jury service for three years. The force of the rebellion was moreover dispelled by improving economic conditions and the election of members of Congress who sympathized with the rebels.

Such views may explain the reaction of Napoleon and his contemporaries, as the products of the Enlightenment, to insurgency. The fact that the citizens of some liberated territories did not welcome the arrival of French armies, and French revolutionary ideas, with open arms, caused some confusion and puzzlement. But all too soon, this was followed by repression, in order that the liberated territories could be turned into clients, and milked of manpower and resources (see Chapter III). As early as 25 May 1796, for example, we find Napoleon issuing a *Proclamation to the Inhabitants of Lombardy* in the wake of his conquest:

> A misguided mob, without any real means of resistance, is committing the wildest excesses, refusing to recognise the Republic, and defying an army which has conquered a succession of kings ... In accordance with the principles of the French nation, which makes no war on the common people, the general in command is anxious to leave open a door of repentance; but those who, within twenty-four hours, have not laid down their arms and taken a fresh oath of obedience to the Republic will be treated as rebels, and their villages will be burnt to the ground. Take warning from the terrible example of Binasco!

These warnings had no effect, for the people of Pavia resisted and imprisoned the garrison. Napoleon ordered the gates of the city broken down:

> I saw the [French] castle garrison appear – they had broken their fetters ... there was not a man missing. If the blood of a single Frenchman had been shed I should have set up on the ruins of the place a column with the inscription 'Here stood the town of Pavia.' As it was, I had the Town Council shot, arrested 200 people, and sent them to France as hostages. Today all is absolutely quiet.

In actual fact, the place was quiet for the simple reason that the French had massacred every armed man they could find. From here on, repression would be the only response. In Cairo in 1798, Berthier was instructed by Napoleon to deal with rebels summarily: 'decapitate all prisoners taken with arms in their hands ... and their headless bodies are to be thrown into the river'. Having unleashed egalitarianism and indeed nationalism, the French then proceeded to stamp on the symptoms of both. And once the Empire had been established, with its system of local, regional and national government; its tiers of bureaucracy and nobility, with the Emperor at its head; with its Civil Code; and with its system of client states ruled by Napoleon's family; then insurgents became traitors once more, rather than freedom fighters. Two of Napoleon's letters show this process in action. In 1791 he writes as a young Jacobin that:

> Europe is divided between those sovereigns who rule over men, and those who rule over cattle or horses. The former thoroughly understand the Revolution. They are terrified of it. They would make pecuniary sacrifices to destroy it ... As for sovereigns who rule over horses, they cannot grasp the Constitution: they despise it. They think this chaos of incoherent ideas spells the ruin of France.

But by 1813, he had a different view. Writing to Davout in the aftermath of the recapture of Hamburg from the Russians in June of that year, he gave orders for severe penalties:

> arrest summarily all citizens of Hamburg who have served as 'Senators of Hamburg ... court-martial the five chief culprits among them, and have them shot. The rest he will send to France, under strong escort, in order that they may be incarcerated in a State prison. He must sequestrate their property, and declare it confiscated: their houses, landed property, and so forth will fall into the Crown domains. He is to disarm the whole town, shoot the officers of the Hamseatic Legion, and despatch to France all who have enlisted in that regiment, in order that they may be sent to the galleys .... draw up a list of five hundred persons for proscription ... choosing the richest and worst behaved. He will arrest them, and sequestrate their property, which will pass into the Crown domain ... Everywhere he must disarm the countryside, arrest the gendarmes, artillerymen, coastguards, officers, soldiers, and officials: all have served against us, and therefore all are traitors.

Napoleon never understood the nature of the nationalism which he had helped to unleash, and which was now the force which drove his enemies on. He did not understand, therefore, that this force was stronger than the forces which divided coalitions of his enemies, and far stronger than that holding his empire together. He did not understand, either, the intense personal loathing that he inspired – and that not just among the sovereigns and aristocrats of the *ancien régime*. As Michael Broers has said, the common people of Europe, in their millions, hated Napoleon *because* he espoused the Enlightenment, just as they had detested the enlightened absolutists who preceded him. This is the major problem besetting those who attempt to set Napoleon in a genuinely European, rather than Franco-centric, context.

VII

Logistics, Pillage and Plunder

General Remarks on Logistics

Murphy's Law – that anything that can go wrong, will go wrong – is always apparent in war, and especially so in logistics. To it should be added Riley's Corollary: Murphy was being hopelessly over-optimistic. Many practitioners believe that logistics is nine-tenths of war, and therefore Sun Tzu's remarks about the necessity for a general to make extensive calculations, is as true now as it ever was. One only has to spend one day in Iraq or Afghanistan, and see the huge scale of the US logistical effort to sustain its force there, to agree with him. Indeed, as at 1 September 2006, about half the US troop strength of 225,000 in the Central Command Area of Operations is tied up in the line of communication. Thus, while it is relatively easy, in either conventional or even asymmetric war, to work out where and when a combat force should be positioned, it is quite another matter to get it there and then sustain it. The risks involved in logistic calculations of this scale are therefore huge.

Current British army doctrine defines logistics as 'the science of planning and carrying out the movement and maintenance of forces,' not too different from Jomini's definition almost 200 years ago, which tells us that logistics is 'the practical art of moving armies'; 'providing for the successive arrival of convoys of supplies'; and 'the establishment and organisation of lines of supplies'. It is a continuous operation, which modern doctrine describes as a function in combat, like firepower, command, intelligence, and protection. Every military unit and formation must therefore undertake it. For our purposes here it may be taken to be synonymous with the business of sustainment – that is, the actual process of maintaining an army during operations. Inseparable from it is administration, which is the management and execution of all military matters, not included in tactics, operational art or strategy.

Logistics, because it deals in resources, be those human, animal or materiel, is one of the factors that generals and their staffs must consider when planning. There are only three of these factors, the others being time and space, and the environment. Some armies consider the enemy as a factor, which must be wrong, since the enemy will be the object of a general's problem, the thing that obstructs the achievement of his mission and, in any case, the three factors bear equally on friend and foe alike. Nor are things like surprise or deception factors: they are effects that the general must seek to achieve.

So, logistics is a factor in planning and in execution, and this applies at every level of war: strategic, operational, and tactical. It is complicated greatly by expeditionary warfare on hostile territory. What supplies are available or can be expected; the available transport by land, sea, and more latterly air; the length, security and nature of the line of communication; the available manpower and the time needed to bring up replacements; the medical arrangements for dealing with wounds, non-combat injuries and diseases; the organization of the force and its general administration, all matter as much or more now as they did to Napoleon. Before any operation can be launched, the general must determine how the army is to be fed, clothed, armed, ammunitioned, resupplied, reinforced and cared for. If he does not do this, his force will rapidly cease to be effective. Lord Wavell commented shrewdly and succinctly on this, saying that:

> The more I see of war, the more I realize how it all depends on administration and transportation (what our American allies call logistics)... A real knowledge of supply and movement factors must be the basis of every leader's plan; only then can he know how and when to take risks with those factors, and battles are won only by taking risks.

Modern doctrine summarizes the factors governing the development of any logistic plans and systems as Demand, Distance, Duration and Destination. By planning carefully according to these factors, operations can be kept within reach of adequate sustainment. Beyond this reach, an army will receive inadequate supply and its operations will culminate rapidly. To expand these slightly in the context of Napoleonic warfare, the system would require, first, a definition of its requirements, underpinned by regulations laying down the allowances of, for example, rations for men and animals, clothing, saddlery and harness, weapons and ammunition. In the French army, as an example, the standard ration was 2 lb of bread or biscuit per man per day provided free and supplemented by meat, cheese, salt fish, or beans as available. In today's British army, the standard supply is the individual 24-hour ration pack, or a four-man box for a tank crew, or a ten-man box for a mechanized infantry section.

These defined requirements, in turn, depended on accurate muster rolls. Napoleonic corps commanders may have complained bitterly about submitting their daily situation reports to the Emperor's headquarters, but it was upon these that the supply of the army was calculated. Today, the equivalents are the daily personnel and situation reports submitted up the chain of command. Standard weapon calibres are the next requirement, so that ammunition can be manufactured in bulk, and its transportation calculated in standard loads. Muskets varied little, if at all, across European armies in the early nineteenth century, so that much use could be made of captured stocks. Artillery calibres did vary to a degree. In the French army, guns ranged from three-pounders with infantry divisions, through six and eight-pounders, up to the twelve-pounders in the corps artillery and reserve. This is without considering mortars, howitzers or the bigger guns of the siege train.

Then came a system of depots and units to transport logistic stocks, and distribute them to the point of use. In Napoleonic times much of this depended on contractors, but the later years of the *Grande Armée* saw a great increase in military supply units. Inseparable from this, is the need to understand the environment in which any campaign will take place. This will inform, for example, a system of route selection, marking, security and maintenance; and the effects of terrain, obstacles, climate, weather and altitude. In expeditionary warfare this is often a huge challenge. Not only are roads of poor quality and few in number, but they are prone to regular attack. The Spanish guerrillas who interdicted the French supply routes in the Peninsula would no doubt have appreciated and understood the tactics used by the Taliban in Afghanistan, or Iranian-backed insurgents in southern Iraq in 2006.

Finally, one must mention medical support, the task of which is to maintain the fighting strength of the army, both by preventing and curing sickness, and by returning the wounded to duty. Good medical services thus contribute not only to the physical strength of the army, but also to its moral strength, by reassuring the soldiers that they will be well cared for in the event of sickness or wounds. This is one area in which modern practice has changed the face of war: in Napoleonic times, a wounded man would expect to die – of blood-loss, shock, thirst or subsequent infection. Nowadays, these factors only apply to irregular combatants such as the Taliban or the Revolutionary United Front in Sierra Leone. Soldiers in regular armies can expect treatment at every stage from the point of wounding to a fully equipped hospital, with systems in place for rapid evacuation. Provided he is identified, and put into the medical system, the odds are that he will live.

Napoleonic Logistics

Although Napoleon's armies were large, they were not unprecedented in size until the Russian campaign. In the seventeenth century, Wallenstein and Gustavus Adolphus had both commanded armies in excess of 100,000 men; the French armies operating against the Netherlands had grown to 120,000; and those of the Habsburgs had reached 140,000. To feed and supply so large a force, Napoleon is often viewed as having reverted to the plundering tactics of the horde, and of living by indiscriminate pillage. This is not so, for he made good use of the systems built up in the French army during the late seventeenth and the eighteenth centuries. It may be argued that his logistic system was the most comprehensive that the world had ever seen, and was not surpassed until the great battles on the Western Front from 1916 onwards. His armies were, however, as Martin van Creveld says, itinerant cities moving at 15 miles a day, and needing sanitation, health care, fresh water, disciplinary arrangements, and route organization, as well as all the other logistical requirements already noted. The chief logistic problem of those days was food for men and fodder for horses. This parallels today in that fuel for vehicles is one of the major bulk commodities that armies have to shift, but it parts company in that ammunition, especially for the artillery, nowadays far eclipses the requirements of rations. We will look at some figures later in the chapter in order to illuminate this.

Napoleonic armies, like their seventeenth and eighteenth-century predecessors, could be fed in garrison by a combination of local requisition, and produce markets. When advancing through friendly territory, the commissariat could buy or requisition from the local area, or draw on the stocks held in depots and fortresses. In enemy territory, organized plunder was the general rule. However, the larger the army, the less effective this was: small armies were easy to feed and needed little in the way of a regular military supply corps – the commissary and the sutlers (contractors) – could do it. The time of year also mattered greatly: was the grain harvest in or not? Were there animals in the fields, or had they been slaughtered? As French armies grew through the seventeenth century, so also grew the system of magazines devised by Michel Le Tellier, who was commissioned by Cardinal Mazarin to reorganize the French army, and his son, François-Michel, Marquis de Louvois, who became Secretary of State for War in 1662.

By 1805, the top level of responsibility for administration in the French army lay with the Minister of War Organization, General Pierre Dejean. His department was responsible for feeding, clothing and equipping the troops, and for supplying transport, but his responsibilities ended at the French frontier. The efficiency of this department may be judged from the events following Napoleon's decision in August 1805, to terminate the project to invade England, and instead turn on Austria. This provided Dejean with a huge problem, but one that could be managed through the existing structure within France and by a complex movement order issued by Berthier. By these means, 170,000 troops were moved in a few weeks from the Channel to the Rhine, and 80,000 new recruits assembled to meet them, and form the eight corps of the *Grande Armée*. Three routes were allocated using the machinery of government down to the prefects of departments, then to sub-prefects and mayors, with billeting and provisions provided at halts. In practice there were problems. As ever, things took longer than planned and there was a good deal of straggling, drunkenness and disorder. But it was good enough to assemble the troops: just enough, just in time.

When deployed on expeditionary operations, logistics were handled within the army by the *Intendant-Général*, for many years General Pierre Daru, who had gained experience as a Commissary with both Massena and Napoleon from 1799 to 1805, before becoming *Intendant-Général*. The *Intendant-Général* himself controlled four staff divisions: first, the *Régisseur des vivres-pains*, who looked after flour, mills and bakeries; second, the *Régisseur des vivres-viande*, who was responsible for livestock, butchery and meat; third, the *Régisseur de fourage*, responsible for fodder; and last, the *Directeur des equipages de transport*, responsible for carts, wagons and draft animals. Below this, at corps level, was a similar but smaller organization under an *Ordonnateur*, and below him, at divisional level, a Commissary. Thus, the home base and the distribution of resources to the troops were well catered for, but there was no control over the line of communication itself, nor the resources along it. This was, at least in part, rectified when Napoleon established the Train Service. This was not just a development of earlier practice, but a departure in which Napoleon was ahead of his contemporaries. The Train Service was not contracted out, but manned by soldiers with military equipment. Such an organization allowed him to break a line of communication into sections which could be patrolled by cavalry, with depots at intervals. As early as 1805, for example, even before the formal establishment of the Train, the line of communication from Strasbourg to Augsburg was divided into 17 sections each covered by 60 four-horse wagons operating a shuttle service. One return journey per wagon per day meant that up to 120 tons of supplies could be moved forward every day. By 1812, the Train Service consisted of 26 battalions, of which 18 were equipped with eighty heavy (1.5 ton) wagons per battalion, and eight with a similar number of light vehicles, along with 6,000 spare horses. This organization was used to build up stocks at Danzig and the depots along the Oder for the invasion of Russia. In January 1812, orders were given to assemble rations for 400,000 men and 50,000 horses for 50 days.

Although, as will be seen later in this chapter, Napoleon broke free from many of the more static aspects of the line of communication established by his predecessors, he did retain some important elements of it, in particular depots and distribution centres. The latter were usually in large defensible cities or fortresses, where routes converged. As a general rule, whenever the army moved six days on, a new centre would be established to keep the tail short. In late May 1813, after the battle of Lutzen, Dresden was to become such a centre, which. Napoleon garrisoned with St Cyr's XIV Corps. The city became a storehouse of ammunition, food and supplies of all kinds, as well as home to field bakeries and hospitals. Napoleon had also ordered the repair and improvement of the fortifications, along with those of the out-lying fortresses of Königstein and Meissen, to make certain they were capable of withstanding an assault.

However, relying solely on supplies carried along the bad roads of early nineteenth-century Europe made the army vulnerable. An important method of securing food for men and horses, therefore, remained requisition. This was an orderly process in which each corps was allocated an area. Random plundering caused not only indiscipline and problems with the population, but was inefficient. In 1805, Soult was told to make good shortages of supply on the march through Heilbronn, and in consequence requisitioned 85,000 bread rations, 3,600 bushels of hay, 1,000 sacks of oats, 5,000 pints of wine and 100 wagons to carry off his plunder; by contrast, in the aftermath of the battle of Jena, Soult was forced to issue severe orders for the prevention of random plunder, and events at Lübeck at the end of the campaign were to show the worst face of the *Grande Armée*. In 1805, the city of Vienna was ordered to provide rations for 80,000 men for three weeks, including 75,000 lb of bread, 25,000 lb of meat, 200,000 bushels of oats, 280,000 lb of hay and 375 buckets of wine *per day*. On 3 September 1812, in Russia, four days before Borodino, Napoleon wrote to Berthier on this subject:

Write to the generals in command of the army corps, and tell them that we are losing numbers of men every day, owing to the disorderly way in which foraging is conducted ... the enemy is taking several hundred prisoners a day; that the soldiers must be forbidden under the severest penalties, to leave the line of march, and that food must be procured in accordance with the army regulations about foraging – that is, by army corps when the whole army is together, and by divisions when it is subdivided; that a general or officer of high rank must be in command of the foraging, and that there must be a sufficient force to protect the foraging parties ... that, so far as possible, when foragers come across inhabitants, they are to requisition whatever they can provide, but not do any more harm to the country.

In modern armies, the use of local purchase, local contracting and local resourcing is really no more than a more refined, less draconian development of Napoleonic foraging.

But requisition was not just a method of feeding the troops; it was also a means of punishing defeated enemies. One soldier, cited by Alan Forrest, wrote from the campaign in 1793 that:

We rounded up all their oxen, cattle and sheep: where a peasant had three cows, we would take two, so that the enemy would not be able to profit from them. After that, we waited until all the corn had been brought in, before taking all the carts belonging to the peasants and transporting their grain to French granaries, with the result that this town is now deserted, abandoned by French and Prussians alike.

At the strategic level, it was also a means of enriching the French exchequer, and of increasing Napoleon's personal wealth and prestige. 'War must be made to pay for war' is a frequently quoted saying of the Emperor in this regard. On 26 June 1796, for example, Napoleon wrote to the Executive Directory on this subject showing the scale of plunder as a matter of national policy:

I enclose the terms of the armistice with the Pope. M. d'Azara, the actual negotiator, had the impudence to offer us five millions in cash and three in kind. I stood out for forty millions. Seeing that I would not come down, he went to the government commissioners, and managed to worm out of them our weak point, namely that we could not march on Rome. After that I could get only twenty millions out of him ... I had made it a condition all along that he should hand over the treasures of Our Lady of Loretto ...

In addition to the rich districts which we still occupy, I find that we have derived from the Papal States the following sums:

In Cash
15,500,000 livres under the treaty
2,000,000 Bologna indemnity
1,200,000 from the Bologna banks
800,000 from the Bologna pawnshops
2,500,000 the Ferrara indemnity
500,000 from the Ferrara banks
2,000,000 found at Faenza and the Ravenna Legation

In Kind
5,500,000 livres under the treaty
2,000,000 Bologna
1,500,000 Ferrara
1,200,000 Faenza and the Ravenna Legation

Total 10,200,000 in kind
  24,500,000 in cash
  34,700,000 grand total

The day after the battle of Jena in 1806, Napoleon issued a decree fixing the war reparations to be levied on Berlin and on every Prussian dependency. Daru was told to have 280,000 greatcoats and 250,000 pairs of boots made ready for winter, at Prussian expense, in the main towns and cities of the country. In addition, six general hospitals were to be organized, with 6,000 mattresses and 9,000 pairs of sheets manufactured in Berlin from commandeered Prussian tents.

This sort of thing was accepted as normal practice at the time – the booty captured in the baggage train of Napoleon's brother Joseph after the battle of Vitoria is another contemporary example – and continued to be so until modern times. The war reparations levied on Germany after the Great War, even though they were never paid in full, are a case in point. The thought that the victor might have some responsibility to rebuild a defeated enemy, as with the Marshall Plan in Germany, or the reconstruction of Iraq, would have seemed nothing short of madness to Napoleon.

Despite the efforts of Napoleon himself and his staff to provide hospitals, the standard of treatment for the sick and wounded remained low – but no lower than in any other European army of the time, except perhaps the British, and certainly better than, say, the Russians. Cramped and unsanitary conditions meant that sickness bred and was rapidly transmitted. Surgical treatment was brutal, and anaesthetics (other than alcohol) and antiseptics in their infancy. Most soldiers regarded hospitals with dread, and would rather remain among their friends than accept the virtual death-sentence of committal to a hospital. Rather than returning men to duty after illness or wounding, therefore, Napoleonic hospitals generally added to the casualty lists after a short delay. Whereas in modern times, a soldier who makes it alive to a field hospital will generally survive, a soldier in Napoleonic times would simply die later.

It is remarkable that Napoleon himself was often absent from the front, especially during marches, concerning himself with logistic problems. Given the road network of the time, the organizations, the available transport and the communications, it must be said that the way in which the army was fed and supplied on many expeditions was a triumph of foresight, planning and execution. It was superior logistic organization that delivered the victories of Ulm, Austerlitz and Jena. The Russian campaign was well set up, as will be shown. But again, a proviso has to be made, that logistics were always comparatively fragile, and the risk involved because of this fragility could only be managed if campaigns were executed swiftly, the enemy remained relatively static, and a decisive battle could be engineered. An enemy who avoided battle rapidly stretched the logistic fragility of the army to breaking point, as was shown in late 1805 after Ulm, and in 1812.

The Problems of Destination and Demand*

Not present in Napoleonic armies were the quantities of technical spares for radios, helicopters, vehicles and so on that modern armies require, nor the specialist natures of ammunition required by air defence artillery, helicopters, or rocket systems. However, some calculations and comparisons are possible. In terms of ammunition, the basic load during the seventeenth century was 100 rounds per gun for a campaigning season, or four to five rounds per gun per day. In terms of transport requirement for the powder and shot, this was insignificant when compared with the requirement for fodder, amounting only to about 2% of an army's transport. By 1805, things had changed as foraging replaced carried fodder. For the campaign against Austria, Napoleon allocated 2,500 of his available 4,500 wagons for ammunition; 300 rounds per gun were allowed, divided between ball, canister and powder, of which 107 rounds were carried with the guns at first line, broken down into 87 ball and 20 canister. In terms of quantities, each division had 16 eight-pounder guns and each corps 24 12-pounders, thus a corps with two divisions would have 60 guns, plus an unspecified number of six-pounders, three-pounders and howitzers: a total of at least 18,000 rounds per division, of which about 6,000 were with the guns. In addition, a division would carry about 100,000 rounds of small arms ammunition. Each division would therefore be allocated about 80 wagons for ammunition. Should a siege train form part of the army, as it did for the Russian campaign, another 1,100 rounds per gun would have to be carried. These figures are not substantially different from those of the German army in 1914, and although direct comparison is difficult, the scale of the problem has not altered in modern times. The standard calibre of the British army, 155 mm

* All figures for modern formations are drawn from either *The Staff Officer's Handbook*, or formation Standard Operating Instructions.

artillery, will fire 500 rounds per gun per day at intense rates. When the requirements of main battle tanks and smaller calibres are added, a single brigade[†] will consume 1,247 pallets of ammunition per day. At ten pallets per supply vehicle,[‡] this is 124 vehicles each day for each brigade.

There was one advantage in Napoleonic times which has largely disappeared today, that of commonality of ammunition. Most European armies used the same calibres of guns and muskets, so that captured stocks were always a useful addition to the stocks. After Leipzig, for example, Napoleon's materiel losses included 325 guns – half the French artillery, 900 fully loaded artillery ammunition wagons, 720 tons of powder, and 40,000 muskets and rifles. Such captures would greatly ease the problems of resupply, especially as the troops could make their own cartridges, given the raw materials of powder, shot and paper.

The problem of feeding the army has probably undergone the biggest change in the intervening years. With the technology to can, dry, condense and freeze food, the field ration requirements for the combat elements of a modern brigade of around 3,000 men will be a mere ten pallets, and thus can be carried on a single supply vehicle. Napoleonic armies, by contrast, have the reputation of being voracious foragers, stripping the countryside bare as they moved. One might expect the inhabitants of the country over which campaigns were fought to plead poverty – 'even the rats starve where the *Grand Armée* marches' was the great cry – but the truth is rather more complex. First, like the general in command, we must consider the situation of the army itself. Even with a system of depots, living off the land was an absolute necessity. An army of more than 100,000 men could not possibly carry all its food for men and horses, without ceasing to do everything else. We will look at some figures later. Second, for an army in the field, a standing crop (other than grass) was not the same thing as food: the army had to spend time gathering raw materials, grinding corn, baking bread, slaughtering animals, salting meat and so on. In Napoleonic times, Martin van Creveld calculated that, given the population density and agricultural practice in Europe at the time, an army of 60,000 men – or in Napoleonic terms, say two corps – could be comfortably supplied with bread by a strip of country measuring 100 miles by 10 miles. The army would consume only 10% of the available food as it passed through this corridor.

The food requirements for men may be of a different order now, but the

---

[†] For illustrative purposes, an armoured brigade will be assumed to consist of its headquarters and signal squadron, two regiments of tanks, two battalions of mechanized infantry, an artillery regiment, engineer regiment, and reconnaissance squadron.

[‡] The supply vehicle used for this purpose is the 8-tonne Dismountable Ramp Off-loading and Pickup System, or DROPS.

fuel problem remains much the same in scale, if not in kind. Just as modern vehicles require fuel, and fuel trucks themselves require other fuel trucks to keep them running; so horses need fodder, and that fodder has to be carried by other horses who themselves need fodder, and so on. The line of communication is itself a consumer of resources, all of which has to be taken into consideration when planning a campaign. Because of the quantities, local supplies of fodder were the most important resource for a Napoleonic army. To minimize this, animals needed to be fed from local forage and, on the same basis as food for men, the requirements for animals can similarly be calculated. Jacques-François de Chastenet, Marquis de Puységur, says in his *Art de la Guerre* of 1743, that 800 acres of fodder each day will be needed to feed 40,000 animals. Therefore, the same strip of 100 miles by 10 miles used as an example earlier will comfortably provide fodder for the military force as it passes through, as its animals will consume only 1/80 of the total area each day. Such foraging is not possible for modern vehicles, which must carry all with them. An armoured division carries 2.95 million litres in its fuel tanks, and another 1.29 million litres in tankers. Tankers are either 12,000 litre or 225,000 litre capacity. An armoured brigade at intense rates – i.e. in combat – requires 117,000 litres per day: six large tankers or 12 small ones. A division of three brigades will, therefore, use up its stocks in tankers in three days, merely topping up the combat elements. If the divisional troops are added, this figure is more like a day and a half. The 136 supply vehicles for a single brigade themselves require 35,000 litres per day – another three small tanker loads.

The examples of Napoleonic practice, of course, assume that the army kept moving: the problem came when movement stopped, for example to undertake a siege or go into winter quarters, and the first resource to be exhausted would then be fodder. Napoleon realized that the eighteenth-century practice of siege warfare was what led to logistic difficulties; with no sieges, the logistic apparatus of an eighteenth-century army became redundant. From Vauban to Napoleon, the French army conducted 200 sieges and 60 battles; Napoleon conducted only two sieges during his entire career, at Mantua in 1796 and Acre, both early in his career. These two experiences and the problem of feeding a static army marked him for life: 'the method of feeding on the march becomes impracticable when many troops are concentrated', he wrote. There were similar problems before Austerlitz in 1805, at Lobau, in Portugal, in 1809, and at Moscow. It was this realization that made him return to the earlier methods of the seventeenth century and before, of a basic ration provided by depots along a line of communication, plus foraging and this, in turn, which gave rise to the much-vaunted 'march dispersed, fight concentrated'. There was no magic in this formula; it was simply a logistic necessity, becoming ever more necessary as the army grew in size, as the calculation already shown proves. It is implicit in the design of his operational manoeuvres of march, battle, and pursuit, with no halts for sieges and no evasion of battle.

There is a major proviso, however, and that is that the agriculture of the country is functioning properly. In Spain, for example, where 'small armies perish and large armies starve' it never worked properly; and where a scorched-earth policy was implemented as in Portugal and Russia, major problems ensued. There are many documented examples of how both static garrisons and field forces in poor areas fared badly. One soldier writing from Metz in 1813, cited by Alan Forrest, complained that his unit had marched for three days on empty stomachs, with nothing to eat except the potatoes they dug up from the fields. They had received no bread for two weeks. Another soldier stationed near Mannheim complained of being reduced to 'a daily ration of two pounds of potatoes which have completely rotted and three ounces of dried peas which have been gnawed by weevils'. Joseph Vachin wrote from remote Moravia that on one occasion his unit had gone for six days with only half a pound of biscuit and a few potatoes. Allowing for the fact that all soldiers, everywhere and in every age, love nothing better than to complain about their food, it is a fact that, combined with cold, damp and poor clothing, the lot of soldiers in Napoleon's armies was one of near-starvation for periods of time, despite the best logistic system that could then be devised.

The Problem of Distance

In terms of movement, the combat elements of a modern armoured brigade will form a column of 40 kilometres in length on a single route, with 50 metres between each vehicle, and will take around two hours driving at normal road speeds of 20–30 kilometres in the hour to pass a single point. Magnified, this means that a modern division will take about ten hours. These figures can increase up to three times if additional combat support formations and logistic traffic is included. Allowing time for rest and refuelling, a division is, on paper, able to cover up to 200 kilometres in the course of a night's move, depending on the time of year. At first sight this seems to bear no relation to what could be done in the early nineteenth century, but is this the case? Moving in this way day after day takes its toll of wear and tear on the vehicle fleet, and mechanical attrition is likely to be more of a factor in reducing combat power than enemy action, even assuming good roads. And as the line of communication lengthens, so do the problems of demand on fuel and spares. In practice, the line of march from Kuwait to Baghdad in 2003 was no more than 400 kilometres, but it took ten days to cover against light opposition, and required several pauses for maintenance, resupply and regrouping.

A Napoleonic corps of two divisions, with organic artillery and cavalry, would contain roughly the same numbers of troops as a modern unreinforced division. On the march, it would form a column about 15 kilometres in length, and again take about four hours to march past a single point – more in the dark. It took ten hours, for example, for Augereau's VII Corps to assemble at Jena in October 1806. The standard marching pace for the *Grande Armée* was 5 kilometres per hour, or 30 kilometres per day. This it could keep up for weeks at a time, something a modern dismounted infantry formation would find immensely demanding, if not impossible, given the cultural factors which have altered people's physical abilities since Napoleon's day. There are a number of celebrated occasions when prodigious feats of marching were made by Napoleon's troops. In 1805, for example, he moved 210,000 men from the Rhine to the Danube, a distance of just over 360 kilometres, in 13 days – not too dissimilar to 2003 rates. In the same campaign, Davout's III Corps marched 140 kilometres in 48 hours – in the same order as our modern division, although of course the much shorter pass time of the Napoleonic corps made a big difference over extended distances. In November 1796, Massena's division made 60 miles towards Mantua between mid-afternoon on the 15th and dawn on the 16th, despite having marched and fought almost without rest for the preceding 24 hours. These timings all include pass time and rest on the march.

The major difficulty in these forced marches was the losses from straggling – the same kind of problem as today's general faces from mechanical attrition. James Dunnigan, in his work on Leipzig, for example, calculated that a Napoleonic corps could lose 80% of its strength over a period of eight months through sickness, disease, desertion and straggling, without firing a shot. Between 1 April and 1 June 1813, for example, counting battle casualties, sick, and stragglers, the *Grande Armée* almost halved in size; from the Armistice of Pleiswitz in late May 1813 up to September, the French lost 150,000 men killed, wounded and taken prisoner in fighting, and another 50,000 sick and straggling.

As well as roads, Napoleon used waterways to good effect to move supplies, although most of the major rivers in Europe flow from south to north and are of limited use to armies moving laterally. In 1807, for example, he made use of the waterways of the Havel, Spree, Oder, Elbe, Vistula and the Bromberg canal to move stores on barges. In 1809 he used the Danube. In October 1813, when his supply situation was also bad, and

Cossack raiding was being exacerbated by deteriorating roads and bad weather, his troops were reduced to only eight ounces of bread per day instead of 28, and had almost no meat. To remedy this quickly, Napoleon ordered the move of large quantities of flour and other stores to Dresden by barge, the transfer of which was to be covered by the move of Marmont and Murat with their entire corps. What he could never do, as could the British, was rely on supplies moved by sea. The Royal Navy's blockade of the Atlantic coast, and its squadrons in the Baltic and Mediterranean, exercised so tight a control that French merchant convoys were always a high-risk enterprise, and an unsafe basis for logistic planning.

The Problem of Duration

The Napoleonic system of war was designed for short campaigns ending in decisive battles, and the logistic system was geared exactly to this: it was campaigning on a logistic shoestring, and yet when it worked, as when such a campaign could be planned and executed, it worked well. The campaign of Austerlitz is a good example. In late August, Dejean was ordered to assemble 500,000 biscuit rations at Strasbourg, where half the army would be concentrated, and 200,000 at Mainz, within 25 days. To move this, 150 wagons were to be brought up from Boulogne, 1,000 provided by a contractor, and 3,500 would be requisitioned. Of these, 2,500 were allocated to the artillery and the rest were to carry food for the army for 11 days. Napoleon's ally the Elector of Bavaria was to provide a further one million rations, split between Würzburg and Ulm. The 700,000 rations in the assembly area would feed the five corps held there for six days; a further four days' bread would take the army into Bavaria and keep it at Ulm for another four. In the event, only half the requirement could be met, not least because the bulk of the wagons did not get forward in time, but also because the Bavarians failed to deliver on time. The deficit had to be made up by requisition, but the system worked sufficiently well for the Austrians to be brought to battle at Austerlitz. Similarly in 1806, Napoleon established bakeries at Weimar and Gera to provide bread in the march to Jena, but mostly the army fed from requisition in the towns of Weimar, Erfurt, Leipzig and Küstrin, and the surrounding rich countryside.

In more protracted campaigns or remote areas, the shoestring often broke. In the spring of 1813, for example, the Emperor wrote to Joseph in Spain, as has been cited earlier in Chapter II, insisting that he should make a demonstration towards Portugal in order to tie down the British. Joseph's objections were chiefly logistic:

I must in the first instance concentrate the troops which is impossible owing to want of victuals. And what is the use of it, if I make such a demonstration? Wellington will not be deceived, for he knows that ... I have had to send large drafts to the Emperor.

Even the British, with a solid line of communication and control of the seas, had difficulties in Spain and Portugal. Again, in the aftermath of Vitoria, Napoleon despatched Soult to recover the position in Spain. He was able to make good much of the deficiency in artillery resulting from losses at Vitoria from the large reserves of cannon and ammunition held in the arsenal of Bayonne, which was able to supply 140 guns of all calibres to the army. He was less successful with supplies, so that the army resorted to uncontrolled plundering in its own country. The condition of the troops can be judged from the fact that they had to be beaten off the bullocks, that Soult had secured to pull his guns over the mountains, to prevent them killing and eating the wretched animals on the spot. When he made his attack plan to relieve Pamplona in late July 1813, Soult allowed only four days in which to capture the stores of the besiegers at Pamplona. It was a daring plan which fully recognized the weaknesses of the allied position, but it demanded surprise, fast marching through difficult country, hard fighting against a determined enemy, and a good system of supply. This last was a fatal flaw from the beginning, for the army was still desperately short of wagons and, if it could not close with its objective and achieve success within that time, then given the lack of forage in so poor a country, the troops would starve. So it turned out.

The preparations for the attack on Russia have already been mentioned, and there is no doubt that although this campaign was foolhardy from the point of view of strategy, it was carefully planned. Napoleon knew from his intelligence preparation that the army would not be able to live by forage, even marching on dispersed routes. 'Without adequate transport', he wrote to Eugène de Beauharnais, 'everything will be useless.' Huge reserves of artillery ammunition were built up. The artillery of the various French corps and the reserve totalled more than 800 guns of all calibres; for the 330 12-pounders, for example, there were available 226 rounds of canister, and 568 rounds of ball per gun. In terms of rations, Napoleon planned for 600,000 men taking 60 days to reach Moscow. This meant 18,000 tons of food for the men alone, or twice what his Train Service could carry; by the time the army reached Moscow, it would be 600 miles from its bases, and require 300 tons of food per day, needing a total of 18,000 tons of wagon capacity. In addition, therefore, to the preparations ordered in January, one million biscuit rations were to be depoted at Stettin and Küstrin in April. The army then took 24 days of provisions with it – four days carried by each man, and 20 on the Train, with the remaining 60 days to be brought forward. There were, in addition, 250,000 horses with the army and the need to gather fodder for them was one of the driving factors in postponing the launch of the campaign to the end of June.

As the campaign unfolded, logistic problems proved to be fatal. After early difficulties, many corps and divisions reported plentiful forage, although the ability to exploit it was impaired by pillaging and indiscipline, as has already been noted. The army was, therefore, in good enough condition to fight at Borodino but, in the longer term, the roads proved even worse than had been anticipated, and the River Vilnya turned out to be too shallow for barge traffic. The army's undisciplined plundering stripped the country too fast, and drove off the local inhabitants. Finally, the Russian army could not be brought to battle quickly, and the Russian government instituted a scorched-earth policy which deprived the invaders of forage, and harried the line of communication mercilessly with Cossack cavalry, making the invaders' situation more desperate the further they penetrated into Russia.

Conclusions

As the comparisons used earlier show, the emphasis in logistics has changed since Napoleon's day, as has the technology. However, the problem has not altered in kind. The degree to which an army can be sustained remains one of the key factors for any general in planning and executing a campaign. Indeed, it may, as in Russia, be decisive. Then and now, it remains a driving factor in the size of forces that can take and keep the field. Napoleon's armies were the largest that the western world had then seen and his method of supplying them had, therefore, to be innovative – hence, his insistence on spreading out and foraging to supplement the depots. There is no information in his correspondence or the archives to show how Napoleon assessed the performance of his logistic system, but in general he seems to have been content, given the few changes he made to it, aside from the major innovation of the Train Service.

It is ironic that, having succeeded in so many campaigns on the basis of just enough, just in time, he should fail in Russia after the most extensive preparations undertaken in the history of warfare up to that point. He knew well that living off the country would be impossible, and he knew the results of staying in one place for any length of time, but even his preparations were insufficient for the demand, distance and duration of the campaign. Even so, had the indiscipline of the troops been checked earlier, it is conceivable that things might have been easier. Those corps with commanders prepared to crack down hard, like Davout, invariably did better than those whose commanders were slack.

Napoleon's logistic system was, therefore, like much else that he did, not so much a revolution as a development of the practice of immediate predecessors or of earlier generals, whose methods he had gleaned from study. The exception is the Train Service. With the same exception, his methods were not dissimilar to those of other European armies of the period. Martin van Creveld, for example, shows that the proportion of supply vehicles in the French and Austrian armies in 1805 was almost exactly the same. All European armies lived off the land, but the French army was particularly proficient, and Napoleon knew how to exploit this skill through organized plunder. The campaign of 1805, like his preparations for Russia, do however show that Napoleon also realized what he had to provide when the army moved through country which would not support large numbers of troops and animals: huge depots and magazines, large numbers of draft animals, columns of wagons and barges, troops tied to securing the routes.

But the Industrial Revolution had yet to reach its full potential, and railways had not yet begun to appear, and it was these factors that allowed armies to grow to the size they did during the First World War, and to remain static for extended periods. It is interesting that in modern campaigns, static operations in theatres like the Balkans, Iraq and Afghanistan have brought their own problems in over-stretching limited military logistic units. Consequently, deployed military forces are once again relying on contractors to provide accommodation, food and food supply, drinking water, fuel and transportation. The situation in modern times is almost the reverse, therefore, of Napoleonic times. Once the line of communication – especially the strategic line of communication – has been established and secured, the use of contracts, and the development of food technology and other commodity storage have made the maintenance of a static force far simpler than that of a mobile one. This must be so, even though modern formations have developed logistic support at unit, formation and theatre levels, thus allowing modern mobile forces to be self-sufficient for longer, and at lower levels of command, than in Napoleonic times. But given the constraints and conditions of his time, therefore, Napoleon must be given credit, whatever his shortcomings in other areas, for making 50 pence do the work of a pound. That he overran most of Europe, and that his armies did not starve in the process, is nothing short of a miracle.

VIII

Case Study 1: Exporting Revolution, 1793–7: Napoleon's First Essay in Generalship

The Boy General

Napoleon Bonaparte attained the rank of Brigadier General on 22 October 1793, three days after the successful conclusion of the siege of Toulon. Although, strictly speaking, the credit belonged to the commander of the besieging troops, General Jacques Coquille Dugommier, it was Napoleon who, standing in as commander of the artillery for his sick mentor, Jean Duteil, had laid the plan for the attack by 38,000 French troops, and directed the artillery. Napoleon's plan had caught the eye of the Committee of Public Safety where two rivals had not, and it succeeded after only two days. It was just as well: 1793 was not a year in which it was acceptable to fail as a French commander.

Napoleon had been lucky. It was not hard for an educated officer such as he was to spot the weak point in Toulon's defences, but the guillotine, exile and desertion had thinned the field of talent, so that rivals capable of even simple analysis were few. He was lucky too in that Duteil was ill, and was in any case well disposed towards his young protégé, Napoleon. As a result, he was mentioned in enthusiastic terms to the Committee. Even better, he had patronage. The *représentant du peuple* – the political commissar of the army – at Toulon was Antoine-Christophe Saliceti: a Corsican, and a friend of the Bonaparte family. It was Saliceti who had recommended Napoleon for the command of the artillery and had backed his attack plan. In this, Saliceti had been supported by another commissar, Paul Barras, who was quick to recognize Napoleon's talents, and who would in the future become a power in the land. This patronage soon made itself felt, for Duteil was guillotined in February 1794, and without connections, the young Napoleon might well have been judged guilty by association.

In January 1794, the Committee followed up the success of Toulon by ordering the Army of Italy to attack the Italian Riviera and capture Oneglia, fifty miles east of Nice, as an additional supply port. In March, Napoleon was appointed to command the artillery, with Saliceti and Augustine Robespierre, younger brother of Maximilien, as commissars. Napoleon at once proposed a plan of attack, which was accepted and put into effect. Oneglia fell on 6 April. Encouraged, Napoleon put forward a new plan on 20 June to invade Piedmont. This plan was the fruit of Napoleon's years of study, being a re-run of the plan prepared in 1744 by General Pierre-Joseph de Bourcet. The remarkable thing about this is not the plan itself, but that Napoleon was bold enough to put it forward, along with a strategic appreciation. Drawing attention to himself in this way, at this time, was either extraordinary confidence or extraordinary rashness – for anything less than complete success would result in an appointment with Madame la Guillotine. Napoleon had not yet learned that the calculation of risk depends on two things: first, the need to take such a risk in order to fulfil a mission, and second, the ability to stand the consequences of failure.

This strategic appreciation described revolutionary France's military situation. She was at war with Great Britain, Austria, Piedmont and Spain – and thus effectively surrounded by land and sea. Her 14 armies were drawn up along the frontiers in a posture of strategic defence designed by Carnot. Since we now know that Maximilien Robespierre was anxious to go onto the offensive, the political climate was clearly ripe for a different view. Robespierre's report to the Committee of Public Safety on 25 December 1793 was explicit about exporting the principles of revolutionary government, which he described as a necessary and provisional form of war against the enemies of liberty. Augustine Robespierre and Saliceti would have known this very well, and perhaps they are the true authors of the appreciation. At the very least, Napoleon would not have proceeded without their support. The appreciation recommended remaining on the defensive in the Pyrenees and in the Low Countries; combining the armies of Italy and the Alps to subjugate Piedmont; then advancing through Lombardy and into the Austrian Tyrol and, in conjunction with the Army of the Rhine, threatening Vienna. Even if Napoleon had not written this himself, he learned fast, for it presages his future approach to making war: 'a well-reasoned and circumspect defensive, followed by a rapid and audacious attack'.

Certainly, it was Augustine Robespierre who took Napoleon's plan to Paris in late June 1794. But, at this point, luck temporarily deserted Napoleon: Maximilien Robespierre was overthrown and executed by the coup of Thermidor (27 July), and the plan was put on ice. Worse, all associates of the Robespierres were suspect. To compound the matter, Napoleon had been sent into neutral Switzerland on an intelligence-gathering mission and this, from Paris, looked suspiciously like intrigue. On his return, he was arrested and locked up. But luck did not desert him for long, for it was Saliceti who was directed to investigate Napoleon's case. He duly reported that there was no incriminating evidence; moreover, he

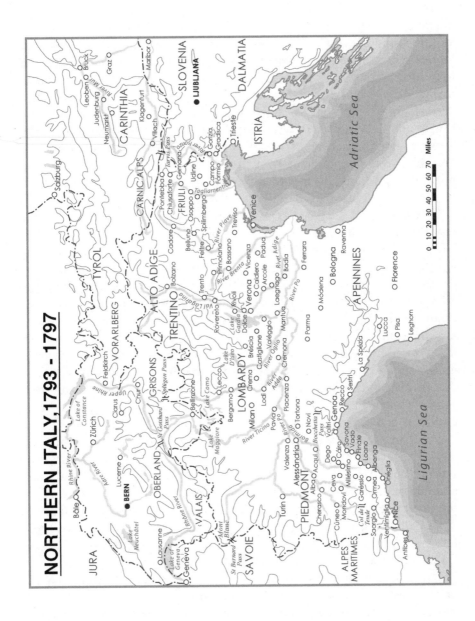

NORTHERN ITALY, 1793 - 1797

reported that Napoleon's services were indispensable to the Republic. After only 11 days, he was released.

From then until March, the Army of Italy was fixed by two limited preliminary operations, one against Corsica which was aborted, and one against Cadibona, which commanded one of the Alpine passes west of Savona. The army was also fixed by a degree of command paralysis, having had three commanders in quick succession, none of whom were exactly firebrands: General Pierre Dumerbion from March to November 1794; Barthélemy Schérer from November 1794 to March 1795; and then François-Christophe Kellermann. In May 1795, Napoleon quitted command of the artillery and returned to Paris, still under a vestigial cloud of suspicion. Offered a minor command he refused and took sick leave, remaining unemployed but in touch with the political situation and developing his contacts – especially Paul Barras.

In August 1795, Napoleon's assiduous nurturing of influential friends resulted in his being assigned on a semi-official basis to the *Bureau Topographique*. This was not exactly what its name implied: it had been set up by Carnot in 1792 and was a somewhat chaotic collection of staff officers, charged with strategic and operational analysis and plans. Napoleon was assigned to the section dealing with Italy. He used this time to develop Bourcet's plan for the invasion of Piedmont. He had wisely made the best of his opportunity in Italy to make personal reconnaissance of the terrain. He knew the Alpine passes, the capacity of the roads, the ports, and the effects of weather and season. He also understood the situation and capabilities of the enemy, and of his own troops. Not for the first time, he was faced with a coalition of enemies, with all the fragilities and mutual suspicions that coalitions can suffer when faced with a single enemy.

Then, on 15 September, having refused the command already mentioned above, he was dismissed from the service by order of the Committee of Public Safety. He was not a civilian for long. The publication of the Constitution of the Year III, which set up the Directory, resulted in mob riots by the Paris Communes and the National Guard – the so-called coup of 13 *Vendémiaire*. Barras, the effective leader of the five members of the Directory, was given extensive powers over public order by the two legislative Councils. Barras at once sent for Napoleon, who in turn dispatched Joachim Murat to secure the Paris artillery park. It was, therefore, troops and guns under Napoleon's command that opened fire in the Rue St Honoré and suppressed the revolt. In gratitude, Barras appointed Napoleon as Commander of the Army of the Interior – that is, all troops not assigned to the frontier commands – on 26 October. Despite his operational experience and his expertise in planning, Napoleon had until then been an artillery commander, and had never commanded any all-arms formation – not even a brigade. Suddenly to command an army was a massive step militarily and politically.

Meanwhile back in Italy, command of the army again changed. Kellermann had conceded ground to the allies and was moved to the Army of the Alps. Schérer returned to the command and by November he had regained the lost ground. Unable to push further, Schérer pestered Paris for reinforcements and supplies, but the treasury was empty. Worn out, Schérer resigned the command in February 1796. At the end of two years of war, therefore, the Army of Italy had been led by a succession of elderly and, at best, adequate commanders. No wonder that it had made little progress against an indifferent enemy. If the situation was to be changed to advantage, then a commander with fire in his belly was clearly needed. The most obvious choice would have been the only really competent and successful formation commander in the theatre of operations, the 37-year-old André Massena. The Directory however took a different view and, as a reward for his loyalty as well as in acknowledgement of his constant demands for action in Italy, Napoleon was given the chance to execute the plan he had made for the invasion of Piedmont. On 2 March 1796, at the age of 26, he was appointed to command the Army of Italy.

The Conquest of Piedmont

On the day of his appointment Napoleon received a detailed directive from the Directory – drafted and refined several times by himself. The directive can be read in Volume I of Debidour *Reueil des Actes du Directoire Executif,* and it lays out the strategic objectives and priorities of the campaign. First, to capture Ceva as a base for further operations; next, to subjugate Piedmont and in so doing, gain access to its much-needed resources; third to advance into the Austrian territories in Lombardy, with Milan as the axis of advance; and finally to secure a frontier with the Austrians – having annexed the rich plain of Lombardy to France. In terms of the operational and tactical execution of this plan, Napoleon was given a free hand but before any campaigning could begin, he had to tackle the desperate logistical situation of the army. The army was well strung out, short of weapons and ammunition of all natures, wagons, mules and horses, bridging equipment, food and fodder. The troops were in rags, and discipline was shaky – in some cases the troops were distinctly mutinous. This was no situation in which to take the field, for there were frictions at work which would wreck such an army before ever the enemy made a move.

The army faced France's largest and most powerful adversary, the Austrian Empire, which on paper at least could field an army of 350,000 men, including 58,000 cavalry. This army was, however, highly multinational with all the problems and tensions attending such a force. It had no real staff system, and it relied on old-fashioned, linear tactics, with little understanding of all-arms co-operation. It was a slow and ponderous army which never moved without copious supplies, in contrast to the speedy and lightly-laden French. Its generals too were old fashioned, and many of them were elderly. Moreover, its main effort lay not in Italy but on the Rhine.

To rectify the French army's situation in Italy, Napoleon made a masterly choice of Chief of Staff: the experienced and capable Alexandre Berthier, who would remain with Napoleon until his exile in 1814. Napoleon wrote of Berthier in his *Correspondance* that:

> He was very active; he would accompany his Commander-in-Chief on every reconnaissance and every journey, without his office work being ever slowed down. He had no decision of character and was quite unfitted for command, but possessed all the qualities of a good Chief of Staff. He ... attended personally to the issue of orders; he was expert at presenting clearly the most complicated movements of an army.

A perfect foil, then, to the young and impatient commander with no time for masses of administrative detail or piles of papers. Berthier had one additional recommendation: he was most unlikely ever to be a rival or a threat to his master. In contrast to Berthier, Napoleon also appointed four young sparks as aides-de-camp: Auguste Marmont, Jean Junot, Joachim Murat, and his own 18-year-old brother, Louis Bonaparte. They were also in contrast to the three senior divisional commanders who greeted Napoleon on his arrival. Jean-Mathieu Serurier was 53. A tall, gloomy man with 34 years' service in the Royal Army, he was methodical, a fierce disciplinarian, and more than a little uncomfortable in the Revolutionary Army – but he knew his business. Charles Augereau, 38 years old, tall and imposing of figure, had also served in the Royal Army, but in the ranks. The son of a stonemason, he was also a murderer and a deserter who had gone on to serve in the Russian army against the Turks, and in the Prussian Guards. He had returned to France in 1792 and a year later was a divisional commander. He has been described as coarse, stupid but cunning, and a bully. There is no doubt, however, that on the battlefield, he too knew his business. Napoleon wrote of him that he had 'plenty of character, courage, firmness, energy; he is accustomed to war, popular with his men, lucky in the field.' The last of the trio was the most able, the 38-year-old André Massena. He too had served in the ranks of the old army until he retired with the rank of sergeant major in 1789. Thereafter he had been a smuggler in the hills of Savoy – a great advantage when it came to knowing the terrain for the coming campaign. In 1792 he had rejoined the French army and had already distinguished himself. Dark, thin and silent, he had a strong taste for loot, money and women. Napoleon's opinion was that he was 'active, tireless, enterprising, grasps a situation and makes up his mind quickly'. Damning with faint praise, perhaps. These three had no great opinion of their young general – a mere bookworm as far as they were concerned – but at their first meeting they were impressed in spite of themselves by his confidence and his willpower.

Berthier's first task was to reorganize the line of communication through France to Nice. Once this was achieved – no mean feat in itself – Napoleon and his staff arrived at the army headquarters in that city on 27 March. There followed a stream of orders concerning the reorganization of divisions, the movement of cavalry, siege and bridging trains, draught horses for the artillery, ammunition, and rations for men and animals. The army he was to command numbered around 63,000 effectives out of an original strength of about 107,000. Of these, 41,000 could be relied on for an offensive campaign. Facing the French were 50,000 Piedmontese under the Austrian General Baron Michel von Colli, of whom half were dispersed to hold the Alpine passes and fortresses, and observe Kellermann's army, with the remainder held as a mobile reserve under General Johann Provera – but again deployed on a 30-mile front. A second operational echelon of 28,000 Austrian troops was held well back and widely dispersed, under the 71-year-old General Baron Johann Beaulieu. Of these, 10,000 were in garrisons; 9,500 in a field force under General Baron Philipp von Vukassovich; and a further 11,500 under General Count Eugen Argenteau based around Acqui, but again well dispersed.

On paper, then, the force ratios were not favourable to the French; moreover, the advance would be constrained by the terrain: northern Italy has a great diversity of terrain, ranging from the fertile plain of Lombardy centred on the River Po and its tributaries, to the foothills of the Alps, and the high ranges of the Apennines. Fighting was bound to focus on control of the mountain passes and the crossings over the rivers, and these were in part dominated by the four major fortresses of Mantua, Perschiera, Verona and Legnano. Napoleon would, for example, have to pass his whole force through the one narrow defile of the Cadibona Pass before making contact with the enemy. The enemy was, however, dispersed by the need to hold a number of defiles and by the requirements of food, forage and billeting – it is easy to criticize the Austrian commanders for dispersal, but we are perhaps prone to forget the limitations of late eighteenth-century logistics. To

succeed, therefore, a French offensive would be based on concentration of
force, surprise, and rapid movement, crushing each enemy formation in
turn before they had time to unite: something which was, in any case, in line
with his instructions. Napoleon also believed that if he could secure the
town of Carcare quickly, this would prevent a junction of his opponents,
allowing him to screen Beaulieu's and Argenteau's forces while he concentrated on Colli. Napoleon's command was in five divisions under their
tough and capable generals: André Massena, Amédée Laharpe, Charles
Augereau, Jean-Baptiste Meynier and Jean-Mathieu Serurier. Napoleon's
tactical organization of these divisions for the campaign in Piedmont shows
the first signs of the *corps d'armée* system that he would later perfect:
Massena was to command a reinforced advanced guard of 19,000 men;
Augereau would take the main body, or *corps de bataille*, of 12,000; and
Serrurier would command the left flank guard of 10,000. The divisions
themselves were not a new organization in the French army, but the French
were well ahead of most other armies in adopting such an organization. The
prototype had been Marshal Maurice de Saxe's Legions of four infantry
regiments, with cavalry, skirmishers and guns. Marshal de Broglie had
adopted a similar organization during the Seven Years War and, in 1795,
Carnot formally adopted the division into the Revolutionary Army as a
combined arms formation. Napoleon himself has been credited with this
innovation, but in fact, as with much else, he merely refined the work of
others. The refinement was the *corps d'armée* system, which we will meet
later.

The original plan had to be modified at this point, following instructions
from Paris to support a diplomatic mission to neutral Genoa by Saliceti.
Massena was ordered to mount a coercive demonstration, which not only
succeeded in thoroughly alarming the Genoese, but was also detected by the
Austrians. Beaulieu misread the demonstration as a full-blown French
advance on Genoa and so moved his troops to secure the Ligurian Apennines and then strike at what he expected would be the open French left
flank as it wheeled south. This unintended deception by the French therefore put the whole Austrian forces in motion. On 10 April, a large Austrian
force appeared unexpectedly at the town of Voltri. The French troops were,
however, able to extricate themselves, and Napoleon made some rapid
changes to his scheme of manoeuvre. Gathering his divisional commanders
together, he issued verbal orders. At first light the next morning, Laharpe's
division were to attack the Austrian force directly, head on, and fix it.
During the night preceding this attack, Massena was to march his whole
force along the Altare ridge west of Montenotte, and fall on the Austrian
right and rear. A long and anxious night followed, but the plan unfolded

exactly as Napoleon had intended. The Austrians, all but surrounded, broke. Napoleon was quick to exploit, ordering a pursuit that not only threatened Ceva, but also prevented any future junction of the allied armies.

Napoleon has been credited with a stroke of tactical genius at Montenotte; in fact, he applied the lessons he had learned from the likes of Bourcet, Guibert and Duteil – and came up with a sensible tactical solution to a problem. This is not to belittle him: at a young age, having never before manoeuvred a combined arms force, he had made the right decisions in a timely manner. He had also placed himself in the right position to be able to make that decision, with the best available intelligence at hand, in order to do the three things that a general must do to discharge his responsibilities: find out what is going on, communicate his intentions to his subordinates, and keep in contact with the staff so that they can solve problems. One can also speculate that Napoleon had realized that, briefly, the initiative had passed to the other side, and that it had to be regained and then maintained. To achieve this he had to do what any commander must do in such a situation: first, seize an opportunity detected by intelligence, or else create one by achieving surprise; have the means available to do the job, and have the will to employ them; act offensively; and last be able to develop a higher tempo* of decision making, action, and logistic sustainability than his opponent.

In the aftermath of Montenotte, Napoleon did not know for certain whether all the Austrian forces had been engaged. He wanted to take on the Piedmontese and capture Ceva, but he still needed to watch his flanks. To guard against the unexpected he therefore created a central reserve at Carcare, and then pushed on. The advance began on 13 April, and from the start, nothing went right. Provera had occupied a blocking position at Cosseria and could not be dislodged. Dego, which Napoleon had thought secure, had also been reoccupied by the enemy. Napoleon gave Augereau the task of screening Provera. The rest of the army then marched to Dego, which was attacked on the 15th. The place was quickly secured and the enemy troops either forced into retreat or taken prisoner. At the same time, word came that the enemy force at Cosseria had surrendered. In the aftermath of their victory, the French troops went in search of plunder, drink, and food. They were thus badly surprised when, early the next morning, a force of five Austrian battalions under General Baron Philipp von Vukassovich arrived, following earlier orders, and unaware of the previous day's events. The Austrians quickly scattered Massena's men, nearly capturing the General himself, seized the village, and fortified a

* In military terms, tempo is the rate or rhythm of activity relative to an enemy.

position. Massena had to collect up his dispersed division and retake the place.

Beaulieu, meanwhile, had remained at Acqui, reassuring Napoleon about the security of his flanks. Napoleon could safely screen him and watch for a while using an economy of force operation, while concentrating on the Piedmontese at Ceva. On 18 April, another enveloping manoeuvre was made by Massena on Colli's entrenched camp, only to find the enemy withdrawn to a strong position. A frontal attack the next day failed, with heavy French losses, but after a pause to bring up more artillery and prepare a new plan, another envelopment the next day did the trick. Colli made a skilful job of disengaging and slipping away before his force was destroyed, but one can only speculate on why Colli had not realized that the envelopment was already Napoleon's favourite tactical gambit. The Piedmontese were herded north by the French cavalry towards Turin until, on 28 April, an embassy from King Victor Amadeus of Piedmont came out to parley with Napoleon at Cherasco, where an armistice was signed.

In 15 days, the French had won six battles and conquered the richest part of Piedmont. This was, by any standards, a great achievement. Napoleon had turned round a poor logistic situation, with a line of communication liable to be severed by force projection from the British fleet in the Ligurian Sea. He had mastered unfavourable terrain, and beaten a well-supplied enemy in superior numbers. He had understood intuitively when and how to seize the initiative, change the situation to advantage, and then win by exploiting local victories. In this way, he translated tactical success into operational success in order to achieve strategic goals. The comparison with Hannibal, who also crossed the Alps, is unavoidable. It is said that Hasdrubal said to him more than once that he knew how to win a victory, but not how to use one. It is, however, true that Napoleon's adversaries were elderly men, who continually misread the situation and at every turn made the wrong decision, from the initial move against Genoa onwards. Even if they had made the correct decisions, it is more than likely that the superiority of French implementation, and the remarkable marching powers of their troops, would have dislocated them.

Many commentators have remarked on the changes in Napoleon's character which began to appear. He had been unpopular as a young officer, often morose and moody. When he was appointed to the command, Massena, Augereau and the others may have been unhappy at serving under such a youth, but after the first battles, his personal authority was no longer questioned. That is not to say that his relations with his subordinates were happy, as will be discussed later.

Lombardy

The Armistice of Cherasco had accomplished France's first two strategic objectives – the seizure of Ceva and the occupation of Piedmont. The next move had to be against the Austrians. Napoleon made good use of Piedmontese wealth to pay, feed and re-equip his troops and make some rapid plans. To reach Milan and drive the Austrians out of Lombardy, the French army would have to cross the Po, one of the great rivers of Europe. Napoleon's preparations to do this were soon detected by the Austrians. Beaulieu had already lost at least 6,000 men and had reported to Vienna that his situation was very bad. However, he put a large force of 21,000 men across the Po at Valenza to forestall the French, and cover the approaches to Milan; beyond this immediate tactical objective there was no operational or strategic vision to defeat the French or to eject them.

Napoleon himself moved up to Tortona on 3 May, and the next day he began preparations for an extensive deception operation. Massena and Serurier were ordered to mount a diversion, and convince Beaulieu that the French would cross at Valenza. Meanwhile, a picked force of six battalions of grenadiers and fusiliers, under the command of Brigadier General Claude Dallemagne, began to march the 55 miles downstream to Piacenza on 7 May, where they would cross. Major Antoine-François Andréossy collected the bridging train and as many barges as could be gathered, and also moved quickly to Piacenza, where he established a crossing. The actual crossing operation was given to Colonel Jean Lannes, who had distinguished himself at Dego and caught Napoleon's eye. Lannes brought off this most difficult operation of war on 7 May without opposition, securing a lodgment on the enemy bank. Laharpe's and Augereau's divisions quickly followed.

Beaulieu quickly realized his predicament, and at once began to march on the bridgehead. On 9 May his advance guard met French troops expanding the original bridgehead, and was halted. A full-blown meeting engagement took place in darkness later that night, during which Laharpe was shot dead by his own men. In the confusion, the French troops began to waver, but they were rallied by Berthier, and beat off the attack. Despite being in superior numbers, Beaulieu lost heart, and slipped away. This operation had been a classic of careful planning, speedy execution, and successful deception. Its only failing was that Beaulieu made good his escape.

The Po runs generally west to east, but it has a number of significant tributaries running north to south into its basin from the Alps. These also would have to be crossed by the French army, and there were few bridges capable of taking the wheeled traffic of an army. The Austrians knew this well, and, as they retreated towards Milan, they left strong rearguards on these defiles. On 10 May, the French made contact with such a guard force on the bridge over the Adda at Lodi, which was taken by storm. This was one of the many occasions on which Napoleon showed a high degree of personal courage, gaining great kudos among the troops who after this gave him his nickname of 'le petit caporel'. This was clearly an occasion on which, of the three elements of command, raw leadership was more important than decision making or resource management, and the commander's personal presence at the point of main effort was a decisive factor in gaining success.

At this point, the strategic scenery shifted – or rather lurched. The Austrians began to withdraw towards the Alps, leaving behind only the garrison of Mantua on the River Mincio south of Lake Garda, and this was soon under siege. The Directory gave orders for the command of the Army in Italy to be split. Kellermann was to take over the passes into Lombardy and hold them. Napoleon, with a reduced force, was ordered to swing south into Tuscany, capture Parma, intimidate Genoa into accepting vassal status, and so increase the flow of strategic resources to France. Subsequent operations might include a march on Rome, or even Naples. This distraction from the business at hand did not please Napoleon. He argued against the orders, and implied resignation – but made sure that a large consignment of booty arrived in Paris at the same time as his refusal. Writing to Carnot he said that:

> Kellermann would command the army quite as well as I do; for I am certain that our victories are due to the bravery and daring of the men. But I am convinced that to combine Kellermann and myself in Italy would be to court disaster. I cannot serve alongside a man who considers himself the best General in Europe. In any case, I am certain that one bad General is better than two good ones.

Losing its most successful general was not something the Directory could contemplate, and the orders were withdrawn.

The Austrians having abandoned Milan without a fight, it was duly occupied by the French. Napoleon had no desire to linger, however, and decided to follow the Austrians into the Tyrol, in order to fulfil the last part of his directive. To do this, he needed to violate the neutrality of the Republic of Venice. This he did without compunction so that, by late June, all of Lombardy and Venetia were secure. Napoleon then set out to do some of the things he had refused to do earlier: bully the Genoese and the Pope in order to gather loot and grants of territory. By July, most of Italy north of Rome was subject to French rule, either directly or indirectly. Only the isolated fortress of Mantua held out.

By this time, the Austrians were alive to the threat posed by the Army of Italy and the need to relieve the siege of Mantua. Although Napoleon had not intended this, Mantua had become the bait which drew successive waves of Austrian attacks. Field Marshal Count Dagobert Wurmser was, therefore, transferred from the Rhine front to Italy. Wurmser was even older than Beaulieu, but he had plenty of fight in him. He brought with him 20,000 men from the Rhine, and to these he added another 27,000 at Trent. The same river valleys that had to be crossed by the French moving from west to east, constrained the Austrian moves from north to south, forcing bodies of troops to march down them. Wurmser divided his force into four columns which were to advance east and west of Lake Garda, down the upper Adige valley, and across the Venetian plain from Vicenza to Verona and on to Mantua. Napoleon's forces were spread out in order to watch a front of 75 miles, and he was unsure of where the Austrian blow might fall. Wurmser began his move on 29 July with his main effort against Massena between the Adige Gorge and Lake Garda. By the end of the first day's fighting, he had pushed Massena back 12 miles. On 30th, a rattled Napoleon wrote that 'I must take serious measures for a defeat ... our communications with Milan and Verona are cut ...' Napoleon had realized that if two or more Austrian columns could unite south of Lake Garda then, not only would the force ratios be highly unfavourable to him, but also Wurmser would do to him what he had done to Colli: execute what subsequently became known as a *manoeuvre sur les derrières*. The next six days were full of crisis and danger; however, Wurmser had revealed his hand, and Napoleon knew that he had to accept risk. Accordingly, he raised the siege of Mantua, abandoning his siege train in the process, and concentrated what forces he could – two divisions – at Castiglione. In doing this, Napoleon came as close to being beaten as at any time in the campaign, but luckily for him, the four Austrian columns were too dispersed to be closely co- ordinated, and it was the ability to beat them individually before they could unite that brought success.

On 3 August, Massena confronted the Austrian column under General Peter Quasdanovich at Lonato, and in a bitter battle checked it. At roughly the same time. Augereau's men fought Wurmser's column to a halt near Castiglione. With Quasdanovich halted and unable to join forces with Wurmser, Napoleon concentrated his forces against Wurmser, who was occupying a strong position on the Castiglione-Solferino heights. Napoleon saw that the Austrian right flank was well anchored, but the left was somewhat hanging: his analysis of the situation led him to what can be seen as a prototype of his future battle system. Napoleon knew that he had to destroy Wurmser if he could: to allow him to reinforce Mantua, or continue

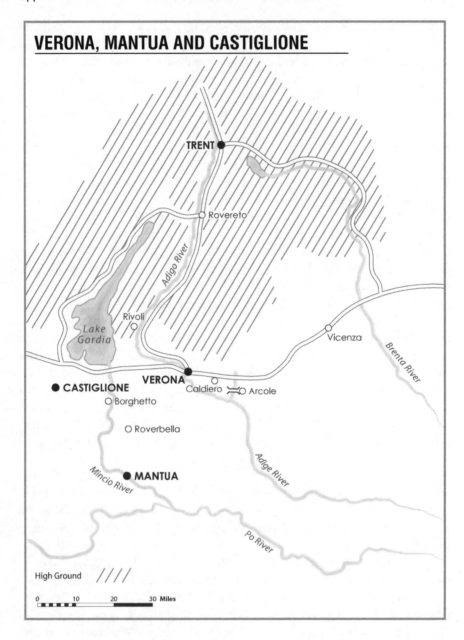

VERONA, MANTUA AND CASTIGLIONE

TRENT

Rovereto

Adigo River

Rivoli

Lake Gardia

Vicenza

Brenta River

VERONA

Caldiero

Arcole

● CASTIGLIONE

O Borghetto

O Roverbella

Adige River

Mincio River

● MANTUA

Po River

High Ground ////

0   10   20   30 Miles

to manoeuvre, could be fatal. Napoleon therefore determined on a pinning attack by Massena against the Austrian right, and a similar pinning attack against the left by Augereau. Meanwhile, Serurier, called from the siege of Mantua, would march round the Austrian left flank and fall on their rear.

This, he hoped, would cause Wurmser to weaken his main battle line, which would then be pierced by a sudden attack using a picked body of grenadiers, with cannon and cavalry in support. This would be followed up by a general attack on the whole position to complete the destruction of the enemy force. Things did not turn out quite as planned, partly because of errors of timing, and partly because Napoleon's subordinates did not fully comprehend the plan – but they were all learning on the job. The result was a tactical draw, but in consequence, an operational success. Wurmser fell back to the line of the river Mincio. There was no doubt that Wurmser had seriously shaken Napoleon, and the loss of the siege train at Mantua was a serious blow. Napoleon had, however, managed to concentrate a superior force against each Austrian column in turn: this was his future method for both campaigns and battles in embryo.

Napoleon sensed the chance to finish the Austrians and, despite the exhaustion of his troops, Massena's division attacked the Austrian outposts, drove them north, and entered Trent on 5 September. But Wurmser did not, as expected, head for home. Instead, he turned west. Napoleon's tired troops followed, and caught the Austrians at the village of Bassano on the 8th, inflicting yet another defeat. But, although pursued hard by the French, Wurmser was able to slip into Mantua with part of his force. Not that this did the besieged any good – rather it brought more mouths to feed from a declining supply of food.

The campaign of 1796 was not over yet. The Austrians determined on one further attempt to relieve Mantua and regain the initiative in northern Italy. Field Marshal Baron Joseph von Allvintzy was given a further 40,000 men and ordered to advance down the Piave valley, in concert with another body of 18,000 troops under General Paul von Davidovich, which would advance down the Adige valley from Trent. The Austrians, slow to understand the threat in Italy, had now committed several times the number of troops available to Napoleon, but in separate packages. Had the entire number been committed concurrently, under a unified command, it is hard to see that even Napoleon could have faced them and won. As it was, Allvintzy was ordered to capture Verona, link up with Davidovich, and relieve Mantua. This move again found Napoleon's forces in a weak position, well dispersed, and with at least 18,000 men sick or in hospital. Allvintzy began his move in November – an unexpected time of year given the Alpine weather – and quickly pushed the French back to the line of the Adige River. On 11 November, he turned south and began a pontoon crossing of the river, south of Verona.

Receiving reports from his cavalry screen, Napoleon realized that he was in danger of surrendering the initiative. He immediately determined on another *manoeuvre sur les derrières.* Napoleon's objective was the Austrian field park and logistic hub in their rear, possession of which would force the Austrians to abandon the drive on Verona. This, in turn, would create the conditions for Napoleon to bring Allvintzy to battle in the marshy terrain between the Adige and Alpone Rivers, where they would be unable to bring their numerical superiority to bear. Only 3,000 men were left to defend Verona, while on 14 November, Napoleon, with 18,000 men in the divisions of Augereau and Massena marched hard for the village of Ronco. At dawn on the 15th, Andréossy pushed a pontoon bridge over the Adige and the exhausted troops crossed and continued on through the marshy country; the going off the roads at that time of year was dreadful, for there had been heavy rain for many days and, even without that, much of the area was either natural marsh, or under rice paddy cultivation. Augereau's men headed for the bridge over the next water obstacle, the Alpone, at Arcola. Massena's division swung to the north, to secure the flank against an Austrian force under Provera, which was thought to be in the area of Porcile.

Allvintzy was still unaware of Napoleon's move, but the bridge at Arcola was defended by tough Croatian troops, who immediately opened fire and halted the French advance. The first French assault was repulsed in bloody ruin; it was renewed, and things looked set to go the same way as before, at which point Napoleon famously seized a regimental Colour and led a charge. In doing so he was swept off the bridge and almost drowned, further enhancing his personal reputation and standing with the troops. Furious with the delay, Napoleon sent troops south to find an alternative crossing, but Allvintzy had by then been warned of the French approach and, retiring from Verona, sent Provera's men against Massena. The chances of cutting Allvintzy off began to look slim, and all direct attacks at Arcola failed. The flanking move did succeed in finding a way across the river at the village of Albaredo and, swinging north, occupied Arcola village. However, night was falling and, afraid of being attacked by Allvintzy, Napoleon withdrew his force behind the Adige River. The next day, the attack was renewed, but the Croats had reoccupied Arcola village, and the work was all to do again. The French made some progress and, unknown to Napoleon, Allvintzy was becoming seriously alarmed. The Croats, despite heavy casualties, still stood firm and, that night, Napoleon again ordered a withdrawal back behind the Adige. On the third day, 17 November, Napoleon decided to change tack. He gave Massena instructions to engage the Austrians in the marshes while Augereau's whole division marched south to cross at Albaredo, and take the Arcola position from the rear.

Massena had first to re-cross the Adige at Ronco, and he had to fight for the crossing. Having got over, he dropped one brigade on the road north towards Porcile and concealed the rest of his men in the marshes. The Austrians made a sally from Arcola to destroy what they thought to be an isolated brigade, and fell into the ambush. Massena was able to occupy Arcola, which was as well, since Augereau had found the crossing at Albaredo held against him, and had only been able to cross after a diversion and a stiff fight. By the end of the day, however, the two divisions had linked up, begun the advance towards the plains, and received news that French troops were moving to join them from Legnano. This was enough for Allvintzy, who ordered an immediate retreat to Vicenza. Napoleon turned his attention to Davidovich's column, and tried to trap him near Dolce on 21 November. Davidovich, however, neatly avoided the trap and retreated towards Trent, having lost 1,000 men and nine guns, and abandoned both his bridging trains. When this news reached Allvintzy, he abandoned any further attempt to relieve Mantua that year.

Rivoli and Venetzia, 1797

From late November 1796, the French government began exploring a compromise peace with Austria, while Napoleon put his army in the best posture he could for defence. In the first days of 1797, despite the snow and cold of mid-winter, the Austrians determined on yet another attempt to relieve Mantua and restore their fortunes. They had, however, signalled their intentions too often, and, given the lie of the land, their lines of advance were predictable. The new Austrian plan called for an advance in three columns: Allvintzy with 20,000 men moving down the Adige river valley; Provera with 9,000 men and a bridging train advancing from Padua towards Mantua; and General Baron Adam von Bajalich with 6,200 men advancing between the other two on an axis from Verona to Mantua. There were, in addition, still around 10,000 men under Wurmser in Mantua. Napoleon knew very well that the Austrians would attack him, and he could deduce where, since he was aware of their concentration areas. The only thing he did not know was when the attack would come. Aside from those investing Mantua, Napoleon's troops were once again holding the same line as when they had been attacked by Wurmser: Augereau with 9,000 men held the lower Adige; Massena with 9,000 was at Verona; Joubert, who had taken command of Laharpe's division after the latter was killed, held the line from the Adige gorge to Lake Garda with 10,000 men; and General Antoine Rey, a new divisional commander, held the area west of Lake Garda with 4,000 men. The only reserve was one brigade, under Colonel Claude Victor, at Castelnuovo.

On 10 January, Bajalich arrived ten miles east of Verona, and at once attacked Massena's troops. The French beat off the attack and Bajalich halted. Allvintzy then attacked Joubert's men between the Adige River and Lake Garda, and drove Joubert back on to the plateau of Rivoli. To destroy Joubert, Allvintzy issued a complex plan involving an attack by six columns: three on the north side of the plateau; two to outflank the plateau from east and west and then fall on the French rear; and one to advance up the gorge of the Adige River.

On the 13th, Joubert sent a dispatch to Napoleon telling him that he could not hold for much longer, but Napoleon was now sure of the Austrian main effort and made a rapid move, seeing that the outcome would depend on who could build up a favourable force ratio fastest. Massena was ordered to leave just enough troops to maintain contact with Bajalich, and march the rest of his division to Rivoli. He was to be there by the morning of the 14th. At the same time, Napoleon ordered Rey's division and Victor's brigade to converge on Rivoli in support. Napoleon himself mounted his horse, and rode the 15 miles from his headquarters to Rivoli, where he arrived at 2 a.m. to confer with the shaken and tired Joubert. In spite of the situation, and confident that Massena would arrive, Napoleon ordered Joubert to go over to the attack in order to reoccupy the small village of San Marco on the north-east corner of the plateau. Occupation of this village would split the Austrian main attack.

Despite serious danger to his left flank, Joubert began the attack and made some progress, but the Austrian fire halted further progress and one of Joubert's regiments actually broke. By now, Massena had arrived and one of his brigades had extended Joubert's line to the west, while Napoleon held the rest in reserve at Rivoli. Bringing up troops from this reserve stabilized Joubert's situation, but the next crisis was already on hand. The Austrian flanking attacks had materialized, and the route for further French reinforcements was cut. A regiment had to be detached from the dwindling reserve to reopen the road.

The Austrian column in the Adige gorge was also progressing well and had to be stopped. As the situation elsewhere on the plateau was under control, Napoleon was able to draw troops and guns from Joubert, and concentrate on the gorge. Heavy fire stopped the Austrians, and a counter-attack pushed them right back down the river. At about the same time, Rey's division appeared from the south and the Austrian flanking attacks were caught between Rey and Massena. With these attacks halted, the main crisis of the day was over.

That afternoon, however, the Austrian division under Provera, unaware of the rough handling given to their compatriots, had crossed the Adige at

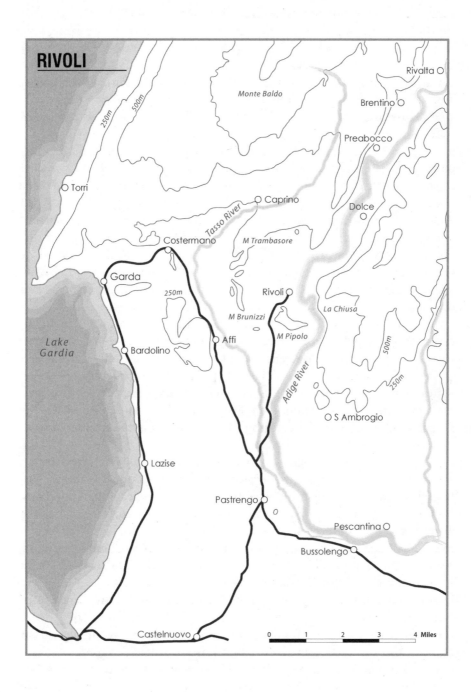

Angiari and were making for Mantua. They were halted by the besiegers just short of the city. Napoleon received the news of this move that evening and, despite the prodigies of marching and fighting that the troops had already completed during the previous 24 hours, he left Joubert to complete the defeat of Allvintzy on the next day. He ordered Victor's brigade and Massena's division to march with him after half an hour's rest. The troops made 30 miles by 8.00 p.m. on the 15th and, exhausted as they were, were allowed only two hours' rest. They then pushed on, losing many stragglers, but arriving in the vicinity of Mantua at dawn on the 16th: a truly amazing feat of endurance. Provera was aware of Massena's approach, and had signalled the Mantua garrison to make a sortie on the 15th. Wurmser decided to delay until dawn on the 16th, by which time it was too late: the French had Provera's men caught between three columns. At noon, Provera surrendered, thus crowning the victory of Rivoli and sealing the fate of Mantua. On 2 February, the ragged skeletons of the garrison hauled down their Colours and marched out. In four days, the French had fought two battles and six other engagements, taken a city, and captured 25,000 prisoners and 60 guns.

The battle of Rivoli and the fall of Mantua opened up Venetia to exploitation. Napoleon, therefore, ordered Joubert to pursue Allvintzy into the Tyrol, supported by Massena and Victor. He moved south with the rest of the army, occupying the Venetian Republic, and threatening the Papal States to the extent that Pope Pius VI was forced on 19 February 1797 to sign the Convention of Tolentino. At a stroke, Napoleon had consolidated the French hold on of all of Italy north of Rome, including the wealthy duchies of Bologna, Ferrara, Romagna and Ancona.

While this was in progress, the Army of Italy was reinforced by an additional division under General Jean-Baptiste Bernadotte. Napoleon was, therefore, able to reorganize his force for the pursuit of the Austrians. Victor, promoted to command a division, was left to secure the rear of the army and get on with the serious business of plunder. Joubert, with 14,000 men, was ordered to continue his advance, pressing Allvintzy into the Austrian Tyrol. In parallel, Massena was to advance up the Piave valley with his 10,000 men. The main body of the army, 23,000 men under Napoleon's own command, would sweep through Venetia and cross the Carnic Alps into Carinthia. The objective was to threaten Vienna and, in so doing, force the Austrians either to capitulate, or conclude terms favourable to the French, thus completing the instructions given by the Directory.

At this point, the Austrian Emperor Leopold summoned his youngest and ablest commander, the Archduke Charles – his third son and, in contrast to the parade of geriatrics employed thus far, a general of almost exactly the same age as Napoleon. Unfortunately, the appointment was not accompanied by any resources of men or materiel, and the result was predictable. Napoleon's army rapidly penetrated into Austria, coming within 100 miles of Vienna within 30 days of marching through rough terrain. On 7 April, an embassy from the Emperor met Napoleon at Judenburg, where an armistice was signed, followed a week later by an interim peace treaty. The eventual Treaty of Campo Formio between Austria and France consolidated not only French gains in Italy, but also gave the Republic all of Germany west of the Rhine, Dalmatia and the Ionian Islands, and the Austrian Netherlands. In compensation, the ancient Republic of Venice was cynically handed over to Austria.

Napoleon had not neglected to maintain his political contacts in Paris even while campaigning hard: if his benefactors were to be swept from power by yet another coup, his victories would count for nothing. In particular, he maintained close contact with Barras, and in July 1797 he sent Augereau to Barras, who made him Military Governor of Paris. Although loud-mouthed and coarse, Augereau was too stupid ever to be a serious rival to Napoleon: a week after his appointment, Barras, with Augereau's troops at his back, took control of the legislature and the executive in the coup of 18ème Fructidor.

Conclusions

Arguably, the tail end of the campaign showed Napoleon at the top of his form. His army was deployed on a lengthy defensive line, with an unreduced fortress at his rear. He had no operational or tactical reserve except a single brigade. He was liable to be attacked by superior enemy forces, who could choose the time and place of their attack and make their initial moves in security. When he was attacked, Napoleon responded with clear thinking and steady nerves, switching troops from areas where he could economize to the areas at greatest risk. He achieved concentration of force and surprise, and he exploited success ruthlessly. What made much of this possible were the superb marching and fighting qualities of the French army, along with excellent leadership at divisional level. Morale had also been improved by things like proper pay and rationing, made possible by looting the captured provinces. Some contemporary reports are telling, stating openly that before Napoleon, the army had received nothing but what it could plunder for two years. There is no doubt, therefore, that success had brought him enormous standing with the troops. Napoleon fostered this with every military trick in the book: battle honours, bounties, and praise for the troops. Madame de

Staël, no Bonapartist, wrote that 'The Army of the Rhine belonged to the French Republic; the Army of Italy belonged to Bonaparte.' Pursuing this, Napoleon is open to criticism for failing to impose stricter discipline on the army, but whether this was a practicable proposition in the 1790s is open to question.

Despite his personal standing and popularity with the troops, Napoleon did not by any means endear himself to his immediate subordinates. Although the mistrust of Massena and the others had been overcome by Napoleon's undoubted ability, Massena and, to an extent, Augereau heartily detested Napoleon throughout his career. Napoleon for his part did little to build their affection, and often put Massena down in official dispatches, much to the latter's fury, despite being well aware of his abilities. On the other hand, Napoleon showed an early tendency to the sort of favouritism which marked the rest of his life: many of those who did gain access to his inner counsels – such as Lannes, Reynier, and Junot – were mediocre commanders. One cannot escape the conclusion that Napoleon feared comparison, and therefore that the company of mediocrities allowed Napoleon's own star to shine brighter in comparison. This need to place his own men in authority comes out clearly in a letter to the Directory written on 20 January 1797:

> As to generals of divisions, unless they be men of distinction, I beg you not to send me any; for our way of waging war is so different from others, that I do not wish to entrust a division to a general until I have tested him out in two or three operations ... It is essential for the Army and the republic to send me young people who are learning how to carry out a war of movement and manoeuvres; it is wars of this nature which have enables us to gain such great successes in this army.

Napoleon was, in every respect, an active, vigorous general pursuing an active policy and strategy from his masters in Paris. He had the additional advantages of inheriting an army, albeit in bad condition, rather than having to create one from scratch, with able subordinate commanders. He had the further advantage, it must be said, of facing elderly and generally inactive enemy generals with no policy directives other than to hope for the best and hold on to the status quo for as long as possible; more active opponents would have punished him for leaving Mantua unreduced while dispersing his forces.

At the tactical level, the state of mind prevalent among the Austrians resulted in failure to co-ordinate moves, failure to look beyond the immediate objective, failure to analyse French tactics, and a willingness to retreat as the default option. Until it was too late, the Austrians saw Italy as an economy of force sector – the Rhine front was everything. But Napoleon's victories in Italy neutralized everything in Central Europe, and made the campaign in Italy the strategic turning point of the War of the First Coalition.

IX

Case Study 2: The Conquest of Prussia 1806: Napoleon at the Height of his Powers

The Strategic Objectives

In December 1805, Austria, having been soundly defeated by Napoleon, made peace by the Convention of Schönbrünn. Not so the remaining members of the Third Coalition, of whom Russia was of most immediate danger to France. In August 1806, the Tsar refused to ratify the peace, as did Great Britain, and together they formed the Fourth Coalition, along with Prussia, Sweden and Portugal. Prussia herself had never contributed troops to the Third Coalition, despite pressure from Russia, and despite also the blatant violation of neutrality by Marshal Jean-Baptiste Bernadotte's corps of the *Grande Armée* as it passed south on its way into Bavaria. The Prussians had been, or so it seemed, waiting to see which way to jump: after Austerlitz it seemed they would jump towards Napoleon.

Such a move was driven at least in part by the Prussian desire to acquire Hanover, which Napoleon had seized from the King of England. Napoleon knew this well and, in return for Hanover, he extracted not only the promise of a formal alliance against Great Britain, but also the Prussian territories of Cleves (Kleve), Ansbach, and Neuchâtel. With Austria subdued and Prussia in alliance, Napoleon next moved to create the Confederation of the Rhine (see Chapter III) on 12 July 1806, and then on 6 August formally to dissolve the old Holy Roman Empire of the German Nation. Such moves were bound to infuriate the Austrians, impotent as they seemed at the time, and Napoleon proceeded to overplay his hand with the Prussians as well, by suddenly offering Hanover back to the British Crown as part of a general peace settlement. The offer was received with scorn in London, but its effect in Prussia was electric. It is unlikely that Napoleon set out deliberately to provoke Prussia: he simply despised it. Although he made no secret of his admiration for Frederick the Great, he also made no secret of his indifference to the present King, Frederick's grandson, Frederick William III.

Despite the gravity of the insult, it seems equally unlikely that Frederick William, or his Francophile chief minister Haugwitz, would have challenged Napoleon, but his beautiful, dynamic, and strong-minded Queen, Louise, had other ideas. She and the rest of the anti-French party at court, which included Count Karl von Hardenburg, the old Duke of Brunswick, and Prince Friedrich Ludwig von Hohenlohe, bullied the King until he could stand no more. On 7 August, the decision for war was taken, and mobilization declared on the 10th. On 26 September, the Prussian war aims were issued in the form of an ultimatum to Napoleon: all French troops were to be withdrawn over the Rhine; the provinces of Cleves, Ansbach and Neuchâtel were to be restored; and the Prussian-led North German League accepted by Napoleon. Not stated, but implicit, were the acquisition of Hanover, and the end of Napoleon's domination of Germany. Napoleon was given until 8 October to agree to these terms, otherwise on this date Prussia would declare war on the French Empire.

French intelligence did not pick up early Prussian preparations for some days, and it was not, therefore, until early September that Napoleon realized the situation, and called up 30,000 reservists and 50,000 new conscripts. It was another ten days until Napoleon became seriously focused on the possibility of war, when he learned of Prussian moves to occupy the Kingdom of Saxony in order to keep it out of the Confederation of the Rhine. Somewhat belatedly, the French Embassy in Berlin issued a démarche to the effect that occupation of Saxony would be considered as a warlike act, and treated accordingly. Napoleon's strategic objectives were, therefore, in direct opposition to those of Prussia: to secure French domination over the Confederation of the Rhine and, implicitly, to extend that domination into Central and Eastern Europe. This was not only to neutralize, now and forever, any threat from Prussia; and not only to extend economic war and further isolate Britain; but also to extend the zone of French allies and clients as far east as possible: Napoleon had at last realized the truth of Talleyrand's advice, that the most potent threat on the continent of Europe was that of Russia.

Planning the Campaigns (1) – Napoleon

Napoleon began planning using information on the Prussian army supplied by his Statistical Bureau, and maps supplied by the Topographical Bureau. Once he was clear on the facts, he examined the alternatives open to him, and formed a plan. The first moves called for a concentration of the *Grande Armée* around Bamberg in northern Bavaria. From there, Napoleon intended to cross the forested ridges of the Frankenwald, and march north into Saxony. He did not, at this stage, form a detailed plan for the engagement of the Prussian army, but laid down as his objective two geographical points, Dresden and Berlin. By achieving these two, he hoped to detach Prussia from Saxony, to interpose himself between the Prussian army and any help coming from Russia; and to draw the Prussian army forward and into a favourable situation for a decisive battle: it was the destruction of this army at the earliest opportunity that was his real operational objective – conquest of territory and a strategic settlement would then follow, as a result of the military defeat of his enemy.

Napoleon communicated this plan to no-one, but instructed his staff to bring the various *corps d'armée*, stationed across southern Germany, up to strength. Route reconnaissance was also ordered, and detailed movement planning begun. In early September, negotiations were opened with his ally the King of Bavaria for stores depots to be established around Bamberg. On 10 September, Napoleon gave orders for his campaign headquarters to be prepared to move, and for the Imperial Guard to prepare for the field. Precautionary orders went to Berthier to concentrate the corps of Marshals Michel Ney, Charles Augereau and Nicolas Davout at Würzburg as soon as he (Berthier) heard of Prussian troops moving into Saxony. This news was also to be passed by telegraph to Napoleon himself, upon receipt of which he would leave for Würzburg.

Napoleon then turned his attention to administrative details, gathering information on the state of his corps and making good various deficiencies. He now revealed a little of his intention to the staff; on 16 September he ordered that Mainz was to be the hub of operations. Ney's corps was to concentrate first at Ulm and then at Ansbach; and Bernadotte's corps, in turn, was to move to Bamberg.

Planning the Campaigns (2) – Prussia

On 10 August the Prussian high command met at Potsdam to plan the coming war. This was no command-led estimate of the situation, but a series of arguments among near-equals, for the army of Frederick the Great had yet to develop the command and staff system that would bring so much grief to its opponents from 1860 onwards. There was no single chief of staff, no contingency plans, and no permanent military structure.

The first task was to bring some sort of organization into being and, after a full month of argument, three field armies began to emerge. The main army was drawn from troops in the military districts of Magdeburg and Berlin, and numbered around 75,000. This was to be commanded by the 79-year-old Karl, Duke of Brunswick, a veteran of Frederick the Great's wars. The second army was assembled around the Saxon capital, and included the

Saxon army. 42,000 strong, it was placed under the command of the 60-year-old General Frederick Louis, Prince of Hohenlohe-Ingelfingen. The third army, around 18,000 strong, was assembled between Göttingen and Mülhausen and commanded by General Ernst von Rüchel, a mere boy of 49. With him, and commanding his cavalry, was General Gebhardt von Blücher. In reserve, near Posen in the east, was a force of 25,000 men under General Anton von L'Estocq.

Deciding on how these forces were to be employed was more difficult than forming them, and five distinct plans were offered. General Gerhardt von Scharnhorst's plan was the one most likely to succeed: to delay, trading space for time, and await the arrival of the Russian armies assembling under General Count Levin Benigsen. This plan offended the sense of honour of several of the more senior officers present, and was not, therefore, pursued. Prince Hohenlohe's suggested course of action was to concentrate the army in the area between Erfurt and Hof, and there wait for the opportunity of attacking the advancing French in the flank. This plan was felt to be insufficiently offensive, and was not pursued. The Duke of Brunswick suggested a concentration of the army, followed by an advance through Erfurt in the direction of Würzburg, and then Stuttgart, aimed at surprising the *Grande Armée* in its likely concentration areas. Hohenlohe then argued against this plan, making a counter-proposal for a move through Hof, towards Bamberg, which would require the army to advance on a front of nearly 100 miles. Neither Brunswick's nor Hohenlohe's proposals found favour. The final suggestion was that of a demonstration through Hof, to the Danube, and then back into Saxony. Since no point at all could be seen in this suggestion, it too was dropped.

Losing patience at last, King Frederick William intervened, imposing a plan that involved the main features of both Brunswick's and Hohenlohe's suggestions – only for Brunswick's scheme to be adopted on 27 September. Hardly were the orders drafted, when the then Captain – later General – Carl von Müffling returned from a scouting mission on 5 October to report that Napoleon himself had left Würzburg with a large army, and was advancing towards Bayreuth, as if intending to invade Saxony. This news halted the planned deployment, and immediately forced the Prussians to begin reacting to French moves: Napoleon had seized the initiative from the start of the campaign. The Prussian army was therefore ordered to concentrate west of the river Saale, in a scheme not far removed from Hohenlohe's original suggestion, so as to be able to threaten the flank of the advancing French army. Brunswick's army was to arrive at Weimar by 9 October, and then move to Blankenheim; Hohenlohe was to reach Hochdorf on the same date, and then move on to Rudolstadt. A cavalry screen, supported by horse artillery and the infantry of the Duke of Weimar, was deployed to try to sever the French line of communication back towards Neustadt – if that was the direction in which it ran – and Rüchel was to support this move by sending detachments to the Fulda gap. Rüchel's main body was to march from Eisenach and co-operate with Brunswick, making a junction with him between Fulda and Gotha. Part of the division of General Friedrich Tauenzien von Wittenberg was left to screen Hof. Finally, the reserve, under the Duke of Württemberg, was to move from Magdeburg to Halle and there wait to be called forward.

These moves were, in the main, sound. However, Hohenlohe went beyond these orders, perhaps believing that it was his original concept that had been adopted. Without reference to the King or the Duke of Brunswick, he ordered the Saxon army corps to the Auma-Schleiz area, and the division of Prince Louis Ferdinand of Prussia to Saalfeld. The result of these moves was to isolate two considerable forces and place them, unsupported, directly in the path of the overwhelming strength of the advancing French.

Napoleon Launches his Campaign

News of Prussian movements and their march into Saxony reached Napoleon on 18 September, and he immediately ordered the Guard to start marching for Strasbourg. His pampered elite did not march, but were carried in carts, unlike the rest of the army. On the 24th he himself left Paris, arriving at Mainz four days later. On 1 October he moved on to Würzburg. There he received the first reports from Marshal Joachim Murat's light cavalry, which had located a Prussian army, 150,000 strong, around Erfurt. On 3 October he officially assumed command of the *Grande Armée*, and reviewed all the corps, which he now had disposed according to his plan (see maps). This plan he outlined in a letter to his brother, King Louis of Holland:

> It is my intention to concentrate all my forces on my extreme right, leaving all the country between the Rhine and Bamberg completely uncovered, in such a way as to have almost 200,000 men united on the battlefield. If the enemy sends detachments into the area between Mainz and Bamberg I shall not be bothered, since my line of communications goes back to Forchheim.

This he further amplified on 5 October in a letter to Marshal Nicolas Soult. The army was to cross the Frankenwald in three columns: Soult was to lead on the right, followed by Ney, and a division of 10,000 Bavarians. Bernadotte, Davout, the Guard, and the heavy cavalry in reserve were to

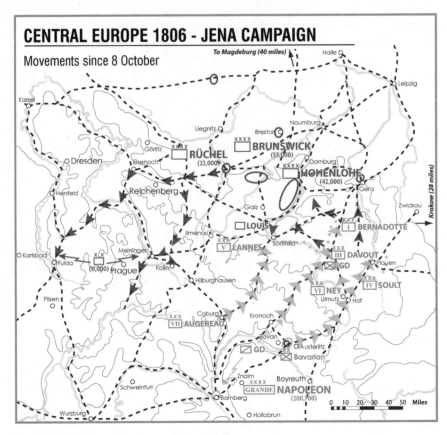

Source: US Military Academy, West Point.

move on the centre route. On the left, the corps of Marshal Jean Lannes was to lead, followed by Augereau. All columns would be led by a light cavalry vanguard under Murat; Napoleon himself would travel with the centre column. These orders, issued through Berthier, were simple and straight-forward, and the disposition of forces revealed is the celebrated battalion square, or *Batallion Carré*, of some 180,000 men, which would enable it to meet an enemy attack from any direction. Napoleon wrote to Soult:

> with this immense superiority of force united in so narrow a space you will realise that I am determined to leave nothing to chance, and can attack the foe wherever he chooses to stand with nearly double his strength.

Moreover, the formation, adopted with only an outline knowledge of the enemy's dispositions, would allow any marshal to fight a defensive meeting battle with his own all-arms corps should this be necessary, with the knowledge first that they would be mutually supported by other corps, and

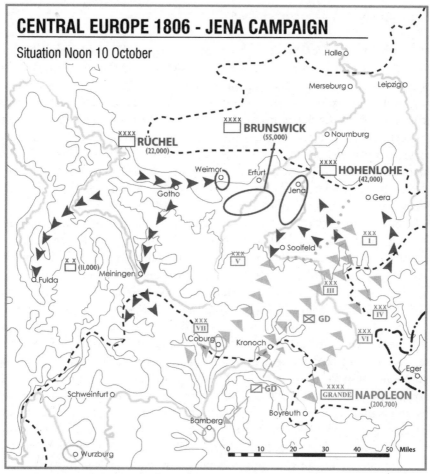

Source: US Military Academy, West Point.

second that Napoleon, having fixed the enemy force by such an engagement, would then manoeuvre the remainder of the army to envelop his opponent. Lastly, by splitting the army into three columns, Napoleon saved at least four days in the vulnerable crossing of the Thuringian forests. Napoleon's mastery of all-round defence at the operational level was never better illustrated. Combined with concentration of force, economy of effort elsewhere, and security, the plan remains a classic demonstration of manoeuvre when faced with a powerful enemy and armed with imperfect information.

The Approach: 8–12 October 1806

At first light on 8 October, the three columns of the *Grande Armée*, having already spent three days marching, crossed the Saxon frontier, led by Murat's light cavalry. A few skirmishes comprised the only activity of the day, and by dusk the columns had reached their designated halting areas around Coburg, Lobenstein and Munchberg. On 9 October the first real engagement took place. Murat and the leading division of Bernadotte's corps encountered part of Tauenzien's division of 6,000 Prussians and 3,000 Saxons at Schleiz and defeated it, opening up the route to Auma and Gera. Elsewhere, the French advance continued and by nightfall on the 9th, Lannes and Soult were approaching Saalfeld and Hof respectively.

From the reports of prisoners taken in the action at Schleiz, Napoleon reached the mistaken conclusion that the Prussians intended to debouch across the Saale and give battle at Gera. In reality, however, the news of Tauenzien's defeat at Schleiz threw the Prussians into renewed confusion. Hohenlohe remained convinced that the correct course of action was a concentration between Kahla and Rudolstadt, followed by an attack across the river. However, his orders to his subordinate, Prince Louis, commander of his advance guard division, were ambiguous. Prince Louis believed that he was to hold Saalfeld to gain time for a move by Hohenlohe towards Auma in support of Tauenzien. By the morning of the 10th, however, Brunswick had forbidden any move across the Saale, and Prince Louis had become isolated. New orders reached him at 11a.m. on the 10th, but it was too late, for at 10 o'clock in the morning, Lannes' corps had closed up to Saalfeld, and battle was joined. After three hours of bitter fighting the French gained the upper hand, and during a desperate attempt to check growing disorder in his forces, Prince Louis himself was killed, and his division fled. Thus perished potentially the best soldier in Prussia.

Once more there was confusion in the Prussian high command. Worried that the French were going to break through towards Leipzig, the Prussian outposts began to fall back, and the army was ordered to re-concentrate at Weimar. Napoleon, however, still had no clear idea of the Prussian dispositions, and no wonder. Unlike his own simple plan, the Prussians had no clear aim and the lack of decision, loose control and frequent redeployments made any assessment of their intentions by Napoleon's intelligence staff almost impossible. The position became clearer on 11 October when reconnaissance reports from the cavalry, and analysis of the actions at Schleiz and Saalfeld, finally convinced the Emperor that his original assessment had been wrong, and that the Prussian main body was located to the west. The conviction grew on him, again wrongly, that Brunswick would offer battle in the area of Erfurt. The orders issued to the Army for 12 October, therefore, called for a wheel to the left to bring it face to face with the enemy and forestall his withdrawal towards the Elbe. The remainder of the campaign up until the close of the battle of Jena on 14 October was based on this wrong conviction, and it was not until then that Napoleon realized his error.

The Swing to the North: 12–13 October 1806

The swing northwards, to bring the *Grande Armée* face to face with the Prussians, illustrates perfectly the advantages of the centralized Napoleonic command system over that of his enemies. Between 2.30 a.m. and 6.00 a.m. on 12 October, on the basis of no more than two reports and some brief map study, Napoleon issued a series of directives to his marshals which culminated in the envelopment and defeat of the Prussian field army at Jena and Auerstadt, even though his perception of its disposition was flawed.

On the left, Lannes (V Corps) was ordered to march directly on Jena. Augereau (VII Corps) was to follow as far as Kahla, where he was to cross the Saale. Murat was to move his cavalry to Zeitz, followed by Bernadotte (I Corps). Davout (III Corps) was to march north to Naumberg and there, with Bernadotte, he was to form the right wing of the army. Soult (IV Corps) and Ney (VI Corps) were to march due west to form the new centre in the area of Gera and Neustadt. Orders were also issued to the Intendant General's department:

> The Emperor's desire is that you should bring to Auma all the corn and bread that is at present on the road, and form a magazine in that town, which is destined to become the central point for our army. Give orders for the immediate establishment of a hospital there.

Confident that his orders would cover all likely Prussian moves, Napoleon himself moved on to Gera, arriving at about 8.00 p.m. on the 12th. At midnight, more news reached him from his marshals which indicated that the Prussian main body was located between Erfurt and Weimar and had abandoned any thought of attacking him. 'The veil is torn at last,' he remarked to Murat, believing that the Prussians must now attempt a retreat towards Magdeburg. He also knew, as the Prussians did not, that Davout was at Naumberg in a position to cut off the enemy's withdrawal route. Thus, Napoleon felt confident that everything was ready for a decisive battle.

Meanwhile, the Prussian advance guard had since been falling back towards the river Saale in the aftermath of the battle of 10 October, while the main army advanced on Weimar. Late on the 12th they learned of Davout's presence at Naumberg and, at a council of war called early on the 13th, an immediate retreat to Leipzig was ordered by way of Auerstadt, Bad Kosen and Freiburg. To form a flank guard, Hohenlohe was ordered to occupy the Kapellendorf feature between Weimar and Jena with Rüchel in support, until the main body was clear of Auerstadt, after which Hohenlohe would follow as rearguard. These orders became effective at 10.00 a.m. on the 13th and thus it was this flank guard, and not, as he believed, the Prussian main body, that Napoleon would meet above Jena.

Napoleon himself issued further orders during the morning of 13th, moving Bernadotte's corps and Murat's light cavalry to fill the gap between Davout and Lannes at Dornburg on the Saale; Ney was to move up to Stadtroda with the leading division of Soult's corps under General Vincent St Hilaire, and the heavy cavalry. The remainder of Soult's corps was to move north-westwards to Kostritz, keeping a watchful eye towards Leipzig. Augereau was to move as fast as possible from Kahla to Jena up the left bank of the Saale. Napoleon himself then set off up the road to Jena, to see for himself what was happening. As he neared Jena at around 3.00 p.m. on 13 October, he received a despatch from Lannes, who reported at least 12,000 Prussian troops on the plateau north of Jena, with 20 to 25,000 more between Jena and Weimar. This was, in fact, Hohenlohe's flank guard with Rüchel in support, but Napoleon still assumed that this was the enemy's main body. Still in the saddle, he dictated the third set of orders that day. Davout was to move his corps westwards from Naumberg to fall on the enemy's left once he heard firing from the south. Bernadotte was to continue to Dornburg on the Saale as instructed, but was to move to assist Davout if attacked. Murat's cavalry was also to move to Dornburg. Soult and Ney were now to march as fast as possible for Jena. Lefebvre with the Guard was to join the Emperor at Marshal Lannes' headquarters beyond Jena as soon as possible. The Emperor then rode on through Jena, and joined Lannes on the Landgrafenberg feature at about 4.00 p.m. Almost three hours of daylight still remained.

On the Landgrafenberg: 13–14 October 1806

On joining Lannes, Napoleon learned that V Corps had occupied Jena that morning and that the leading division under Suchet had then crossed the Saale and climbed the Landgrafenberg, where contact had been made with the forward elements of the Prussian flank guard, part of the division of

Tauenzien. The Prussian pickets had been driven back into the villages of Lutzeroda and Closewitz. Still certain that he faced the main Prussian army, Napoleon gave orders for the remainder of Lannes' V Corps and the Guard to strengthen the position on the Landgrafenberg as soon as possible. He knew that, by 10.00 a.m. on the 14th, he would be reinforced by Augereau's VII Corps and St Hilaire's division of Soult's IV Corps. By noon the rest of Soult's corps, Ney's VI Corps, and the heavy cavalry reserve should have arrived, bringing his strength to over 90,000 men. In addition, I and III Corps with Murat's light cavalry were within striking distance to the north. Thus within the space of 24 hours, Napoleon was able to concentrate 145,000 men at the decisive point.

The Prussians could have swept Lannes' troops away at this early stage if they had chosen to do so; however, Hohenlohe was convinced, unwillingly, that he should adopt a purely defensive posture to cover the withdrawal of the Prussian main army – an extremely fortunate decision for Napoleon. Having not used his light cavalry to cover the Saale crossings, and having lost contact after his pickets had been driven in, Hohenlohe was blind to the true scale of the enemy force opposed to him. The French, therefore, continued to build up their bridgehead unmolested. In particular, artillery batteries were ordered up to secure the Windknollen and this posed a considerable problem. The track leading up to the Landgrafenberg was narrow and rough – it is little changed even today – and soon, a massive traffic jam had developed at the foot of the hill. Napoleon himself supervised the solution. Baron Marbot wrote that:

> He at once sent for 4,000 pioneering tools from the wagons of the engineers and artillery, and ordered that every battalion should work in turn for an hour at widening and levelling the road, and that as each finished its task it should go and form up silently on the Landgrafenberg while another took its place. They were lighted at their work by torches, but this illumination was hidden from the enemy eyes by the blaze of Jena beyond.

By about 3.00 a.m. on 14 October, 25,000 men and 42 pieces of artillery had reached the summit. Napoleon himself, satisfied that things were moving, had moved back to the summit to his tent, pitched in the centre of a square formed by the Grenadiers of the Guard. Here he wrote his orders for the next day's action. His plan called first for the expansion of the bridgehead on the Landgrafenberg to make possible the deployment of the main force of the *Grande Armée* – four corps, the heavy cavalry and the Guard, and then a classic envelopment would be launched. To do this, Lannes was to attack at 6.00 a.m. on the 14th and secure a line running from Lutzerode to Closewitz. The committal of other troops would depend on

the timing of their arrival but, provisionally, Ney was to support Lannes in
the centre; Augereau was to advance on the left up the covered valley of the
Muhlbach stream to turn the enemy's right; and Soult was to move towards
Rodigen to turn the enemy's left. The Guard and the heavy cavalry would
remain in reserve on the Landgrafenberg. With the whole plateau secure, the
second phase of the battle would end in the destruction of the Prussian
main army a day later by a flank attack of I and III Corps from the north-
east. This intention was communicated to his marshals in the form of
written orders, the last which were to be issued. From here on, the battle was
controlled by verbal messages.

Unknown to Napoleon, however, the main body of the Prussian army
was already marching hard towards Auerstadt so that, in fact, a divided
Prussian army was about to meet a divided French army. Both French and
Prussian generals were to be substantially surprised by the events of the 14th.

Schlacht bei Jena: Morning, 14 October 1806

That morning, the battlefield was covered by a dense fog, but even so, by
dawn, French strength on the Landgrafenberg had increased to 46,000 men
and 70 guns. Marbot again recalled that:

> The term 'massed' was never more correct, for the breasts of the men of each
> regiment were practically touching the backs of those in front of them, but the
> troops were so well disciplined that in spite of the darkness and the packing of
> 40,000 men onto that narrow platform, there was not the least disorder, and
> although the enemy were only half a cannon shot off, they perceived nothing.

As dawn broke, Napoleon completed his personal reconnaissance. He
then visited as many battalions as possible, to stimulate the men's courage
and determination. In the Prussian lines, many of Tauenzien's units had not
recovered from the alarms and panics of the last two days; some units were
no more than half strength, and all were hungry and miserable. Their
fighting ability was, however, to be surprisingly good despite this state of
affairs.

The initial French attack was launched as ordered at 6.00 a.m. on the
14th. Lannes' two divisions, Suchet on the right and Gazan on the left,
supported by 28 guns, advanced, and, despite fierce fighting, by 9.00 a.m.
Suchet had cleared Closewitz. Gazan fared less well around Cospeda.
Initially repulsed, his men in turn threw back a Prussian counter attack.
Seeing that he was greatly outnumbered, Tauenzien ordered the evacuation
of Cospeda, Closewitz and Lutzeroda, leaving only a strong force of

skirmishers in the wooded areas. The Prussians at first fell back on their reserves near the village of Vierzehnheiligen and, as the French followed up, Tauenzien flung his men into a violent counter-attack between the two villages of Lutzerode and Closewitz, which again sent the French reeling back in confusion – and indeed split Lannes' corps into two: half around the Isserstedt woods and half between Closewitz and Vierzehnheiligen. But instead of pressing their advantage, the Prussians halted, turned about and began marching off to the north-west towards Kleinromstedt. To understand why they did this we must turn to the flanks. On the French left, Augereau's VII Corps was observed moving up the Muhltal towards the Weimer road. This caused considerable alarm to Tauenzien, both because he was aware of the danger of his southern flank being turned, and also because his communications with Rüchel were about to be cut.

Moreover, while Lannes' Corps had been engaged on the Landgrafenberg, St Hilaire's division had moved through Lobstadt and Zwaten and into the woods beyond. Here it came into violent contact with some troops of General Friedrich von Holtzendorff's division, moving southwards from Dornburg on the Saale. Von Holtzendorff had assembled his troops at Dornburg on hearing firing around Closewitz and was marching to the sound of battle. Seeing that he was outnumbered, he withdrew towards Nerkewitz, and St Hilaire continued his advance towards Rodigen. This action had again been reported to Tauenzien, and this made him decide to withdraw.

By 10.00 a.m., therefore, the first part of Napoleon's plan had been achieved, and the ground needed for the deployment of the *Grande Armée* had been accomplished. Napoleon himself, therefore, moved up behind Lannes and ordered a pause in the centre and left, to allow the rest of the army to close up. But if a temporary cessation of activity took place on the left and centre, the same cannot be said of the right. Moving up towards Rodigen, St Hilaire's advance guard battalion reached a position just short of the village at about 10.00 a.m., with the rest of the division formed up in dead ground to the rear. Holtzendorff decided that he must gain time to complete his withdrawal across the steep valley in front of Nerkewitz in good order. He, therefore, ordered half his infantry, supported by *jaegers* and cavalry, to stage a limited attack, to cover the withdrawal of the remainder of the infantry. He also withdrew his 12-pounder artillery battery into a covering position at Nerkewitz. As the attack moved forward with the infantry in echelon, St Hilaire, in a masterpiece of tactical timing, launched his division directly into the flank of the Prussians from the dead ground. Within a short space of time the Prussians began to retire, in an orderly withdrawal, across the stream towards Nerkewitz. St Hilaire was now joined by the cavalry brigade of Soult's corps which crashed through the Prussian lancers and covering *jaegers*, fell on one of the retiring columns, and cut it to pieces: 400 prisoners, six guns and two Colours were taken.

Holtzendorff managed to rally his shaken men for a further effort near Nerkewitz, but the French worked around to his left and then charged frontally with cavalry. This was too much for the Prussians who made off, abandoning most of their guns, towards Apolda. Holtzendorff, to his credit, succeeded in rallying one battery of artillery and what remained of the cavalry, which he sent to join Hohenlohe at Kleinromstedt. He then set off to rally the infantry which had remained in good order, but his troops took no further part in the battle. He was, in fact, saved from pursuit and complete destruction by events in the centre, which forced Soult to rein St Hilaire in, ready for a flank attack on Hohenlohe.

Looking back from the Prussian point of view at the initial French deployment, and attacks by Lannes' corps from the bridgehead towards Closewitz and Lutzerode, it must have appeared that the French had appeared almost by magic in a dominating position, which had been made more so by the Prussian withdrawal. By around 9.00 a.m. Prince Hohenlohe had begun to realize that he was facing rather more than an attack by a French detachment. The arrival of Tauenzien and his report only served to emphasize this, and so he immediately sent a messenger to Rüchel asking for assistance. He then ordered Tauenzien to draw up his survivors to the rear, and sent three Saxon brigades to form up along the Weimer road, with orders to keep it open at all costs. Finally, he strengthened his main position around Vierzehnheiligen with a further Saxon brigade and some Prussian troops from the division of General Julius von Grawert, which was in reserve.

By 11.00 a.m., Prussian strength around Vierzehnheiligen had grown to 11 battalions in line facing Lannes' corps; a Saxon division in support on the right; 45 squadrons of cavalry; and considerable artillery support. Suddenly, an unexpected struggle flared up to the south of the village – Marshal Ney's impatience for action had got the better of him and, taking his vanguard of two battalions of infantry and two regiments of light cavalry, he plunged between Lannes' left and Augereau's right – instead of to the right of Lannes as Napoleon had intended. Ney's force at first surprised the Prussian horse artillery battery 'Steinmetz', took its guns, and threw back its cavalry escort and parts of two heavy cavalry regiments. However, these troops quickly rallied and counter-attacked. They broke the French light cavalry, rode through Ney's infantry which hastily found square, and pressed on towards the Guard. As Ney was now beyond reach of both Lannes and Augereau, he was cut off.

Fortunately for Ney, Napoleon, who was well forward behind Lannes, realized what was happening and sent forward his total available cavalry reserve, two regiments. Lannes was ordered to press on, into and through Vierzehnheiligen, to re-establish contact with Ney, and Augereau moved his leading division up to Isserstedt to support Ney's left. These moves did succeed in taking the pressure off Ney, but were not immediately successful in other respects. As Lannes' skirmishers moved into Vierzehnheiligen they met a counter-attack by Prussian *jaegers*. Casualties on both sides were heavy, but the mist still concealed the French main body. The morale of the Prussians was at this point high, for the success of the cavalry counter-charge had led them to believe that the action of Saalfeld was about to be avenged. Hohenlohe, therefore, ordered his troops to attack Vierzehnhei-ligen. The infantry formed up in echelons of two battalions and advanced, meeting the oncoming main body of Lannes' corps and throwing the French back into Vierzehnheiligen, while Ney's troops pulled back to consolidate near Isserstedt.

Schlacht bei Jena: Afternoon, 14 October 1806

The crisis of the day had now come, and Hohenlohe was presented with the opportunity to make good the losses of the morning. However, when his troops reached a point 500 paces short of Vierzehnheiligen, the Prince ordered a halt: he thought it unwise to move off into the unknown in what was still a thick mist. Furthermore, his orders were to cover the main army's withdrawal and not become decisively engaged, even though his own instinct told him to storm the village. At this point, General Grawert rode up and congratulated Hohenlohe on winning the battle! The Prince declined the congratulations and told Grawert that he intended to attack the village. Grawert asked for a delay, pointing out that the fighting so far had cost serious casualties and that it would, therefore, be more advantageous to await the arrival of Rüchel. Hohenlohe, believing that Rüchel would arrive shortly and that General Holtzendorff's troops would also join him, accepted Grawert's advice. He would later regret this decision.

The line of Prussian infantry, which had already been pounded for nearly two hours, now remained a further one-and-a-half hours exposed to the merciless fire of the French who, concealed in the village and in the furrows of potato fields around it, offered no mark for return fire. In places, the fronts of companies were marked only by individual soldiers still loading and firing, while all their comrades lay dead or dying around them. General Ludwig von der Marwitz reported later that 'Along the entire line, one battalion volley followed another, with no effect in many places. The area around the entrance to the village was the scene of the most terrible blood letting and slaughter.' Lannes attempted to end the battle there and then by launching simultaneous attacks on the Prussian front and left. Hohenlohe at once withdrew his left, but it seemed that the French attack would succeed, until some Saxon cavalry squadrons charged, and reversed the situation by driving Lannes' men back into the village in some disorder. Once again Hohenlohe failed to follow up his success, and once again the French were threatening to envelop his flanks.

On the Prussian right, some of Ney's infantry and a brigade of Lannes' corps moved forward through Isserstedt wood and on to the Weimar road, cutting off the three Saxon infantry brigades stationed there. And back towards Jena, the Prussian commander could see the approach of fresh French formations – these were, in fact, the heavy cavalry and the rest of Ney's corps – and to the south-east in front of Closewitz, he could also see the corps of Soult. Under such circumstances any further advance seemed foolish, and Hohenlohe therefore moved up his last reserves to fill the gap between the centre and his right, where an attack by the cavalry brigade of the French VII Corps had buckled Grawert's flank, and opened up a gap of more than a mile in the Prussian line. By 1.00 p.m. every formation of Hohenlohe's command, with the exception of Tauenzien's remnants, was committed to the line, ₁nd Hohenlohe was left waiting anxiously for the arrival of Rüchel – of whom there was as yet no sign.

By this time, Napoleon had 42,000 men in reserve and available for committal to the battle, in addition to 54,000 troops actually engaged. He therefore ordered a general attack against the whole Prussian line. On the French right, St Hilaire was to follow up Holtzendorff's remnant; on the left, Augereau was to drive the Saxons off the Weimar road. The centre was to be attacked by the entire corps of Ney, Lannes, and the cavalry, once the flanking attacks had got under way. Augereau was ready by 11.30 a.m. but St Hilaire was not in position until 1.00 p.m., when Napoleon signalled the general advance by all except the Guard which, to its collective chagrin, was held back.

Leading Augereau's advance were the 7th and 20th Regiments of Chasseurs, and an extract from the history of the 7th Chasseurs tells something of the action:

> The 7th charged uphill against the Prussians, and penetrated both the first and second lines but, losing touch with the 20th, were unable to realise completely the fruits of one of the most audacious charges of the day... Major Castex [an officer of the 20th who had been placed temporarily in command of the 7th

during the sickness of its Commanding Officer, Colonel Lagrange] handled the
7th brilliantly, but was not able to occupy the road which the regiment had
crossed as the Prussians, who had laid down in the face of the initial charge,
had reformed. Castex led a charge into the flank of a Saxon battalion which at
once crumbled and fled.

All across the front, the French artillery moved into canister range and
poured a devastating hail of shot into the exhausted Prussian line. Then
came the main attack, as almost three French corps smashed into the
decimated Prussian and Saxon battalions. Soon the Prussians began to
waver, the flood of retreating units grew, and Hohenlohe, seeing defeat
staring him in the face, ordered a general retreat towards Gross and Klein
Romstedt. It was, however, no easy task for Hohenlohe to disengage from
the French attack, for Lannes' corps artillery continued to pour a heavy fire
on the retiring Prussian columns. Even so, the withdrawal was at first
executed in good order. But as the French cavalry joined in the attack, panic
began to set in and the withdrawal became a rout. Part of the Prussian force
fled west towards Weimar, and the fact that any escaped was largely due to a
single Saxon grenadier battalion under Colonel Winkel, which formed
square and retired in good order, covering the flight of the rest. Another
part of the army fled north towards Apolda and fortunately for it, was
covered by the remains of Tauenzien's division, which held off the pursuit,
even allowing Grawert to re-form some of his command. Even so, the
Prussians lost 2,500 prisoners, 16 guns and eight Colours.

But the Prussian fugitives on the road to Weimar came up unexpectedly
near Kappellendorf with the 15,000 men of Rüchel's command, whose
failure to arrive at Vierzehnheiligen had been a contributory factor to the
severity of the Prussian defeat. Rüchel's best course of action would probably have been to take up a defensive position on the Suhlbach stream and
there either rally the retreating army, or at least cover its escape until dark.
Instead, he deployed his men with insecure flanks halfway between Kot-
schau and Grossromstedt in echelon, ready for an attack. Hohenlohe then
arrived and led these troops, with part of his own cavalry, in a futile
advance, to gain time for the withdrawal of the rest of his army. The leading
echelon reached almost as far as Grossromstedt before coming into action
against the cavalry and guns of Lannes' corps, almost beating them back.
However, St Hilaire's division attacked the Prussian left flank, while the
French artillery and cavalry returned to the attack. With his position
untenable and losses mounting, Rüchel ordered a retreat. At first this went
well enough, covered by his Prussian and Saxon cavalry, but again, French
artillery firing in mass broke the cohesion of the covering force. This done,

the French heavy cavalry charged, and soon Rüchel's men too were a mass of fugitives fleeing down the Weimar road. The French took a further 4,000 prisoners, and five Colours.

By 3.00 p.m. the victory of Jena was complete, and by 4.00 p.m. Murat's light cavalry pursuit was fully under way. At 5.00 p.m., Ney himself entered Apolda. Only Tauenzien maintained any sort of order, but elsewhere it was only the early fall of night that saved the survivors. For the loss of 5,000 men, Napoleon had inflicted 25,000 losses, including 15,000 prisoners, and he was certain that on the 15th this number would rise – for he still believed that Davout and Bernadotte were moving on Apolda across the line of retreat of the Prussian survivors.

Napoleon rode back to his original bivouac on the Landgrafenberg, and at dusk reached his new headquarters in an inn in Jena, from where he organized the pursuit of the beaten enemy, which was to take him in a little more than a week to Berlin. But there at the inn he found waiting for him a Captain Tobriant, an officer of Davout's staff. At first, Napoleon could not believe the news Tobriant had brought – Davout claimed to have fought and defeated the main Prussian army ten miles away near Auerstadt. 'Your master must have been seeing double, he snapped, in an unkind reference to Davout's short-sightedness. But gradually he began to realize that while he, with 96,000 men, had been engaging only the flank guard of the Prussian army, Davout with only 26,000 men had faced Brunswick's main army. It must have been hard for a man like Napoleon to swallow the error under which he had laboured for the past week – but swallow it he did. But what had happened to Davout?

Auerstadt

It will be recalled that on the 12/13 October, the Duke of Brunswick had positioned Hohenlohe's command near Jena to act as a flank guard, while he himself with the main army marched hard for the Saale crossing at Bad Kosen. From there he hoped to make his escape towards Leipzig. Meanwhile, Davout and Bernadotte had been ordered to cross the Saale at the same place and envelop the Prussian army, thought by Napoleon to be at Jena, from the north. Neither Davout nor Brunswick had any clear idea of the other's presence until shortly before battle was joined, and so in contrast to the set-piece, attacking battle of Jena, one can view Auerstadt as a classic meeting engagement.

The battle was desperately hard fought. Napoleon wrote in his *Bulletin* on the 15th that:

Marshal Davout's corps performed wonders. Not only did he contain, but he pushed back and defeated for more than three leagues the bulk of the enemy's troops, which were to debouch through Kosen. This Marshal displayed distinguished bravery and firmness of character, the first qualities of a warrior.

Upon receipt of the Emperor's orders at 4.00 p.m. on the 14th, Davout had at once despatched a copy to Bernadotte, and then prepared his own corps to advance from Naumburg to Apolda. As at Jena, dense fog covered the area, and Davout had little idea of the enemy strength in front of him. However, his cavalry reconnaissance had informed him of large troop movements to the west, and prisoners had revealed that they belonged to Brunswick's command. Davout's order of march was, therefore, a light cavalry screen, followed by an advance guard infantry division under General Etienne Gudin, supported by divisional artillery and a cavalry regiment; these were followed at some distance by the remaining two divisions under Generals Louis Friant and Charles Morand with the corps artillery.

The troop movements revealed by Davout's cavalry were of course Brunswick's army, 60,000 strong. The army was divided into three large infantry divisions under Generals Karl von Schmettau, Hermann von Wartensleben, and the Prince of Orange, with a cavalry division under Blücher, all supported by 16 artillery batteries containing 230 guns. In the dark, foggy night of 13 October, a massive traffic jam developed on the narrow roads, and the army was ordered to bivouac near Auerstadt. Here, a cavalry patrol brought in a few French prisoners who revealed that Davout's advance guard was already in control of Bad Kosen. Instead of launching an early attack to force these troops aside – the French strength at Kosen at this stage was only one-and a half infantry battalions and two cavalry squadrons – Brunswick decided to evade any action – first because he believed that Napoleon himself was at Naumberg, and second because of the undoubted confusion in the army. He therefore ordered that the army should move west on to the high ground near Hassenhausen, with Schmettau's division, supported by cavalry, in the lead.

Thus matters stood at dawn on 14 October. From then until noon, Davout's corps of three divisions faced and outfought the Prussian main army until, with both his flanks either disintegrating or withdrawing, King Frederick William had no choice but to order a withdrawal of his whole force, hoping to rejoin Hohenlohe and Rüchel at Jena, whose forces he still believed to be intact. By 12.30 p.m. the Prussian army was in full flight west and north. Blücher attempted to form a rear guard to gain his compatriots time to escape, but was rapidly enveloped and swept aside. The pursuit continued until 4.30 p.m., when Davout was compelled to halt his exhausted infantry on the crest of the Eckartsberg. His three regiments of cavalry and a single reserve battalion continued to harass the enemy, but were not strong enough to inflict serious casualties on the fleeing masses. As it was, Davout had inflicted 13,000 casualties, including 3,000 prisoners, and captured 115 guns. The cost was high – the corps lost 7,000 out of its 26,000 men. Thus ended the twin battle of Jena–Auerstadt, but there is one postscript aside from the pursuit.

What happened to Bernadotte?

Going back to 13 October, at 3.00 p.m. Bernadotte had been ordered to move south from Naumburg to Dornburg on the Saale, thus filling a gap in the French line as it wheeled northwards, and where a crossing of the Saale was possible. But when Napoleon had issued new orders, he had no knowledge of whether or not this order had been obeyed. Consequently, in his later orders to Davout, which instructed him to move on Apolda, he included the following sentence: 'If Bernadotte is still with you, you can march together. The Emperor hopes, however, that he will be in the position which he has assigned to him at Dornburg.'

So it was that, as Davout came into contact with the Prussian army at Hassenhausen and sent urgent messages to Bernadotte for help, those messages were ignored. Bernadotte later claimed that the orders were ambiguous, and indicated to him a direct order to occupy Dornburg. Clearly, he failed in two respects. First he failed to appreciate Napoleon's intention; second he failed, on receipt of Davout's message, to understand that the tactical situation had now changed and that his duty was to assist Davout. The dictates of common sense, his own experience, and the intimate knowledge that he had of the workings of Napoleon's mind should have told him this intuitively. His failure on the 14th almost carried him to a court martial and firing squad. It certainly cost him Napoleon's continued trust, despite his recognition of Bernadotte's abilities. Napoleon is reported to have remarked on the 15th: 'Bernadotte has behaved badly. He would have been enchanted to see Davout fail ... which does him (Davout) the greatest honour, all the more so because Bernadotte had rendered his position difficult.' The one benefit from Bernadotte's behaviour was that Napoleon had a fresh corps with which to support Murat's cavalry in the long pursuit northwards to Berlin.

The Pursuit

Napoleon's plan for the exploitation of his victory was to envelop the fleeing Prussian army, and thus complete the destruction of which he had thus far been cheated. Murat, Soult, and Ney were ordered to press the Prussian rear guards, while the remaining four corps (I, II, V and VII) were to march through Halle and Dessau, and descend on the Prussian line of retreat. Of these, only Bernadotte's I Corps was fresh and intact, and Bernadotte had some ground to make up in more senses than just geography. His men made a march of more than 25 kilometres by the 17th to reach Halle, where his leading division met the Prussian reserve under the Duke of Württemberg. The Prussians lost 5,000 men and 11 guns.

For the Prussians, it was now a case of saving whatever could be saved. King Frederick William ordered Prince Hohenlohe to re-form what force he could muster at Magdeburg on the Elbe, and defend the line of the river. But there was no coherent body around which to re-form and, with only 40,000 men under arms, and few guns, Hohenlohe decided to ignore these orders. He pressed on north towards Stettin, hoping to effect a junction with General Benigsen's Russian army. Blücher, commanding what troops had managed to break clean after Auerstadt, was retiring through Brunswick, carrying with him most of the artillery.

On 18 October, Napoleon switched his line of communication from Würzburg to a new logistic centre at Mainz. On 21st, Davout's corps crossed the Elbe at Wittenberg over the intact bridge, while Lannes' troops repaired the damaged bridge at Prenzlau, and crossed. By 22nd, Napoleon had two corps-sized bridgeheads over the main river obstacle before Berlin, while two more corps, IV and VI, were closing on the great arsenal and fortress of Magdeburg. Ordering Ney to invest the place, Napoleon himself pressed on with the main army. Potsdam was entered on the 24th and Berlin on 27 October, where Davout's corps had the honour of leading the entry to the city. Two days later, the mass of Prussian prisoners taken at Jena and in the days following was brought to the city, and paraded in humiliation through their capital.

While French troops paraded in triumph in Berlin, others continued the pursuit. III and IV Corps marched east, and were joined by IX Corps – mostly Bavarian troops – under Jerome Bonaparte, who had been summoned from Dresden in order to form a corps of observation on the Oder River, to guard against the possible approach of Benigsen's Russians. Bernadotte, with his own corps and four cavalry divisions, continued to press the Prussian retreat. On the 26th, he came up with part of Hohenlohe's force at Zehdenick, and smashed it. On the 28th, Hohenlohe surrendered his command. On the 29th, the French cavalry closed up to Stettin, where the garrison was bluffed into surrender. Two days later, V Corps arrived to garrison the place, effectively closing the lower part of the Oder. The only Prussian forces now remaining in the field were the garrison of Magdeburg, and Blücher's force: the latter was marching hard for Lübeck on the Baltic where he hoped to co-operate with forces from Swedish Pomerania. Marching equally hard, and on his heels, were Bernadotte, Soult, and part of Murat's cavalry. Closing from beyond Hamburg in the west were Marshal Mortier's X Corps and the Dutch army under Louis Bonaparte.

Lübeck was at this time a free, Hanseatic city, lightly garrisoned. Blücher, ignoring the city's status, forced an entry but had no time to put the place in a state of defence before the corps of Bernadotte and Soult closed up. The French immediately stormed the city, and, according to the custom of the time, sacked and burned the place. Von Scharnhorst surrendered 10,000 of Blücher's command; at least 3,000 plus an unknown number of civilians died. Perhaps 8,000, including Blücher himself, managed to escape but were cornered on the following day at Ratkau, and forced to surrender. From this time onwards, Blücher hated Napoleon like the devil, and could not rest until he was finally defeated and exiled. With him also surrendered a division of Swedish infantry under General Count Moerner, which, as Baron Marbot recounts in his memoirs, had just disembarked. The Swedes received courteous treatment from Bernadotte, in stark contrast to the humiliation handed out to the Prussians, and from this chance meeting came the election of Bernadotte as Crown Prince of Sweden in 1810. The final remaining Prussian force was the garrison of Magdeburg. On 10 November, with no hope of relief, the dispirited General von Kleist surrendered his 22,000 men, 500 guns, and ample provisions to Ney.

Aftermath and Conclusions

On his arrival in Potsdam on 25 October, Napoleon went on a personal pilgrimage to the tomb of Frederick the Great, where, according to witnesses:

> he stopped at the entrance in a grave and meditative attitude. His glances seemed to penetrate the gloom which reigned around those august ashes, and he remained there nearly ten minutes, motionless and silent, as if absorbed in profound thought.

Well he might do so, for the army of the great Frederick had been humbled by Frederick's pupil. Napoleon rubbed the message home – and spoiled the effect he had made at Frederick's tomb – by stealing Frederick's sword, sash, orders, and the Regimental Colour of the Prussian Guards, which had been carried in battle during the Seven Years' War. He had already ordered the destruction of the battle monument at Rossbach as he passed over the field.

From the point of view of the operational art in a purely military context, the achievement of Jena ranks among the greatest feats of arms in history. Napoleon had pre-empted his enemies, taken risks with a bold advance through rough country, and exercised effective command through a staff and corps system which allowed the *batallion carrée* to function flexibly. He had seized and maintained the initiative throughout, despite wholly incomplete intelligence and even faulty deductions from what there was, and he had ruthlessly smashed Prussian military power. At the operational level, therefore, the reforms he had instituted in organizing the corps system, in the organization of the headquarters, in the insistence on daily reports from the corps, and in devolving authority to his corps commanders had paid off. And apart from Bernadotte, his subordinates had done well: Lannes, Soult, Murat, and especially Davout, had all shown that they could understand their master's intentions and translate orders into actions on the battlefield.

This is not to suggest, however, that Napoleon wanted independently minded subordinates: he did not. He, and not his staff, remained the driving force in planning and executing war, and therefore his command system remained centralized, not decentralized, and reliant on obedience and interpretation, rather than initiative. The stream of messages issued by him personally is an indication of just how centred the command system was on Napoleon himself. There is no sign of any prioritization, or sequencing by the staff, and no system of copying orders to one subordinate around the others in order to maintain what would now be called situational awareness. Napoleon himself, therefore, carried a huge burden of work, and a huge span of command. But when viewed from the present, one is inclined to forget that the structure of the *Grande Armée* was new; that it was probably only really understood by Napoleon himself and Berthier; and that the idea of methodical, uniform, written staff work, by a staff trained in a staff college, was still in the future. It is not surprising, therefore, that in this campaign as in others, orders miscarried, or were misinterpreted, or simply were not understood; nor that intelligence was thin and badly interpreted. It was as well for Napoleon that he had been faced in 1806 by a divided Prussian command, a staff system not worthy of the name, and with aged, second-rate generals. That the Prussian soldiery had fought as hard as they did should have given him pause for thought.

Moreover, Napoleon's attempt to force a decisive battle had failed. Jena-Auerstadt had been ruinous for the Prussians, but any enemy is only beaten when he admits it – and Frederick William was not ready to admit defeat. It was to take two further campaigns into 1807, and two major battles at Eylau and Friedland (see Chapter V), before both Prussia and her ally Russia acknowledged defeat. Nor did the battles of 1806 bring unbounded joy at home. On his arrival in Berlin – where Davout's corps had the honour of leading the triumphal entry on 27 October – Napoleon was met by a delegation of the Senate from Paris. The Senate had sent not congratulations, but an urgent request for a general peace: great though their emperor's achievements were, the French people had already begun to realize that *la gloire* had to be paid for in blood and treasure. Nor would the Prussians ever forget or forgive Napoleon's behaviour in Berlin. Humiliated they might be, but in 1806 were sown the seeds of *Befreiungskrieg* in 1813. Once again, Napoleon missed the opportunity to turn a defeated enemy into a friend and ally.

The effective neutralization of the Fourth Coalition still brought no lessening in the hostility of Britain, and Napoleon's sojourn in Prussia gave birth to the Berlin Decrees (see Chapter II), which instituted the strategically fatal Continental System. From it came the long war in Spain, the calamitous war in Russia, the alliance of all the powers of Europe in the Sixth Coalition, and defeat.

X

Case Study 3: From Dresden to the Battle of the Nations, 1813: The Beginning of the End

The Ten Weeks' Truce

After the inconclusive battle of Dresden in May 1813, both Napoleon and the allies of the Sixth Coalition needed an operational pause: casualties, stragglers, logistic difficulties and general exhaustion made it impossible for either side to continue the fight. Both were, therefore, willing to accept the offer of mediation from the Austrian Chancellor, Metternich. The truce which resulted, known to history as the Armistice of Pleiswitz, was therefore a matter of convenience, rather than a genuine attempt to reach a negotiated peace. During its ten weeks, however, the Austrians concluded the Treaty of Reichenbach with the allies. By the terms of this treaty, Metternich agreed to present allied demands to Napoleon as the basis for a general settlement, which would be negotiated at a congress in Prague. If the Austrian mediation failed, however, Austria would join the allies.

Allied Plans

The lengthy processes of allied negotiation during the period of the truce arrived at a general operational plan for fighting Napoleon when the truce expired. This plan, known as the Trachenberg-Reichenbach plan, laid down allied operational objectives. First, it would be an offensive campaign, with Napoleon's centre of operations, Dresden, as the first objective. A most important proviso was that a general action against Napoleon himself would be avoided, unless under highly favourable conditions and force ratios. French forces were only to be attacked when divided, and when the allies were superior in numbers. If any allied army was itself attacked by the French, it would break contact, while other allied formations converged on the French flanks and rear. Any fortresses encountered would be masked, but not invested. This process would be accompanied by attacks on the

French rear area by Cossacks and other irregulars. It was hoped that by this process of attrition, eventual victory would be surer than by risking another major battle.

To put these plans into effect, the allies formed four multinational armies. The main effort was with the Army of Bohemia, commanded by Prince Karl von Schwarzenberg, since the allies believed that Napoleon was most likely to attack southwards towards Prague. This army consisted of 220,000 Austrian and Prussian troops. Schwarzenberg was to threaten either Hof, or Eger, or Silesia, as circumstances dictated – or if necessary to retire to the Danube if Napoleon attacked. In the last case, General Jean-Baptiste Bernadotte (now Crown Prince of Sweden) would then attack Napoleon's left flank and rear. Bernadotte's Swedish Army of the North was therefore reinforced, by Russian divisions, to a strength of 100,000. He was to leave 20,000 Swedes to screen Hamburg, and then be prepared to advance, either in support of Schwarzenberg, or towards Leipzig. If he was attacked he was to retire, while the remaining allied armies closed in on the French from the flanks and rear as before. The third army, the Army of Silesia under General Gebhard von Blücher, was some 95,000 strong and composed of Russian and Prussian formations. Blücher was ordered to follow any French retirement towards the Elbe, cross the river, and unite with Bernadotte – but not risk a battle unless he was sure of winning it. Last, the Russian Reserve Army in Poland under General Count Levin Benigsen was to advance towards Glogau ready either to attack the French main army in co-operation with the other allied armies, or else block the route into Poland.

Although no written Trachenberg plan survives, this clearly shows that Napoleon's opponents had at last learned something from him, in particular the focus on the enemy army. But their deliberate avoidance of Napoleon's favourite device, the decisive battle, gave the plan – as originally conceived – little chance of achieving victory except by attrition. Supreme command was vested in Schwarzenberg, who in the absence of the Archduke Charles was Austria's senior general, and who enjoyed Metternich's confidence.

On 7 August, in accordance with this plan, Russian troops began marching from Silesia to join the Army of Bohemia. Five days later, bonfires on the hills around Prague proclaimed that the peace conference was disbanded, and that the armies of Austria would march with their Russian and Prussian allies.

Napoleon's Plans

While the allies consulted, Napoleon had been making good his losses as fast as only he could. By August he had formed Eugène's army in Italy, along with Count Wrede's Bavarians, to a strength of almost 200,000 men. This force would, he hoped, tie down the bulk of the Austrian armies if and when she entered the war. In addition, the Elbe fortresses and other garrisons accounted for another 50,000 men. In the Central European theatre his main field army was reinforced to almost 400,000 men with 1,300 guns, but only 40,000 cavalry. This army, like that of the allies, was becoming more and more multinational and now included formations of Danes, Poles, Italians, Saxons and other Germans, as well as a host of individuals from all corners of the Empire. The difference was that Napoleon remained in complete command, with no requirement to consult his allies, and was thus able to leave the formulation of his plans to a relatively late date: it was 12 August before he completed them. He then took, for him, the unprecedented step of asking the opinions of his marshals. This may have been inspired by the loss of Ney's chief of staff, Jomini, who had defected to the allies. More likely it was due to the circumstances, which were like no others which Napoleon had ever faced.

Napoleon had no intention of retiring behind the Rhine to await the attack of the combined armies of Europe. Nor could he, given the force ratios, launch an all-out offensive. It seems from his correspondence that Napoleon expected the allied main effort to be with the Army of Silesia, possibly reinforced from Austria. Alternatively, he felt that the Austrian army might try to unite with the Army of Silesia. What he did not expect was what the allies actually did – reinforce the Army of Bohemia from that of Silesia. His intentions, in the light of these expectations, were set out in letters to Marshals Jean Ney, Auguste Marmont and Nicolas Oudinot, on 12 August, in which he said that:

> It seems to me that the present campaign can only lead us to a good result if, to begin upon, there is a great battle … in order to have a decisive and brilliant affair, there are more favourable chances in holding ourselves in a more concentrated position and awaiting the arrival of the enemy … I need not say that, whilst disposing yourself in echelons, it is indispensable to threaten to take the offensive.

For the first time in his career, therefore, Napoleon was contemplating an operational, if not a tactical, defensive. But it was a movement which would contain and, he hoped, be the precursor to, further offensive action.

Napoleon's plan required a division of his forces – again most unusual for one who generally sought concentration – and given the strength of the allies this was risky. In the north, Oudinot was given an independent command consisting of the IV, VII, XII, XIII and III Cavalry Corps; General Jean-Baptiste Girard's division; and General Jan Henryk Dombrowski's Polish division. This was a total of 120,000 men. Oudinot's task was to attack towards Berlin, destroy Bernadotte's army, and then advance on Stettin. The choice of Oudinot was a strange one. Soult would have been the obvious choice, but Soult had left for Spain. As well as Marmont and Davout, there remained Marshals Claude St Cyr, Pierre Augereau or Edouard Mortier. All were proven all-arms commanders, and Mortier certainly knew Germany as well as any French general. Certainly Napoleon owed Oudinot a debt after the crossing of the Beresina, but his choice was to prove disastrous, and the command was too large for his abilities.

However, while Oudinot carried out this attack, the main effort would be placed in an operational defensive between Görlitz and Dresden. With his left flank and his rear firmly anchored on the Elbe, on which he held every crossing and every fortress, Napoleon felt that he could rest secure, and could exploit any allied mistakes with 300,000 men formed into the I, II, III, V, VI, XI and XIV Corps; the Guard Corps; and the I, II, IV and V Cavalry Corps. Thus the Elbe was not to be simply a line of defence: it was, with the city of Dresden which was fortified and developed as the centre of operations, a base for subsequent offensive movements. As he wrote in his correspondence, 'What is important to me is not to be cut off from Dresden and the Elbe; I care little for being cut off from France.'

What the plan seems to show is that by 1813, and probably since the Danube campaign against Austria in 1809, Napoleonic armies had become too large and unwieldy for even Napoleon's skill to command. The staff work involved in controlling so many subordinate formations, and the systems for issuing orders in a timely manner, stretched the technology of the time to a huge degree. But leaving aside the choice of Oudinot, the plan had much to recommend it. The position of Austria remained uncertain until 12 August and, had Napoleon decided to attack straight away in the south, he would probably have had to deal with an allied withdrawal deep into Poland; if he had followed, the other allied armies would have closed in behind him. Given the length of his communications, the state of his army, and the threat to his southern flank, it was not something that recommended itself.

Dresden and After

Only two weeks later, after much marching and counter-marching by both armies, the allies risked battle at Dresden on 26 and 27 August. They failed. After fighting a defensive action with inferior forces on the first day, Napoleon brought up reinforcements and went over to the attack. By 3.00 p.m. on 27 August it was over. Napoleon, soaked to the skin, his famous cocked hat plastered round his ears, rode into the city followed by 1,000 prisoners. Another 12,000 followed, along with three generals, twenty-six guns, and thirty ammunition wagons. Napoleon had gained a most remarkable, if almost his last, victory. The allies had made many mistakes, but Napoleon had once again shown a flash of his old genius. He had at once realized the advantages which the terrain and his interior lines offered, and he had boldly denuded his centre in order to create local superiority on the flanks, on what was the first occasion in his career when he had not managed to assemble a force numerically equivalent or superior to that of his opponents. For Napoleon this was indeed an innovation. As von Caemmerer said,

> When an army of 120,000 men, in the presence of 180,000 enemies, deploys from a bridgehead, then surrounds the enemy on both wings, and seriously damages both; when it compels a whole division to lay down its arms in the open field, when it brings in immediately from the battlefield 1,300 prisoners, fifteen standards and twenty-six guns, that is a quite undeniable victory.

But Dresden was followed by the defeat of Napoleon's lieutenants. Oudinot was smashed at Grossbeeren, Vandamme at Kulm, Macdonald at the Katzbach, and then Ney at Dennewitz. It seemed that the allied plan of defeating Napoleon's lieutenants was vindicated. Far from having lost the initiative at Dresden, the allied Army of Bohemia was intact and its morale revitalized; the Army of Silesia and the Army of the North were threatening from the north and east, and the Reserve Army of Poland would soon be hastening westward. For all its success at the tactical level, Dresden had become, at the operational level, a wasted victory.

By 23 September, reviewing the state of his army and the events of the past three weeks, the unpalatable facts must have become clear to Napoleon. Another period of intense marching, during which the allies had avoided a great battle, had only served to exhaust his dwindling troops, and achieve nothing. The allies' refusal to offer battle to Napoleon himself, but wear down his subordinates was succeeding remarkably well – so much so that Napoleon was being kept off-balance, and was compelled to dash hither and thither to assist one or other of his marshals to react to an allied move, but then usually arriving too late and with too little force to achieve any decisive result. Faced with this situation, the Emperor came to the decision to abandon all territory, including the garrisons on the Oder and Vistula, and to pull his army back behind the Elbe, maintaining strong bridgeheads at Königstein, Pilnitz, Dresden, Meissen, Wittenberg-Elbe, Torgau and Magdeburg. Husbanding his remaining 260,000 men and 784 guns he would watch the allies, and, if they took the offensive, he would concentrate and force them to fight.

The allies too had recast their ideas and were about to embark on the series of moves which would lead them to victory. The Army of Poland was now on the move, and Benigsen was ordered to unite with the Army of Bohemia. This combined army would then advance through the Erzgebirge towards Leipzig, cutting Napoleon's communications. Blücher was ordered to cover Benigsen's flank, and then to move north and join Bernadotte. This united army would then cross the Elbe and oblige Napoleon to withdraw

By 15 October, the possibility of the various allied armies uniting at Leipzig was very real, if not imminent, and various despatches made clear to Napoleon that he had to act quickly. Napoleon also realized that the allies' strength was so great that he had no choice but an operational and a tactical defensive. On 12 October, Marmont had been sent with the VI Corps and the Guard to Taucha near Leipzig, with orders to support Murat. Napoleon believed that Bernadotte was some distance away and given that, he might be able to destroy the Army of Bohemia before the arrival of the Army of the North. At 3.00 a.m. on 14 October, therefore, he issued orders to all corps for a general concentration of the army at Leipzig, and specific orders to Macdonald to move with all speed:

> I hope you will arrive here [Düben] in good time today. It is necessary to cross the river at once. There can be no doubt that during tomorrow – the 15th – we shall be attacked by the Army of Bohemia and the Army of Silesia. March with all haste.

Napoleon entered Leipzig at noon on 14 October and immediately rode to join Murat, who had succeeded in retaining control of much of the ground of tactical importance in the vicinity of the city. Napoleon's reconnaissance soon convinced him that an allied assault was imminent: his concentration was not a moment too soon. By nightfall on 14 October, 157,000 French and allied troops had closed on the city, while a further 18,000 under General Jean Reynier were expected within 48 hours. But Davout was still in Hamburg with 25,000 men, and St Cyr in Dresden along with the other Elbe garrisons deployed at least another 30,000 who were being effectively masked by 20,000 men whom Benigsen had detached.

The Army of Bohemia, immediately south of Leipzig, now numbered 203,000 Austrians, Russians and Prussians. Blücher was approaching from Halle with 54,000 Russians and Prussians, while Bernadotte's 85,000 Russians, Swedes and Mecklenburgers moved in from the north-east. Benigsen too was within striking distance. Schwarzenberg, King Frederick William of Prussia, and Bernadotte remained uneasy about fighting Napoleon, but the fiery Blücher and Tsar Alexander won the argument. The time had come for a major, and probably decisive, engagement on terms advantageous to the allies.

Leipzig – The Plans

The main feature of Leipzig's location was the various water obstacles. These were the Elster, Pleisse and Parthe rivers, which divided the ground around the city. To the east and south, between the Parthe and Pleisse, lay a series of low ridges which were suitable for the defence. Here the country was open, so cavalry and guns could move freely, although there were some ponds and marshes. The highest feature was the Galgenberg, although the Kolmberg was crowned by an old Swedish redoubt from the Thirty Years' War. Most of the villages outside the suburbs lay in this area, of which the most important were Markkleeberg, Sommerfeld, Liebertwolkwitz and Stötteritz. South and south-east of the city, between the Pleisse and Elster, lay marshy ground protecting the defences of the city. The two streams were interconnected by marshy channels, with woods and gardens in between, making this a very difficult area indeed for troops, and virtually impassable for wheeled vehicles and guns. As the Elster flowed north-west of the city, it made a right-angled turn towards the west and was joined by the Luppe, and the combined stream then flowed through an area like that between the Elster and the Pleisse. Further west, towards Lindenau, the country became almost a level plain, while to the north, between the rivers Elster and Parthe, the land was also relatively flat and well drained except along the banks of the Elster, which were marshy.

Another feature of Leipzig was the convergence of routes from all directions. Of most significance was the road west through Lindenau, which afforded the only real withdrawal route for the French. Over the marshy ground this route was carried on a causeway which had five bridges in a space of one-and-a-half miles. There were other bridges too, further south, but in order to make the ground between the Elster and the Pleisse even more of an obstacle, these had been demolished. Napoleon had ordered the existing defences of the city and those in the suburbs to be improved, and some earthworks and small redoubts had been constructed around Linde-nau. Altogether the position did provide the French with the opportunity to fight on interior lines with a strong defensive position at their backs, while the allies would have to approach over some very difficult ground.

Even when outnumbered, Napoleon had no intention of fighting a wholly defensive battle. On 16 October he would have about 160,000 men available, including 27,000 cavalry and 690 guns. His plan was to hold off the expected advance of Blücher, and possibly Bernadotte, in the north with the III, IV, VI and VII Corps, all under Ney's command, while the garrison of Leipzig, about 7,000 Germans and Italians under General Arrighi, would hold open the line of communication through Lindenau. His main effort would be placed between the Pleisse and Parthe, where almost 120,000 men would be assembled for an attack on the expected approach route of the allied main army. The II, V and VIII Corps, supported by the III Cavalry Corps, would fix the allied army by a frontal attack, while the XI and the II Cavalry Corps, under Macdonald, would turn the allied right and draw off the reserves. The *coup de grâce*, a smashing blow in the centre, would be delivered by the Guard Corps, the IX Corps, either the IV or VI Corps drawn from Ney's command at the appropriate moment, and the I and V Cavalry Corps, all supported by as many guns as could be assembled. If it went to plan, this would be a classic example of the Napoleonic battle system.

The allies, too, planned to attack. Schwarzenberg's first scheme placed the allied main effort in the constricted and marshy ground between the Elster and the Pleisse. This met with violent opposition, and eventually the Tsar told Schwarzenberg that he could do as he pleased with the Austrians, but that the Russians must come east of the Pleisse. The modified plan ordered the reinforced corps of General Ignatius Gyulai to assault west of the Elster and seize the Lindenau position, cutting the French communications. The corps of General Count Maximilien von Meerfeld would attack towards Leipzig between the Elster and the Pleisse, while Blücher's army attacked from the direction of Halle. The main effort was placed against the line of the villages Markkleeberg – Wachau – Liebertwolkwitz, which would be the objective of a column under Field Marshal Mikhail Barclay de Tolly. The Russian and Prussian Guards were held in reserve at Rotha, but the Austrian reserves under General Vicenz Bianchi were to stay west of the Pleisse. This plan contained several major problems. First, as the armies of Bernadotte and Benigsen, and some Austrian formations as well, had not yet arrived, allied strength was only just over 200,000 including 40,000 cavalry, a force ratio of only 1.25:1 over the French – although the allies deployed nearly twice as many guns. Second, a significant proportion of the allied troops were to be kept in reserve, where they would not be able to affect the main effort. Third, while two-thirds of Napoleon's forces would be massed for his main effort, the allies would commit only one-third – about 77,000. However, one bitter lesson of Dresden had not been learned, for the Elster cut off Meerfeld's corps from the rest of the army.

The Battles of 16 October – Wachau, Lindenau and Möckern

The planned deployments occupied both sides during 15 October. That night, the French troops witnessed the sky illuminated by a blaze of rockets – a signal announcing the imminent union of all the allied armies. At 9.00 a.m. next day, Napoleon arrived at the Galgenberg and saw that the allies had pre-empted his plan of attack. He therefore decided to let the allied attack expend itself, before going over to the offensive himself.

By 9.30 a.m. the division of Eugen of Württemberg had penetrated as far as Wachau. The French II Corps immediately counter-attacked, supported by heavy artillery fire. Wachau changed hands several times, but by 11.00 a.m. Eugen was forced to withdraw. On his left, Kleist's corps stormed and took Markkleeberg, but could exploit northwards. On Eugen's right, General Prince Andrei Gortschakov's Russians had advanced on the south side of Liebertwolkwitz, but without support could make no progress in the face of the French artillery, and fell back. By 11.00 a.m., with the allies halted, Eugen could see the ominous signs of a French advance developing: he asked for help from General Carl von der Pahlen's cavalry, and received 14 squadrons.

Napoleon had every reason to feel satisfied. The main allied attack had been held, Macdonald and the II Cavalry Corps were moving into position for his planned attack, and he expected the arrival of the corps of Souham and Marmont to reinforce his main effort. He now prepared to pass from the defensive to the offensive. Macdonald was ordered to storm the Kolmberg and then turn the allied right. Once this was done, Napoleon intended to let loose a general attack, supported by the fire of a great battery of guns, positioned between Wachau and Liebertwolkwitz, which would shatter the allied centre, thus winning the battle. Macdonald began his attack just before noon. By 2.00 p.m. only Eugen of Württemberg, with two-thirds of his division dead or wounded around him, still held his ground: the allies had been, to all intents and purposes, driven back to their starting points. It was Dresden all over again, and it seemed that all that was needed now was for Napoleon to complete another stunning victory. The I Cavalry Corps and the Guard cavalry were massed around Meusdorf; Oudinot and Lauriston formed attack columns between Wachau and Markkleeberg; and south of Liebertwolkwitz, Victor formed up the Old Guard behind him. Although there was still no sign of Bertrand, or Marmont, or Souham, Napoleon was so confident of success that he sent word for the bells of Leipzig to ring for a victory.

At 4.00 p.m. Macdonald's troops resumed the attack in order to complete the turning of the allied right. Some progress. But an unexpectedly stiff fight was put up by the Austrians, and by dark, the French advance had been effectively stopped. On the allied left, too, the fortune of battle began to change. General Prince Poniatowski's VIII Polish Corps and Augereau's IX Corps advanced against Kleist, and forced him back. But the Austrian cavalry reserve arrived from over the Pleisse, and at the same time, the French Guard cavalry and part of the III Cavalry Corps also appeared. The Austrians at once charged, driving the French back, but suffered heavy losses themselves, and were in turn driven back on the village of Cröbern. The French infantry pressed forward again, but fortunately for Kleist, the Austrian reserve infantry under Bianchi, following up the cavalry, arrived just in time to halt the French attack. Meerfeld too was able to advance again. At 5.30 p.m. Napoleon was forced to commit a division of the Old Guard and one division of Souham's corps to save the dire situation on his right flank. Meerfeld's men were stopped, and again thrown back. Meerfeld himself, being rather short-sighted, rode into the midst of some Poles of the VIII Corps, whom he mistook for Hungarians, and was captured.

While all this was happening on the flanks, Drouot's great French artillery battery continued to fire on the allied centre. Behind the battery, the I Cavalry Corps was waiting for the moment. At 2.30 p.m. General Jean-Pierre Doumerc, who was standing in for the wounded General Michel Latour-Maubourg, ordered a charge. His cuirassiers destroyed part of Eugen of Württemberg's line, and captured 26 guns – but it did not stop there. The cavalry rode up to the Wachtberg, where Tsar Alexander and the King of Prussia were watching the battle. It seemed both would be captured, but in the nick of time, the French were themselves charged by the Cossacks of the Tsar's bodyguard, followed by 13 squadrons of cuirassiers from the Russian reserve. Those Frenchmen who managed to escape, fled back behind the battery.

The Tsar now ordered the assembly of a battery of 94 Russian guns, bigger even that Drouot's battery, and there the Russian and Prussian Guards from the Grand Duke Constantin's Reserve Corps were marching. This was enough to stabilize the allies' situation. The result of the day's fighting on the southern front was, therefore, a bloody draw: had Napoleon been reinforced as he expected, it would have been a different story, but that was often the case on the Napoleonic battlefield. So, what had gone wrong?

West of the Pleisse, Gyulai's corps had closed up to Klein Zschocher by about 10.30 a.m. The Austrians pressed on to where the French garrison troops under General Jean Arrighi were drawn up across the Lutzen. Gyulai's repeated attacks, however, failed in the face of the French artillery. On Gyulai's left, however, the Hessen-Homberg division slowly worked its way through the marshy country and stormed the causeway, only to be beaten off by a counter-attack.

At 10.00 a.m., as Gyulai's attack was developing, Ney had despatched Bertrand's corps south to support Napoleon as he had been ordered. The corps was on its way when Bertrand received a message from Arrighi, asking for help. Since Arrighi was clearly worried about losing the line of communication, Bertrand moved with his whole corps to Lindenau – one brigade would have been enough. It was Bertrand's men who repulsed the Hessen-Homberg division. After this, the action around Lindenau was confined to artillery fire until dusk, when Gyulai withdrew his corps to Markranstadt. He had not severed the French communications, but he had diverted Bertrand's corps, and this was probably a more important, if unintended, effect.

But the bloodiest of the three battles of the day was fought out to the north of Leipzig, between the corps of Marmont and Blücher. Marmont had chosen a defensive position between Lindenthal and Breitenbach, in order to protect the northern approach to the city – but he was uneasy in having only his own corps. Napoleon had therefore promised Marmont that, if he was attacked, Bertrand's and Souham's corps would support him – although he had, of course, no intention of doing this as he had other plans for these two corps. On the evening of the 16th, Marmont's cavalry screen reported that Prussian troops were marching from Halle. At 10.00 p.m. that night, he watched the glow from the camp fires of the Army of Silesia: he at once sent the news to Napoleon, and again received the promise of support. But early next morning, Napoleon's orders were that, as no major enemy force opposed him, Marmont was to march south to join the main army, and his place was to be taken by Bertrand. Marmont had no choice but to obey.

Blücher, meanwhile, knew very well that he would get no help from Bernadotte for at least another day. Even so, he decided to press on. His intention was to occupy the higher ground around the village of Radefeld with his four corps: General Count Louis Langeron's Russians in the first echelon, General Count Fabien Sacken's Prussians in the second, General Guillaume St Priest's Russians in the third echelon, and General Graf Yorck von Wartenberg's Prussians covering the northern flank. He would decide on subsequent moves once he could see the French positions. The attack did not begin until 10.00 a.m., but Langeron had no difficulty in occupying

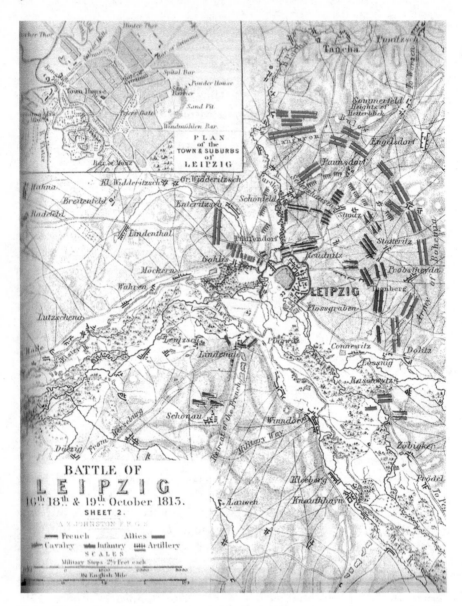

LEIPZIG, 1813
Source: Simon Forty and Michael Swift
Historical Maps of the Napoleonic Wars
(London, 2003)

Radefeld, since Marmont had withdrawn his advanced guard. Blücher then ordered Langeron to press on so as to be able to dominate the Düben road. Yorck, meanwhile, pushed the French out of Stahmeln and Wahren. Marmont realized that if he maintained his withdrawal, the allies would fall on Napoleon's rear. He therefore occupied a hasty blocking position between the village of Möckern and the Rietzsche stream. He hoped for support from Souham's III Corps, but he knew that Bertrand's men had moved south.

It was 2.00 p.m. before Blücher realized the relative weakness of the French position. By 3.00 p.m., Marmont's Polish division had been driven from the village of Wiederitzsch in disorder, when Marmont's Saxon cavalry charged the Russians. The Poles rallied, turned back, and threw the Russians out of the village. Once again the Russians attacked and once again the Poles were driven back, when General Antoine Delmas's division of the III Corps appeared, escorting a baggage train. The division was less than 5,000 strong, but the size of the baggage train made it seem like a corps. The Russians held off until Langeron realized the true situation, and returned to the attack. This time, it succeeded. Yorck, too, had realized the true nature of the enemy position and moved on Möckern and the surrounding area. There followed one of the bloodiest struggles of the entire campaign, for the possession of this village. Initial Prussian attacks were repulsed with great slaughter, but as the French prepared to counter-attack, several ammunition wagons blew up in a tremendous explosion, spreading panic. Seeing this, the Prussians returned to the attack, but again the French rallied and drove their enemies back. The climax of the battle in the north had now come. Marmont personally led his infantry to attack and destroy Yorck's corps, but Yorck brought up cavalry which charged furiously forwards. The Prussian horsemen swept away Marmont's leading battalions and their cavalry, and crashed into the midst of Marmont's artillery. The fighting was hand-to-hand until, at last, the French broke and ran. With Möckern gone, Marmont could do nothing but retire, as the whole of Yorck's corps moved forward. Only night brought an end to the fighting, and Marmont's exhausted men bivouacked where they stood. They had lost over half their strength in killed, wounded and prisoners; but Yorck's corps had lost nearly 8,000 men, or one-third of its strength, and Langeron had lost 1,500.

South of Leipzig, the battle of 16 October appeared to be a draw. The allied attack early on had achieved some tactical surprise and Napoleon's main attack had been held. At Lindenau, the French had held open their communications, but Gyulai had successfully prevented Bertrand from reinforcing Napoleon's main effort. At Möckern, Blücher had shut Napoleon in from the north. Anything less than total victory was in reality a defeat for Napoleon, and he had barely held his own. He could expect little in the way of reinforcements – only Reynier's 18,000 and this, after the losses of the day, would give him only 170,000 men. The allies, on the other hand, could expect Colloredo, Bernadotte and Benigsen, giving them 320,000 men.

17 – 19 October: The Defeat of Napoleon

That night should have seen Napoleon planning a rapid withdrawal to the Rhine. Instead, the night found the *Grande Armée* in wet and hungry bivouacs on the battlefield. Once his tent had been pitched, Napoleon ordered the captured Meerfeld to be brought in. Napoleon knew Meerfeld, spoke to him briefly then, and called him back again later. Napoleon asked how strong the allied army was. Meerfeld told him that it was more than 350,000 men. Napoleon then asked whether the allies realized that he was there, and whether they would attack again. Meerfeld answered yes to both questions. Napoleon is said then to have asked him

> Shall this war last forever? It is surely time to put an end to it. Austria should speak the word of peace, and not listen to Russia, because Russia is under the influence of England, and England wishes for war. I am ready to make great sacrifices.

Meerfeld replied that the Emperor of Austria would not make a separate peace from his allies, and that Great Britain wished only for a Europe free from domination by a single power. Napoleon said: 'Let England give me back my [West Indian] islands and I will restore Hanover, Holland and the Hanseatic cities.' But he would not agree to dissolve the Confederation of the Rhine or to give up of his empire in Italy and the north-western Balkans. Meerfeld then told him that the Bavarians had changed sides. Napoleon replied that they would be sorry. He then suggested another armistice and negotiations for peace, during which he would withdraw west of the Saale, while the Russians retired east of the Elbe, and the Austrians into Bohemia. Saxony would stay neutral. Meerfeld told him plainly that the allies would never agree to those sorts of conditions, and that they would not leave Germany even if they could not drive the French back across the Rhine. Napoleon replied that they would have to beat him in another battle to do that, and that they had not yet won the present battle. Napoleon then said goodbye to Meerfeld, and sent him back under safe-conduct with a letter for the Emperor Francis. Francis was delighted to see Meerfeld again, as he had thought him dead, but said that he could speak to him only in the presence of the Tsar and King Frederick William. Once they had heard Napoleon's terms, they agreed that having come this far, they would have none of Napoleon's tricks.

Once Napoleon had learned the extent of his losses, and realized that his ammunition stocks were low, he knew that he could not last out another day like 16 October. Torn as he was between military necessity and holding on to his empire in Germany, he decided to withdraw. Even so, probably for domestic political reasons, he was determined to continue the battle for one more day. No additional bridges were built to supplement the single route over the Lindenau causeway. Napoleon's orders were not issued until 7.00 p.m. on 17 October, after a day of skirmishing, for the allies had decided to postpone their attack until 18 October in order to make sure that they had the greatest possible force available.

Napoleon ordered Bertrand to leave Lindenau late on 17 October and secure the crossings over the Saale and the Unstrut Rivers. The rest of the army began to move to new positions at 2.00 a.m. on 18 October, in pouring rain: Napoleon had decided to defend a line much closer to Leipzig, but he had no plans for any further offensive action. The army was divided into three parts. The right wing of the army was placed under Murat's command. This consisted of the II, VIII and IX Corps, part of the Guard, and the I, IV and V Cavalry Corps. The centre was placed under Macdonald who, in addition to the XI Corps, was given the V Corps and the Guard cavalry. Ney continued to command the left wing with the III and IV Corps, Reynier's VII Corps which had just arrived, and two cavalry divisions. Dombrowski's Polish division with two cavalry divisions was ordered to block the approach from Gohlis into the north of Leipzig, while Mortier, with the Old Guard and Arrighi's division, kept open the line of retreat through Lindenau.

Schwarzenberg's attack plan for 18 October called for an assault in six huge columns. The main effort would be with the attack from the south, with two columns commanded by General Count von Colloredo and Field Marshal Barclay de Tolly, towards the villages of Markkleeberg, Lösnig, Wachau, and Liebertwolkwitz. Next, Benigsen's Russians would attack the French left around Probstheida and Holzhausen. Third, Blücher's four corps would attack on the north-east side of the city; Bernadotte's Swedish army would fill in between Blücher and Benigsen. Finally, Gyulai would once again attack Lindenau and the French line of communications from the south. By 8.00 a.m. the attack was well under way. By 2.00 p.m., Colloredo's men were fighting in the main French position at Connewitz. On Colloredo's right, Tolly had closed up to Probstheida. Benigsen too had reached the French main position between Zuckelshausen and Paunsdorf. Blücher's troops, too, were fully engaged and were pushing Marmont's depleted corps back into the city, but there was no sign of Bernadotte. Away east of Leipzig, Bertrand's corps had burst out of Lindenau, and by the same time, 2.00 p.m., Bertrand had cleared the route towards Weissenfels and his men were marching hard for the Saale.

Between 2.00 p.m. and 5.00 p.m., the main allied attack was launched. The struggle in many places was truly heroic, but at 5.00 p.m., the allied sovereigns received the news that Benigsen's troops had captured the villages of Zweiaundorf and Molkau. Here 4,000 Saxon troops deserted to the allies. It had been the arrival of Bernadotte which had allowed Benigsen to make such good progress, even though Bernadotte committed only his artillery. These Russian and Swedish guns also saved the day for Langeron: his own ammunition was exhausted, but the arrival of additional fire-power forced Ney, his last reserves spent, back into Leipzig town, with what remained of his command. By dusk, although the French were still holding some positions, their ammunition was almost exhausted, food and water were scarce, and casualties were heavy. They were thus hardly in a condition to continue the battle, and it was fortunate for them that Schwarzenberg did not at once exploit the situation.

While the battle of 18 October was in progress, the French retreat had begun. Napoleon had ordered the move to begin at 11.00 a.m. and from that time, a stream of traffic began to move down the Lindenau causeway. Everything not immediately needed for the fight was despatched: baggage, artillery parks, camp stores and wagons; and at 4.00 p.m., I, III and V Cavalry Corps were ordered west of Lindenau. By evening, news of the retreat reached Blücher and so, while the rest of the army bivouacked, Yorck's corps was despatched to occupy the passages of the Saale at Halle and Merseberg. Marching all night, the Prussians gained their objective early on 19 October – but there was no concerted attempt by the allied high command to forestall the French retreat by occupying Freiburg, Kösen or Naumberg, or by destroying bridges. The only formation sent in pursuit, apart from Yorck's corps, was General Bubna's Austrian light division. Possibly the allies were only too glad to offer Napoleon the chance to disappear, so as not to have to face him in person when the attack on Leipzig was resumed.

Napoleon, meanwhile, had issued orders for the retreat of the rest of his army. The city of Leipzig itself would continue to be defended by Baden, Saxon and Italian troops. Macdonald, with what could be saved of the VII and VIII Corps, which contained large numbers of Poles and Germans, and his own XI Corps, was ordered to act as rearguard. The causeway at Lindenau was to be mined, and was to be blown once the rearguard had broken contact and withdrawn. The rest of the army began thinning out from its forward positions at 2.00 a.m. on 19 October; by 5.00 a.m. the allied patrols began to bring news of their departure. It was a year to the day since Napoleon had marched out of Moscow.

At 7.00 a.m. the allies began to advance on the city, and by 10.00 a.m. they stood outside the suburbs. By 11.30 a.m. the French had been everywhere driven in to the *Altstadt* and, with Napoleon himself gone, the troops' thoughts turned towards safety. As the allies advanced, the only escape route looked in danger. Fighting was desperate at the gates of the city and around the Parthe bridge, with fearful losses on both sides, but by 12.30 p.m. the allies were in the city and all hope for the French rearguard had gone. Shortly before 1.00 p.m. Napoleon, who was sleeping at Lindenau, was awakened by the roar of a huge explosion: the causeway had been blown too early. Thousands of troops left on the far side surrendered, others tried to swim, of whom many drowned. Macdonald managed to swim the Elster on his horse, but Poniatowski, who had only received his Marshal's baton from the Emperor's hands on 15 October, was drowned. Just after 1.00 p.m. the Tsar and the King of Prussia, with Schwarzenberg and their staffs, rode into Leipzig marketplace. Cheering troops lined the streets, bands played, swarms of ecstatic civilians came out from their shelters in cellars. In the marketplace, the sovereigns met Bernadotte and Bennigsen; Blücher and Gneisenau arrived a little later, followed by the Emperor of Austria. The only other monarch present was Napoleon's captured ally, the King of Saxony. The unfortunate king had refused to accompany Napoleon and had remained in the city to meet his fate. He was arrested in the Tsar's name and later sent to Berlin as a prisoner of war.

The Battle of the Nations was over. The allies had lost, by most estimates, something like 50,000 killed and wounded. Napoleon's losses were still heavier: the allies had taken 15,000 prisoners and 5,000 deserters, many of whom were Poles and Germans. Another 15,000 were sick in the hospitals, but at least 40,000 had been killed and wounded – most estimates make the total around 75,000. These losses included six marshals and generals killed, 11 generals and marshals wounded, including Ney, Macdonald, Marmont, Souham, Latour-Maubourg and Sébastiani; and 36 generals and marshals captured, including Lauriston, Reynier and Prince Maximilien. French materiel losses included 325 guns – half Napoleon's artillery – 900 ammunition wagons, 720 tons of powder, and 40,000 muskets and rifles.

Aftermath

Napoleon crossed the Rhine with an army of 80,000 men, of whom perhaps 60,000 were fit to fight. There can be no doubt, despite Napoleon's own attempts to disguise the fact, that the French army was comprehensively defeated at Leipzig; only the inadequacies of the allied pursuit allowed the campaign, and the war, to go on into 1814. But even in adversity, Napoleon was already looking ahead. There was a sense of defeat permeating the *Grande Armée*, especially among the clients and allies, which had to be overcome. General Henryk Dembinski later recalled that:

> Several days later, when we reached the Fulda, our corps approached the main route at the same time as the Emperor was passing ... He addressed us for a long time, urging us not to abandon him. 'Read the *Moniteur* ... you will see that Poland existed in my thoughts ...' The conversation continued for over three-quarters of an hour, always in a tone of confidence and reproach.

Meanwhile, Bertrand had reached Weissenfels late on 18 October and word was sent to him to occupy all the country between Kösen and Merseberg, as well as Freiburg, and watch the passages over the Saale. He was also to collect all available stores and position these in depots along the army's withdrawal route. At the same time, Kellermann, in Mainz, was ordered to collect all available troops, including recruits, at Erfurt and Würzburg, and to provision the latter city. Kellermann was also ordered to call out the National Guard for the defence of France itself, for Napoleon was sure that an invasion was imminent. Last, orders were sent to St Cyr at Dresden to escape as best he could.

The rest of the army retreated on Weissenfels. Napoleon, not unnaturally, feared an allied attack but he need not have done. At Erfurt he rested two days before continuing westwards. At Hanau on 28 October he was intercepted by a force under Count Wrede, of 27,000 Bavarians and 25,000 Austrians who until recently had faced each other as enemies. In a remarkable feat of arms, getting a beaten army to win only 11 days after a colossal defeat, Napoleon pushed the opposition aside. The army then marched on and reached Frankfurt am Main late on 31 October, and Mainz on 2 November. The allies reached Frankfurt two weeks later, and there they halted. Napoleon was given enough breathing space, therefore, to recover his army and to fight another campaign in 1814.

XI

Conclusions

Scope of the Chapter

Absolute pronouncements on whether or not Napoleon was a good general
are not, to my mind, helpful. Nor are they appropriate. In each chapter I
have offered some analysis of Napoleon's strengths and weaknesses. In this
final chapter, therefore, I intend to return to the more general thesis on
generalship offered in the opening chapter, look at Napoleon's personal
qualities, examine his legacy and, in particular, his impact in the years
following his downfall, and see where his example helps – if it does.

The Mask of Command: Napoleon's Personal Qualities as a General

War, as Clausewitz reminds us, is made up of danger, exertion, uncertainty
and chance. To succeed in it requires moral and physical courage, firmness,
energy, strength of character and will, intellect and knowledge. To what
extent does Napoleon meet these requirements, and measure up to the
criteria identified in the opening chapter of this book? He must, of course,
be assessed against his results, and against his contemporaries. Tempting as
it may be to compare him with others, either before or after, and true as it is
that the human condition does not change, the mores of the time will have
influenced his behaviour, and make comparisons of this sort meaningless.

Let us begin with courage. On the evidence, there is no doubt that
Napoleon was morally and physically courageous, even when his judgement
was misplaced: it is a theme running through every episode of his life, and
something on which even his detractors remark. In eighteenth- and
nineteenth-century warfare it was still very much accepted that, when
required, the place of the general was at the head of his men. Napoleon
knew this, and there are plenty of examples throughout his career, from
Arcola to Waterloo, which show him braving personal danger in order to
inspire the troops. Not for nothing did Wellington remark that 'his presence
on the battlefield was worth 40,000 men'; and the dreaded cries of '*Vive
l'Empereur!*' which heralded his appearance on many a European battlefield
came to strike fear into the hearts of his enemies, and courage into the

hearts of his own men. Marmont, for example, remarked of him as late as the battle of Lutzen in 1813 that

> This was probably the day, of his whole career, on which Napoleon incurred the greatest danger on the field of battle. He exposed himself constantly, leading the defeated men of the III Corps back to the charge.

There is no doubt too that Napoleon exercised enormous personal charm, or magnetism, which may have been a sub-set of his strong will, reinforced by the habit of constant command. This is seemingly at odds with his personal appearance and habits. He is described as being short, but in fact he was slightly above the average height for a French man at the time: 1.68 metres, or 5 feet 6 inches in imperial units. In later life, he ran to fat and this may have made him appear shorter; he was, too, often accompanied by grenadiers of his guard, who were invariably 6 feet tall or more. The lampoons of Gillray and Cruikshank, portraying him as 'Little Bony' may also partly account for the myth of his short stature. He was brutally frank in his personal dealings, and often outspoken to the point of rudeness. He had no social graces at all, but despite all this, he could reduce almost anyone to admiring submission in a short time – a power which never left him. Many people remarked on his large grey eyes, which seemed to fascinate them.

There were a few exceptions: Metternich never succumbed, describing Napoleon's character as consisting of egotism and nepotism. Talleyrand appears to have been deferential in public, but unimpressed in private. He once said to Tsar Alexander that 'The French people are civilised, their sovereign is not'. Sir Hudson Lowe, the Governor of St Helena, also appears to have remained unmarked by Napoleon's appeal, to the point of indifference. His personal magnetism was reinforced by the great gift, of immense value to a general, of being able to recall the names and faces of individual officers and even private soldiers, which increased further the devotion of his *moustaches*. The nickname of *le petit caporal*, often taken as an indication of Napoleon's stature, is more likely an endearment, like *petit ami*. His charm did not, however, stop him abandoning his troops ruthlessly, as he did in the East in 1798 and in Russia, nor of spending their lives in huge numbers. He would probably have responded that command is not a popularity contest, and that a general may well have to give orders that result in carnage. He would have known of, and approved, Frederick the Great's reprimand to the cowering grenadiers: 'Dogs! Would you live for *ever*?'

It is also certain that Napoleon was possessed of a remarkable intellect, and a keen memory, not only for faces and names, but for facts and figures. His recall of orders of battle, places, geography and events was almost, it seems, photographic. His mind was always active, seeking new ideas on almost any subject, and he was clearly able, through careful application and study, to comprehend a problem in its entirety, analyse it, and come rapidly to an intuitive solution. He then had the strength of will and the moral authority to carry through his decisions. This derived very largely from his professional expertise in almost every area of land warfare – although he never mastered naval tactics nor understood the marine environment. On the battlefield, though, this often served him well. His rapid orders in the saddle at Lutzen are a good example.

His powers of concentration were reflected in his appetite for work: 18 or 20 hours a day were not unusual, and on campaign, he was known to go for days at a time with little or no sleep. His energy was enormous, and as John Terraine has said: 'Its particular outlet was war, its sanction was victory.' The appetite for work developed in him the tendency to attend to almost every task himself: the breadth and depth of his correspondence shows this to a remarkable degree. But while the general must lead the development and execution of the plan, so too he must be able to delegate, both to the staff and to his subordinates. Napoleon was remarkably bad at this, with several ill effects. First, the work of the staff was frequently unco-ordinated and, as a result, situational awareness throughout the army was low. Second, when tired or under stress, he could be subject to fits of rage which brought him to screaming pitch – such as that reported by Metternich in the Marcolini Palace in Prague in 1813. These rages, when combined with the power vested in him, made things extremely uncomfortable – indeed at times terrifying – for those who had to serve him. In contrast, he was noted for his calmness in the face of danger, and his ability to control his emotions in the face of extremities of suffering.

Overwork affected Napoleon's health and physical strength, a key element in maintaining a clear focus for mental activity: Baron von der Goltz reported of Napoleon in youth that 'He passed half the day in the saddle or in his carriage, made all dispositions for his great army, and then dictated to his aides-de-camp ten, twelve, fourteen or more long letters.' In 1806 Napoleon writes to Josephine: 'I manage to do some fifty miles a day on horseback, and in my carriage. I lie down at eight, and get up again at midnight ...' By the time he was aged 41 he complained of a lack of his former vigour. Not surprising, given the amount of time he spent travelling hard and living rough. By 1812, he was clearly suffering from bad digestion, piles, and the early stages of duodenal-pyloric cancer. Despite the conspiracy theories, the latter probably killed him.

An additional trait which resulted partly from his personal work ethic was that he seldom confided in his marshals, and did little or nothing to develop their own qualities of generalship. He would probably have responded that there is a great gulf between a commander-in-chief who controls a whole army, or a theatre of operations, and a subordinate general subject to control and supervision. The latter has nothing of the freedom of action nor the scope for intellectual agility enjoyed by his master, especially when, like Napoleon, he is also a politician, statesman, and diplomat. Napoleon would probably also have said that it was not for him to tell his marshals how to dispose their troops for battle, nor to dictate minor tactics; however, it is clear that Napoleon would brook no rival, nor near equal, and that what he wanted was functionaries who understood just enough of his mind to be able to interpret his orders, but who were not innovators. As the Napoleonic Wars progressed, it is arguable that experience should have made the French Marshalate better, despite the effect of casualties. This is demonstrably not the case: the marshals of 1813–15 were by no means the equal of those of 1805–6, despite the fact that most had been brigade and divisional commanders for many years. Napoleon never instituted any sort of staff college, nor re-shaped the higher command system of the army. He never seems to have acknowledged that appropriate talent is needed at every level, and that since no general is immortal, he needs to groom successors against the day that the hazard of battle goes against him. Metternich's charge of nepotism, however, is a fair one. Not only did Napoleon consistently advance those who had served him well, despite their lack of ability (Ney for example), but he also placed his family in positions of power with complete ruthlessness: Joseph as King of Spain, Louis as King of Holland, and so on. This trait might seem rather at odds with his failure to invest in the future, but on reflection, it was probably simply a feature of his desire to retain total control of the French state, its allies and clients, and the armed forces.

Frequently, his lack of confidence in his subordinates led to near disaster, especially when generals or marshals of limited imagination – Ney and Bernadotte in particular – were involved. What he could do with such methods when armies of no more than 200,000 were deployed was simply not possible with larger forces or more extended theatres of operation, nor as his opponents finally mastered his battle system and produced generals – and armies – better able to compete on equal terms. There are, accordingly, many examples of his being left waiting for someone to turn up on a battlefield and their failing to appear – Bautzen in 1813, and Ligny in 1815 are two that spring to mind – often because Napoleon had not properly explained his intentions. On the other hand, he had a tendency to blame his marshals when things went wrong: Ney for Dennewitz, Macdonald at the Katzbach, and Vandamme at Kulm, for example. This sort of attitude not only drove away the likes of Massena, Bernadotte, Moreau and Jomini, but

CONCLUSIONS 201

also made co-operation with powerful allies, such as the Tsar, impossible for any length of time.

Mastery of his profession and long hours of study, allied to his powers of intellect, also without doubt produced in Napoleon an unrivalled ability for rapid, intuitive decision-making. Napoleon was noted for his ability to make the right *tactical* decision, quickly, and he is evidence of the truth of Einstein's remarks that: 'The intellect has little to do on the road to discovery. There comes a leap in consciousness, call it intuition or what you will, the solution comes to you and you do not know why or how. The truly valuable thing is intuition.' He had the remarkable gift, as the Duke of Wellington put it, of being able to see the other side of the hill. It is questionable, however, whether Napoleon's timing in strategic decisions was quite so sound, as has been discussed in Chapter II. But when on campaign he could, with a few moments' thought, analyse a series of reports, assess a complex situation, and issue orders to retain control of a situation or seize the initiative: the swing to the north before Jena, cited in Chapter VIII, is but one example. Not that he was always right – but he often avoided disaster simply by being able to react more quickly than his opponents – as at Aspern-Essling. This, as much as anything, contributed to the legend of his genius which, as time went on, he believed more and more strongly.

What is interesting about Napoleon in his early period of command was that he had very little experience, and yet his intuitive decision-making was excellent. How was this possible? In Napoleon's case, he seems to have been able to substitute vicarious experience through study, for the real thing. He had attended the *École Militaire* at the age of 15 and had worked so hard that he had graduated in only one year instead of three. At the age of 19 he had then been stationed at Auxonne, where his regiment acted as the depot for the School of Artillery. The School was then under the command of Major General Baron Jean-Pierre Duteil, the most distinguished gunner officer in the French army. Here, Napoleon had studied gunnery, and learned the theories of concentration firepower, and the co-operation of all arms. Duteil had, for example, been instrumental in the adoption of horse artillery into the French army in 1791, following the example of the Prussians. He also studied de Guibert on tactics, and de Bourcet's *Principes de la Guerre des Montagnes*. But, more widely, during his 15 months at Auxonne he studied the works and campaigns of Alexander the Great, Hannibal, Cyrus the Great, Julius Caesar, Turenne, Luxembourg, Prince Eugen, and especially Frederick the Great. To the end of his life, Napoleon maintained his devotion to these great commanders, Frederick's *Secret Instructions* of 1748 being one of his favourite sources of inspiration. He remarked in his memoirs on St Helena: 'Read and meditate upon the greatest captains. This is the only means of rightly learning the science of war.' In addition, he was tutored in mathematics and social sciences. He is known to have studied the history of England, and been much taken by Jean-Jacques Rousseau's *Social Contract*. Later on, by about 1806, his intuitive powers can be largely ascribed to wide experience, and by what Fuller describes as 'a creative mind'; that is, originality, the ability to surprise an opponent and disarm him morally, and in addition, an understanding of what responsibilities and decisions rest with the commander, what with the staff, and what with his subordinates. He commented: 'I have fought in sixty battles and I have learned nothing which I did not know at the beginning.' Hardly a true statement – if it were, it would not say much about Napoleon as a general.

And what of luck? Napoleon is quoted as having demanded subordinates who were lucky; but perhaps successful generals make their own luck: through careful calculation before a campaign in order to minimize chance, and through allowing their intuition full rein. Where Napoleon can be said to have been supremely lucky was in being in the right place, at the right time, and in the right circumstances, to launch his career. It is probable that only the conditions of revolutionary France could have allowed someone of Napoleon's youth, provincial status, and lowly connections to rise so far, so fast. Under the *ancien régime*, to command an army at the age of 26 was remarkable enough, but even those rare cases had been limited to kings, princes of the blood, or the highest ranks of the nobility: the Archduke Charles has been mentioned already; other examples of men who achieved high command at an early age include Charles VIII of France, aged 24 in 1491; Prince Maurice of Nassau, aged 33 in 1600; Gustavus Adolphus, 36 in 1632; the Condé D'Enghien, 22 in 1643; and Charles XII, 26 in 1708. Revolutions create opportunities for talent through necessity, regardless of birth. They first break down traditional structures and the hierarchical pyramids of rank and experience that go with them. The older generation, usually loyal to the old regime through vested interest, is killed, imprisoned, or driven into exile, leaving a gap which has to be filled if the revolution is to be defended from its enemies. Frequently – but not exclusively – that gap will be filled by youth, and men of low station. Nathaniel Greene was 33 at the start of the American Revolution; George Monck 36 at the outbreak of the English Civil War. In the twentieth century, the generals of the Red Army in Russia in 1917, those of the Republican forces in the Spanish Civil War, and those of the Iranian Army after the fall of the Shah, were generally young men without patronage under the old regimes. Many of these failed; others achieved competence by learning their lessons the hard way; a few, through connections, luck, and sheer competence, achieved greatness.

Leaving luck aside, any complex activity, and especially war, if carried out well, requires intellect, dedication, and strong intuitive powers – what Clausewitz calls genius, which is really a highly developed mental aptitude for a particular calling. Willpower and the ability to dominate enhance it, along with courage and luck. These give, as they did to Napoleon, the ability to deal with adversity and limit the agonies of doubt that so oppress many who hold great responsibilities. Napoleon feared hesitation more than risk-taking, for he believed in careful calculation before any campaign in order to minimize risk. But as with any man who wields supreme power, he believed more and more, as the years went by, what he wished to believe. His strong will, frequently remarked on by Napoleon himself and by others, turned to obstinacy. Even as late as November 1813, after the debacle of Leipzig, he could have secured a negotiated peace that would have left France with more territory than she had in 1789 – but he did not know when to stop. This tendency was fuelled by the anxiety of his courtiers to please him, and report only what suited him; Adolf Hitler, Slobodan Milosevic and Saddam Hussein are more recent examples of this process in action. This sort of delusion caused him to continue his military adventures well beyond the point at which it was logical or even reasonable to do so. Napoleon's finance minister, Count Molé, remarked that 'Although Napoleon's common sense amounted to genius, he could never see where the possible left off.' To paraphrase Lord Acton, he clearly believed that power is wonderful, and absolute power is absolutely wonderful.

Napoleon's Legacy

When one looks at the curriculum for military history at the British Army Staff College in 1913 – and indeed its equivalent in the USA, the Command and General Staff College – one is struck by the emphasis on the Napoleonic Wars, and the American Civil War, in spite of the more recent example of the sequence of wars in Europe between Prussia and her rivals. The dominance of Napoleon was marked and, in France, probably amounted more to worship than mere dominance. Every general clearly wanted to be him: to crush his enemy's army, march into his capital, and thus attain the goal of decisive victory. This elusive ideal has persisted right down to the present. What does not seem to have dawned on those responsible for teaching the military class of the future is the simple fact that, in the end, *Napoleon lost*.

Of course, Napoleon himself on St Helena, and his many admirers later, did all they could to disguise this. It was Basil Liddell Hart who reminded the world of the uncomfortable truth that 'it is as well to remember that St Helena became his destination'. To get him there took more than 20 years of ruinous war – mainly against poorly co-ordinated coalitions, inefficient armies, and elderly, second-rate generals. Faced with this sort of opposition, Napoleon did not have to be faultless: he just had to be better than the other side. Tempo in military terms is helpfully defined in this context: it is the rate or rhythm of activity *relative to the enemy*. But given this sort of opposition, and given the edge that superior French organization and a unified command brought, it is not surprising that the legend grew to the size it did.

Because of this legend, the evolution of the nature of modern warfare over the next century has become obscured. European armies after Napoleon were almost invariably large organizations raised through conscription, and the full impact of the Industrial Revolution – which was not felt until after 1815 – equipped them with weapons far closer to those of today's battlefield than to those of Leipzig or Waterloo. Aircraft, the railway, the telephone and telegraph, the steam and petrol engines, aircraft, smokeless powder, breach loaders and repeating weapons were all in place by 1914. It is, of course, true that military technologies do not advance in complete capability leaps: armies do not replace all their weaponry and equipment in one turn – cutting-edge technologies and legacy systems continue to co-exist,* and this gradual process of technical innovation, to an extent, obscures tactical or operational innovation. But there is, in warfare, a relationship between the introduction of new technologies, and the employment and deployment of troops. This relationship is not constant, and needs careful and frequent revision. When it is not attended to, trouble follows. Thus by the American Civil War, although the armies were equipped with powerful, rifled muskets and heavy artillery, and could be moved by rail, the tactics were still those of Waterloo. The results, for generals seeking the Napoleonic grail of the decisive battle, were the casualty rates of battles like Antietam, Fredericksburg and Gettysburg, and the acceleration of trench warfare. One can argue that the same process continued through the Franco-Prussian war, the early stages of the South African War, and the first four months of the Great War, which cost the French army 800,000 casualties. It was not until 1918 that this relationship was adjusted – and Blitzkrieg was born. Even then, the spirit of Napoleon still lived.

Even today, armies still operate within what is described as a Napoleonic staff model, and a corps structure, at a time when once again, the

---

* For example, the pilot of an *Apache* helicopter – twenty-first-century technology – will wear laces in his boots – Roman technology. A divisional command post may be equipped with digital tracking systems which give a sophisticated view of the battlespace in real time, but men will still fight with bayonets.

employment-technology relationship is shifting. The revolution in information should mean that the staffs of generals are organized in a way that cuts across traditional divisions in order to provide superior (not necessarily faster) information, and thus produce superior decisions. The most likely opponents of Western generalship today are not states, but non-state groupings, whose command structure, as far as they can be said to have one, operates in the virtual realm. Bringing an army corps into action may succeed in taking ground, but as the Israelis discovered in south Lebanon and the Coalition has found in Iraq, the action is not necessarily going to be decisive. But the focus on destroying an enemy force as *the* decisive act remains. This is, however, the wrong lesson to draw from Napoleon's legacy in the context of modern warfare. Napoleon may have been successful on many – but by no means all – his battlefields, and he may have been a master of campaigning. However, in strategic terms he was a failure. One of the principal reasons for his failure was that he never succeeded in transforming a defeated enemy into a willing ally: he won wars, *but he never won the peace.*

Appendix

Composition of the *Grande Armée* in 1812

Formation	Commander	Troop numbers	Nationalities
Imperial Guard	Lefebvre	41,000 infantry (38 battalions), 2,400 cavalry (16 squadrons)	
Old Guard	Lefebvre		French
New Guard	Mortier		French
Middle Guard	Roguet		French
Hessian Guards	Claparède		1 regiment each French, Polish, Dutch Hessian
Artillery	Sorbier	112 guns	French, Swiss, Prussian
Cavalry	Bessières		French, 1 regiment Polish
I Corps	Davout	68,000 infantry (88 battalions), 3,400 cavalry (16 squdarons)	
1st Division	Morand		French, 1 regiment Baden
2nd Division	Friant		French, 1 regiment Spanish
3rd Division	Gudin		French
4th Division	Dessaix		French
5th Division	Compans		Mecklenberger
Artillery	Pernety	150 guns	French
Cavalry	Girardin		French
II Corps	Oudinot	34,300 infantry (48 battalions), 2,800 cavalry (16 squadrons)	

6th Division	Legrand		French, 1 regiment Portuguese
8th Division	Verdier		French
9th Division	Merle		Swiss, 1 regiment Croat
Artillery	Dulauloy	92 guns	French
Cavalry	Corbinbau		French
III Corps	Ney	35,000 infantry (45 battalions), 3,500 cavalry (24 squadrons)	
10th Division	Ledru		French, 1 regiment Portuguese
11th Division	Razout		French, 1 regiment Portuguese
25th Division	Marchand		French, 1 regiment Illyrian
Artillery	Foucher	86 guns	French
Cavalry			French
IV Corps	Eugène	42,000 infantry (54 battalions), 3,300 cavalry (20 squadrons)	
Italian Guards	Lecchi		Italian
13th Division	Delzons		French, 1 regiment Croat
14th Division	Broussier		French, 1 regiment Spanish
15th Division	Pino		Italian
Artillery	Danthouard	116 guns	French, Italian
Cavalry			French
V Corps	Poniatowski	32,000 infantry (33 battalions), 4,100 cavalry (20 squadrons)	
16th Division	Zayonczek		Polish
17th Division	Dombrowski		Polish
18th Division	Kaminiecki		Polish
Artillery	Pellerier	70 guns	Polish
Cavalry			Polish

VI Corps	St Cyr	32,200 infantry (28 battalions), 1,900 cavalry (16 squadrons)	
19th Division	Deroy		Bavarian
20th Division	Wrede		Bavarian
Artillery		55 guns	Bavarian
Cavalry			Bavarian
VII Corps	Reynier	15,000 infantry (18 battalions), 2,100 cavalry (16 squadrons)	
21st Division	Lecocq		Saxon
22nd Division	Defunck		Saxon, 1 regiment Wurzburg
Artillery		34 guns	Saxon
Cavalry			Saxon
VIII Corps	Jerome/ Vandamme	15,800 infantry (18 battalions), 2,000 cavalry (12 squadrons)	
23rd Division	Tharreau		Hessian
24th Division	Ochs		Westphalian
Artillery		34 guns	Westphalian
Cavalry			Westphalian
IX Corps	Victor	31,600 infantry (43 battalions), 1,000 cavalry (12 squardons)	
12th Division	Partouneaux		French
26th Division	Dändels		Berg, 1 regiment Baden
28th Division	Girard		Polish, 1 regiment Bavarian
Artillery		80 guns	German
Cavalry	Fournier		German
X Corps	Macdonald	30,000 infantry (36 battalions), 2,400 cavalry (16 squadrons)	

7th Division	Grandjean		1 brigade and 2 regiments Polish, 1 regiment each Bavarian, Westphalian
Prussian Division	Grawert		Prussian
Prussian Division	Yorck		Prussian
Artillery		84 guns	Polish
Cavalry	Massenbach		Prussian
XI Corps	Augereau	50,000 infantry (45 battalions), 700 cavalry (4 squadrons)	
30th Division	D'Heudelet		French, 1 regiment Westphalian
31st Division	Lagrange		French, 1 regiment Wurzurg
32nd Division	Durutte		French
33rd Division	Destrées		Neapolitan
34th Division	Morand		French
Artillery		60 guns	French
Cavalry	Fournier		French
Austrian Corps	Schwarzenberg	26,800 infantry (26 battalions), 7,300 cavalry (44 squadrons)	
1st Division	Trautenberg		Austrian Empire nationalities (cannot separate)
2nd Division	Bianchi		As above
3rd Division	Siegenthal		As above
4th Division	Frimont		As above
Artillery		60 guns	As above
Cavalry			As above
I Cavalry Corps	Nansouty	12,000 (54 squadrons)	
1st Light Division	Bruyère		Polish, 1 regiment Prussian
1st Heavy Division	St-Germain		French
5th Heavy Division	Valence		French
Horse Artillery		30 guns	French

II Cavalry Corps	Montbrun	10,400 (52 squadrons)	
2nd Light Division	Sébastiani		1 brigade each Polish, Württemberg, Prussian
2nd Heavy Division	Watther		French
4th Heavy Division	Defrance		French
Horse Artillery		30 guns	French
III Cavalry Corps	Grouchy	9,600 (50 squadrons)	
3rd Light Division	Chastel		Bavarians, 1 regiment Saxon
5th Heavy Division	Doumerc		French
6th Heavy Division	De la Housaye		French
Horse Artillery		30 guns	French
IV Cavalry Corps	Latour-Maubourg	7,900 (40 squadrons)	
4th Light Division	Rosinski		Polish
7th Heavy Division	Lorge		1 brigade each Saxon, Polish, Westphalian
Horse Artillery		24 guns	Polish

Bibliography

Primary Sources

Archives de la Ministère des Affaires étrangères (Paris)

Barras, Paul, *Mémoires de Barras,* ed. G. Dupuy (4 vols, Hachette, 1895).

Bourrienne, Louis de, *Memoirs of Napoleon Bonaparte*, ed. R. W. Phipps (4 vols, New York, 1891).

Bonaparte, Napoleon *Commentaires de Napoléon Ier* (6 vols, Paris, 1867).

Bonaparte, Napoleon *Correspondance de Napoléon Ier*. Publiée par ordre de l'Empereur Napoleon III (32 vols, Paris, 1858–70).

Bonaparte, Napoleon *Correspondance inédite de Napoléon Ier* (3 vols, Paris, 1912–13).

Bonaparte, Napoleon *Mémoires et Correspondance politiques et militaires du Roi Joseph* (10 vols, Paris, 1855).

Bonaparte, Napoleon *Supplément à la Correspondance de Napoléon Ier*. Lettres curieuses omises par le comité de publication. Rectifications. Ed. Baron Du Casse (Paris, 1887).

Bonaparte, Napoleon *Lettres inédite de Napoléon Ier* Publiées par L. Lecestre (2 vols, Paris, 1897).

Bonaparte, Napoleon *Le Registre de l'Isle d'Elba*. Lettres et ordres inédites de Napoléon Ier, 28 mai 1814 – 22 février 1815. Publiés par L. G. Pélissier (Paris, 1897).

Bonaparte, Napoleon *Lettres, Ordres et Décrets de Napoléon Ier*, en 1812–3–4 non inserées dans la 'Correspondance'. Recueillis et publiées par L. de Brotonne (Paris, 1898).

Bonaparte, Napoleon *Lettres Inédites de Napoléon Ier*. Collationnées sur les textes et publiées par L. de Brotonne (Paris, 1898).

Bonaparte, Napoleon *Dernières lettres inédites de Napoléon Ier*. Collationnées sur les textes et publiées par L. de Brotonne (2 vols, Paris, 1903).

Bonaparte, Napoleon *Supplément à la Correspondance de Napoléon Ier*. L'Empereur et la Pologne (Paris, 1908).

Bonaparte, Napoleon *Lettres de l'Empereur Napoléon* du Ier août au 18 octobre

1813, non inserées dans la 'Correspondance'. Publiées par X ... (Paris, Nancy, 1909).

Bonaparte, Napoleon *En Marge de la Correspondance de Napoléon Ier*. Pièces inédites concernant la Pologne, 1801–1815. Ed. A. Skalkowski (Warsaw, Paris, Lvov, 1911).

Bonaparte, Napoleon *Ordres et Apostilles de Napoléon*, 1799–1815, ed. A. Chuquet (4 vols, Paris, 1911–12).

Bonaparte, Napoleon *Correspondance inédite de Napoléon Ier*. Conservées aux Archives de la Guerre. Publiée par E. Picard et L. Tuety (4 vols, Paris, 1912).

Bonaparte, Napoleon *Inédites Napoléonien*, ed. A. Chuquet (2 vols, Paris, 1913–19).

Bonaparte, Napoleon *Lettres de Napoléon à Joséphine*, ed. L. Cerf (Paris, 1928).

Bonaparte, Napoleon *Maximes* (Paris, 1874).

Borgo, Pozzo di *Correspondance Diplomatique* (2 vols, Paris, 1890).

Bulletins de la Grande Armée, ed. A. Goujon (2 vols, Paris, 1822).

Burke, E., *Reflections on the Revolution in France* (1790, reprinted by OUP, 1998).

Caemmerer, R. von *Die Befrieungskrieg 1813–1815* (Berlin, 1907).

Caulincourt, Armand de *Mémoires du Général de Caulincourt, Duc de Vincenza* (3 vols, English pocket edition, London, 1950).

Caulincourt, Armand de *With Napoleon in Russia* (English edition, New York, 1935).

Caulincourt, Armand de *No Peace With Napoleon* (English edition, New York, 1936).

Debidour *Receuil des actes du Directoire Exécutif* (2 vols, Paris,).

Goltz, Baron Colmar von der *The Nation in Arms* (English edition, London, 1906).

Jomini, Baron (tr. H. W. Halleck) *Life of Napoleon* (New York, edition undated).

Las Cases, Count *Mémorial de Sainte-Hélène* (2 vols, Paris, 1842).

Masson, F. *Napoléon Inconnu* (Paris, 1895).

Menéval, Baron C. F. *Memoirs of Napoleon Bonaparte* (English edition, 3 vols, New York, 1910)

Montholon, C. J. F. T. de *Mémoires de Napoléon* (Paris, 1823).

d'Odeleben, Baron *Relations Circonstanciés de la Campagne de* 1813 en Saxe (ed. M. A. Vitry, Paris, 1817).

Paine, Thomas *The Rights of Man* (London, 1791).

Puységur, Jacques-François de Chastenet, Marquis de *Art de la Guerre par Principles et Règles* (Paris, 1743).

Robespierre, Maximilien *Œuvres Complètes*, ed. E. Déprez (10 vols, Paris 1910–1967).

Tukhachevskii, Mikhail *New Problems in Warfare* (unpublished MS, 1931 printed by the US Army War College, 1983).

Wellington, Field Marshal Lord *The Dispatches of the Field Marshal the Duke of Wellington*, ed. J. Gurwood (12 vols, London, 1834–9).

Books

Argyle, Michael *The Social Psychology of Everyday Life* (London, 1992).

Beardsley, E. M. *Napoleon: The Fall* (London, 1918)

Belloc, Hilaire *Napoleon* (London, 1932).

Blumensen, Martin and Stokesbury, James L. *Masters of the Art of Command* (New York, 1975).

Broers, Michael *Europe Under Napoleon* 1799–1815 (New York, 1996)

Browning, Oscar *The Fall of Napoleon* (London, 1907).

Cassirer, Ernst *The Philosophy of the Enlightenment* (Princeton, USA, 1979)

Chandler, David *The Campaigns of Napoleon* (London, 1966).

Chandler, David *Napoleon's Marshals* (London 1984).

Clausewitz, General Carl-Maria von (tr. and ed. Michael Howard and Peter Paret) *On War* (Princeton, 1986).

Connelly, Owen *Napoleon's Satellite Kingdoms* (London, 1965)

Connelly, Owen *Blundering to Glory: Napoleon's Military Campaigns* (Wilmington, Delware, USA, 1987).

Creveld, Martin van *Supplying War. Logistics from Wallenstein to Patton* (CUP, 1977).

Creveld, Martin van *Command in War* (London, 1985).

Danilewski, Lieutenant General Mikhailovski *Military Operations of the Emperor Alexander against Napoleon from* 1805 (St Petersburg, 1886).

Darwin, Charles *The Origin of Species* (London, 1859).

Dixon, Norman *On the Psychology of Military Incompetence* (New York, 1976).

Dixon, Norman *Our Own Worst Enemy* (London, 1987).

Dodge, Theodore *Napoleon* (4 vols, New York, 1932).

Dunnigan, James F. *Leipzig* (Simultaneous Publications Wargame, 1971).

Earle E. M., Craig G. A. and Gilbert F. (eds) *Makers of Modern Strategy: Military Thought from Machiavelli to Hitler* (Princeton, USA, 1943).

Ellis, Geoffrey *The Napoleonic Empire* (London, 1990)

Elting. John R. *Swords Around a Throne: Napoleon's Grande Armée* (London, 1989).

Esdaile, Charles *The Wars of Napoleon* (London, 1995).

Evans, Michael and Ryan, Alan (eds) *The Human Face of Warfare. Killing, Fear and Chaos in Battle* (St Leonard's, Australia, 2000).

Forrest, Alan *Napoleon's Men. The Soldiers of the Revolution and Empire* (London, 2002).

Fortescue, Sir John, *History of the British Army* (13 vols, London, 1899–1930).

Forty, Simon, and Swift, Michael *Historical Maps of the Napoleonic Wars* (London, 2003)

Fregosi, Paul *Dreams of Empire. Napoleon and the First World War 1792–1815* (London, 1978).

Fuller, J. F. C. *Generalship – Its Diseases and Their Cure* (Harrisburg, Penn, USA, 1936).

Fuller, J. F. C. *Decisive Battles of the Western World* (2 vols, London, 1956).

Gat, Azer *War in Civilisation* (OUP, 2006).

Gawain, Shakti *Developing Instinct* (London, 2001).

Gawain, Shakti *Intuition: The New Frontier of Management* (2001).

Gay, Peter *The Enlightenment: An Interpretation* (New York, 1996).

Gregory, Richard L. *The Oxford History of the Mind* (OUP, 1991).

Griffith, Paddy *The Art of War in Revolutionary France 1789–1802* (London, 1998).

Hall, Christopher D. *British Strategy in the Napoleonic Wars* (Manchester UP, 1992).

Herrold, Christopher J. *The Age of Napoleon* (London, 1970).

Houssaye, H. *Jena et la Campagne de 1806* (Paris, 1912)

Howard, Michael (ed.) *The Theory and Practice of War* (London, 1965).

Israel, Jonathan I *Enlightenment Contested. Philosophy, Modernity and the Emancipation of Man 1670–1751* (OUP, 2006).

Jedlika, Ludwig 'Erzherzog Karl, der Sieger der Aspern' in *Gestalter der Geschichte Osterreichs*, ed. Hugo Hantsch (Vienna, 1962).

Jones, William *The Principles of Psychology* (Henry Holt, 1890).

Jordan, David *The Revolutionary Career of Maximilien Robespierre* (London, 1985)

Keegan, John *The Face of Battle* (London, 1976)

Keegan, John *The Mask of Command* (London, 1987)

Kerchnawe, Hugo *Feldmarschall Karl Furst zu Schwarzenberg* (Vienna, 1913).

Kissinger, Henry *A World Restored* (New York, 1964).

Kraehe, Enno E. *Metternich's German Policy: I. The Contest with Napoleon, 1799–1814* (Princeton, 1963).

Lefebvre, Georges *Napoleon: from Brumaire to Tilsit 1799–1807* (London, 1969).

Lefebvre, Georges (tr. A. Anderson) *Napoleon: from Tilsit to Waterloo – 1807* (London, 1933).

Lettow-Warbeck, D. von, *Der Krieg von 1806 und 1807* (2 vols, Berlin, 1899).

Liddell Hart, Captain B. H. *The Ghost of Napoleon* (London, 1933).

Liddell Hart, Captain B. H. *The Strategy of the Indirect Approach* (London, 1954).

Luttwak, Edward N. *Strategy. The Logic of War and Peace* (Cambridge, Mass, USA, 1992).

Markham, Felix *Napoleon* (London, 1963).

Marshall-Cornwall, James *Napoleon as Military Commander* (London, 1967).

Maude, F. N. *1806: The Jena Campaign* (London, 1905).

Moran, Lord (C MacMoran Wilson) *The Anatomy of Courage* (London, 1945).

Mowat, R. B. *The Diplomacy of Napoleon* (London, 1924).

Muir, Rory *Britain and the Defeat of Napoleon* (London, 1996).

Muir's *Historical Atlas* (London, 1974)

Nicholson, Harold The *Congress of Vienna 1812–1817: A Study in Allied Unity* (London, 1946).

Parry, Clive and Hopkins, Charity *Index to British Treaties, Vol. I* (HMSO, 1970).

Petrie, F. Loraine *Napoleon and the Archduke Charles: the Campaign in the Valley of the Danube in 1809* (New York, 1991).

Petre, F. Lorraine *Napoleon's Last Campaign in Germany 1813* (London, 1974).

Petre, F. Lorraine *Napoleon's Campaign in Prussia 1806* (London, 1990).

Reber, Arthur S. *The Penguin Dictionary of Psychology* (London, 1995).

Ridley, Matt *Nature versus Nurture. Genes, Experience and What Makes us Human* (London, 2003).

Riley, J. P. *Napoleon and the World War of 1813: Lessons in Coalition Warfighting* (London, 2000).

Saxe, Compte Maurice de *Mes Rêveries* (2 vols, Paris, 1757).

Schom, Alan *Napoleon Bonaparte* (New York, 1997).

Scott, Franklin D. *Bernadotte and the Fall of Napoleon* (Cambridge, Mass., USA, 1935).

Secher, Reynauld *A French Genocide: The Vendée* (University of Notre Dame Press, USA, 2003).

Simpkin, Brigadier Richard E. *The Race to the Swift. Thoughts on 21st Century Warfare* (New York, 1985).

Smith, Digby *The Decline and Fall of Napoleon's Empire* (London, 2005).

Smith, General Sir Rupert *The Utility of Force; the Art of War in the Modern World* (London, 2005).

Sorel, A. *L'Europe et la Révolution Française* (Paris, 1904).

Steiger, G. *Die Schlacht bei Jena und Auerstadt 1806* (Cospeda, 1981).

Sun Tzu (ed. James Clavell) *The Art of War* (New York, 1983).

Szatmary, David *Shay's Rebellion: The Making of an Agrarian Insurrection* (University of Massachusetts Press, 1980).

Urban, Mark *The Man Who Broke Napoleon's Codes* (London, 2002)

Wartenburg, Count Yorck von *Napoleon as a General* (English edition, 2 vols, London, 1902).

Webster, C. K. *The Foreign Policy of Castlereagh, 1812–1815* (London, 1931).

Wilkinson, Spenser *The French Army before Napoleon* (OUP, 1915).

Woolf, Stuart *Napoleon's Integration of Europe* (London, 1991).

Articles, Papers, and Journals

Breakwell, Glynis and Spacie, Keith 'Pressures Facing Commanders.' *Strategic and Combat Studies Institute Occasional Papers* no. 29 (1997).

Byrd, Melanie and Dunn, John 'A Document on Napoleon and his Polish allies in 1813', *Journal of Slavic Military Studies* vol. 10 no. 1 (March 1997).

Coker, Dr Christopher 'The Unhappy Warrior', *RUSI Journal* (December 2005).

Professor Sir Lawrence 'War', *Foreign Policy*, issue 137 (July–August 2003).

Hughes, Dr Thomas 'The Cult of the Quick', *Aerospace Power Journal*, vol. XV no. 4, (Winter 2001).

Luttwak, Edward 'The Operational Level of War' in *International Security* vol. 5 no. 3 (Winter 1980/81) .

Lehrman, D. S. 'A Critique of Konrad Lorenz's Theory of Instinctive Behaviour', *Quarterly Review of Biology*, 28 (1953).

Weston, D 'The Army: Mother, Sister and Mistress', *Journal of the Society for Army Historical Research*: no. 74 (1995).

Websites and Electronic Material

Robinson, Lynn A., *Divine Intuition* <www.lynnrobinson.com>

Stout, James Hervey, *Instinct* <www.stout.mybravenet.com>

Interpretations <www.sociology.org.uk>

Plymouth University *The Role of Nature and Nurture in the Development of Behaviour* <http://salmon.psy.plym.ac.uk>

The Wrong Reality – 1:2 Advance of Intelligence <www.humantruth.org>

Military Manuals and Publications

British Army Doctrine Publication Volume 1: *Operations* (HQDT/18/34/46 June 1994).

British Army Doctrine Publication Volume 2: *Command* (HQDT/18/34/61 April 1995).

British Army Doctrine Publication *Land Operations* (DGDD AC 71819, 2005).

British Army Doctrine Publication Volume 5: *Soldiering. The Military Covenant* (HQDT/18/34/71 February 2000).

RMA Sandhurst Study on Morale, Leadership and Discipline, 1950.

Serve To Lead (RMA Sandhurst).

US Marine Corps Doctrine Publication *Campaigning* (MCDP 1–2 August 1997).

US Marine Corps Doctrine Publication *Command and Control* (MCDP 6 October 1996).

Lectures and Broadcasts

General Sir John Hackett *Looking for Leadership*, BBC Home Service, February 1968.

Professor E. R. Holmes *Cultural Asymmetry*. Lecture to the Higher Command and Staff Course, Joint Services Command and Staff College, 21 March 2003.

F. M. Slim 'Courage and Other Broadcasts', BBC Home Service.

General Sir Rupert Smith *Lecture to the Higher Command and Staff Course*, Joint Services Command and Staff College, 3 April 2003.

Major General Julian Thompson *Lecture to the Higher Command and Staff Course*, Maritime Warfare Centre, 10 February 2003.

Index of Persons

Monroe, James, later 5th President of the USA (1758–1831) 38

Montgomery, Field Marshal Bernard Law, Viscount (1887–1976) 6

Moore, General Sir John (1761–1809) 33

Morand, General Count Charles Antoine Louis Alexis (1771–1835) 173–174, 206, 208

Moreau, General Jen-Victor-Marie (1763–1813) 200

Mortier, Marshal Adolphe Edouard Casimir Jospeh, Duke of Treviso (1768–1835) 176, 182, 193, 206

Müffling, General Friedrich Karl Ferdinand, Freiherr von (1775–1851) 158

Murat, Marshal Joachim, Grand Duke of Berg and Kleve, King of Naples (1767–1815) 88, 91–92, 93, 105, 126, 134, 135–153, 159, 160, 162–164, 174–175, 177, 193

Nelson, Admiral Horatio, Viscount (1758–1805) 8

Ney, Marshal Michel, Duke of Elchingen, Prince of the Moscowa (1769–1815) 64, 65, 67, 70, 71, 75, 80, 89, 92–94, 157–175, 180–192, 193, 195, 200, 207

Orange, William IV, Prince of (1748–1806) 173

Oudinot, Marshal Nicolas Charles, Duke of Reggio (1767–1847) 67, 70, 92, 95–99, 180–192, 206

Pahlen, General Carl Ernst Wilhelm Phillip von der (1775–1834) 187

Paine, Thomas (1737–1809) 108–109

Picton, General Sir Thomas (1758–1815) 87

Poniatowski, Marshal Prince Josef Anton (1763–1813) 188, 195, 207

Provera, General Johann, Marquis (1740–1804) 138–140, 146, 150

Quosdanovich, General Peter Vitus von (1738–1802) 143

Reille, Marshal Honoré Charles Michel Jospeh, Baron (1771–1860) 64, 107

Reizenstein, Sigismund Karl Johann, Freiherr von, Baden Minister of State 47

Rey, General Antoine Gabriel Venance 147, 148

Reynier, General Jean Louis Èbénézer (1771–1814) 152, 184, 192, 193, 208

Robespierre, Augustin (1763–1794) 131–132

Robespierre, Maximilien (1758–1794) 131, 132

Rousseau, Jean-Jacques (1712–1778) 108, 202

Rüchel, General Ernst Friedrich Wilhelm Phillipp von (1757–1823) 158–175

Sacken, General Fabien Gottlieb von der Osten, Count (1752–1837) 189–190

St Cyr, Marshal Laurent Gouvion, Marquis (1764–1840) 118, 182, 184, 196, 208

Ste-Hilaire, General Vincent Joseph le Blond (1766–1809) 165, 167–168, 170–171

St Priest, General Guillaume Emmanuel (1776–1814) 189–190

Saliceti, Antoine-Christophe (1757–1809) 131–132, 138

Saxe, Marshal Maurice, Comte de (1696–1750) 7, 138

Sébastiani, Marshal Horace François Bastien de la Porte, Count (1742–1851) 195, 210

Sérurier, Marshal Jean-Mathieu Philibert (in some references spelled Serrurier) (1742–1819)